The Good European

IAIN BAMFORTH graduated from medical school at Glasgow University in 1982, and has since followed an idiosyncratic career which at one point took him from a position as chief resident in the American Hospital of Paris to a year in a base hospital in the Australian outback. Besides working as a general practitioner, he has also been a scientific translator and editor, literary journalist and lecturer in comparative literature. He has published three books of poetry with Carcanet, and a literary history of medicine, *The Body in the Library* with Verso. His varied interests have finally led him to Strasbourg, where he currently lives with his German wife and two children when not working as a health consultant in rural areas of Asia.

Also by Iain Bamforth from Carcanet

Sons and Pioneers
Open Workings
A Place in the World

IAIN BAMFORTH

The Good European
ESSAYS AND ARGUMENTS

Art is something so lucid that nobody understands it.
Karl Kraus

CARCANET

For Felix and Claire

First published in Great Britain in 2006 by
Carcanet Press Limited
Alliance House
Cross Street
Manchester M2 7AQ

A CIP catalogue record for this book is available from the British Library
ISBN 1 85754 765 9
978 1 85754 765 8

The publisher acknowledges financial assistance from Arts Council England

Typeset in Monotype Centaur by XL Publishing Services, Tiverton
Printed and bound in England by SRP Ltd, Exeter

Contents

By Way of a Prologue

As this revolution of the *Strasburgers* affairs is often spoken of, and little understood, I will, in ten words, says *Slawkenbergius*, give the world an explanation of it, and with it put an end to my tale.

Every body knows of the grand system of Universal Monarchy, wrote by order of Mons. *Colbert*, and put in manuscript into the hands of *Lewis* the fourteenth, in the year 1664.

'Tis as well known, that one branch out of many of that system, was the getting possession of *Strasburg*, to favour an entrance at all times into *Suabia*, in order to disturb the quiet of *Germany* – and that in consequence of this plan, *Strasburg* unhappily fell at length into their hands.

It is the lot of a few to trace out the true springs of this and such like revolutions – The vulgar look too high for them – Statesmen look too low – Truth (for once) lies in the middle.

What a fatal thing is the popular pride of a free city! cries one historian – The *Strasburgers* deemed it a diminution of their freedom to receive an imperial garrison – so fell a prey to a *French* one.

The fate, says another, of the *Strasburgers*, may be a warning to all free people to save their money. – They anticipated their revenues – brought themselves under taxes, exhausted their strength, and in the end became so weak a people, they had not strength to keep their gates shut, and so the *French* pushed them open.

Alas! alas! cries *Slawkenbergius*, 'twas not the *French*, – 'twas

CURIOSITY pushed them open — The *French* indeed, who are ever upon the catch, when they saw the *Strasburgers*, men, women, and children, all marched out to follow the stranger's nose — each man followed his own, and marched in.

Trade and manufactures have decayed and gradually grown down ever since — but not from any cause which commercial heads have assigned; for it is owing to this only, that Noses have ever so run in their heads, that the Strasburgers could not follow their business.

Alas! alas! cries Slawkenbergius, making an exclamation — it is not the first — and I fear will not be the last fortress that has been either won — or lost by NOSES.

The End of Slawkenbergius's Tale in
Tristram Shandy (Volume IV)

The Continuing Adventures of Mr Ross Hall, Esq. (& Madam Zell)

WHAT should we make of him? Like William Godwin, father of Mary Shelley, he was a pedagogue incapable of practising what he preached. He wrote a treatise known to every educated person at the end of the eighteenth century on how to educate a young boy and left his own five children with the Foundling Hospital in Paris. Edmund Burke observed that his often-expressed 'love of humanity' was a charade which excused him from any real concern with the suffering of men and women. Contemporary humanitarianism follows his impulse, allowing the heart and not history to lead it towards causes that can do no wrong: it doesn't care for human beings too much but it likes to take care of them. As Flaubert had to remind his mistress Louise Colet half a century later: 'Don't imagine that the pen has the same instincts as the heart.' Rousseau was hopelessly dependent on his *gouvernante* Thérèse Levasseur, not to speak of poor Madame de Warens, and yet proclaimed his proud 'Roman courage' and his defiant independence: if he had a need it was for a lack of binding attachments. What we think of as ordinary sociability was for Rousseau the hell of mutual dependence: too many people aping each other. In spite of his preference for cultivated upper-class young ladies, with their soft skin and ribboned hair, at the age of 33 he made Thérèse, an illiterate laundry maid met at the Hôtel Saint-Quentin in Paris, his lifelong companion: her malapropisms were so notorious Rousseau himself made a list of them to amuse Mme de Luxembourg. She could neither tell the time nor count, yet Rousseau claimed she possessed a stock of uncommon good sense which could be relied upon in times of difficulty. Many of his friends thought his helpmate a simpleton, though the ever rampant James Boswell, after a tryst with her in a boarding house in Dover, praised her 'amatory skills'. She looked after Rousseau until his death, at the age of 66, in July 1778. He was as ready to praise the ordinary people like Thérèse for their spontaneity of feeling as, with his next breath, to curse them for being lackeys to their masters. It was ever thus with Rousseau. The coolly subtle dialectician of *The Social Contract* becomes the radical free spirit of *La Nouvelle Héloïse*, whose 'true voice of feeling' when first heard in 1761 made readers, especially young women, swoon. Mary Shelley's famous phantasmagoria of the nursery owes more to him than it does to the men who told her ghost-stories in Geneva. The moonlit occasions of romantic love, as practised novelistically by Julie on St-Preux, and Rousseau himself on Sophie d'Houdetot, were thrilling and deeply flattering. Love feeds, and feeds upon, the emotional needs aroused by its being physically thwarted: the kind of celestial transcendence written about by the Christian mystics has become the bubble of air in a spirit level inclining this way and that. Hundreds of letters addressed to the author confirm that his novel had caused a swell of emotional emancipation in the reading public; Goethe's *Werther* was to do the same a few years later. The reaction of Mme de Polignac, who confessed in a letter to Mme de Verdelin that while she had no urge to meet Rousseau the philosopher Rousseau the novelist was a different matter, was typical of many urbane spirits: 'In my first impulse I was on the point of getting out the horses and going to Montmorency to see him at all costs and telling him how much his tenderness seems to me to elevate him above all other men; to make him show me the portrait of Julie and to kneel before the image of that divine woman.' Both Kant, the legislator of rationalism, and his townsman Hamann, the first rebel against universal reason, took him to be one of their own; indeed, Rousseau's was the only portrait to be seen in Kant's austere study. Much later, Claude Lévi-Strauss, in a famous phrase in *Tristes Tropiques* was to call him 'our master and our brother'. Although he had no formal schooling and moved from job to job with regularity (he was at one time or other engraver, tax cashier, servant, clerk, personal tutor, piano teacher, diplomatic secretary in Venice and music copyist, which latter occupation brought in most of his earnings), the *philosophes* made him their darling. In return, he spiked the pages of their Encyclopaedia with little thought-bombs: his only and otherwise conventional article, on a non-musical subject, *Economie politique*, contained a passage which rather than upholding Locke's doctrine of the natural right to property suggests that legality is a mere patina concealing the worst kind of exploitation and injustice: 'Let us sum up in a few words the social contract of the two estates: "You need me, because I am rich and you are poor; let us therefore make an agreement between us; I will allow you to have the honour of serving me, provided you pay me the little that remains to you for the trouble I take to command you".' Diderot was most amused that, in an orthodox exposition of liberalism, Rousseau should be so hostile to the notion of property, a 'natural right', as to suggest it was injustice institutionalised. He stood at a crux in human affairs: the practical use of the mind which, from the beginning of recorded time, had been exclusively at the service of the body's needs, was about to wreck havoc on nature in order to satisfy the appetites that living together in society had awakened in human beings. 'It was iron and corn which first civilised men, and ruined humanity': the Fall of Man must have occurred in the Neolithic Age then. In the *The First Discourse on Inequality* he first voiced his conviction that man is naturally good but corrupted by society, further asserting that the sciences and arts had been instrumental in making that corruption widespread; they should not be abolished, however, for they might serve to mitigate the evils of viciousness. It was the *Second Discourse*, in 1753, which became the chapbook for the Revolution and altered the way people thought about themselves and the larger world. In it he took issue with Hobbes, whose vision of the war of man against all men in the state of nature was, he claimed, a projection not from nature but society. Hobbes regarded human self-centredness as a fact of nature; Rousseau as a product of civilisation. And this civilised man is alienated: 'The savage lives within himself; socialised man always lives outside himself; he knows how to live only in the opinion of others, and it is from their judgement alone that he derives the sense of his own existence.' Rousseau was celebrating the hunter-gatherer before the word existed, though he was no simple primitivist: the idea of the noble savage was a *fable convenue* and the state of nature, as he said in the preface to his discourse, a 'hypothesis' which enabled mankind to determine how far it had sunk from the ideal. Natural man might be praiseworthy, but he wasn't a full moral being. Seneca had said it before him: primitive man might be admirable but was a Stoic by instinct only – it was better to know a way of life to be virtuous and to pursue it knowingly than to pursue it without knowing why. So where were the full moral beings in this late age? Paris made him famous and he hated it; Geneva's iron moralists chased him away, and he claimed it was the finest place on earth. His patriotic father Isaac had brought him up in the belief that Geneva was the only city in the modern world which had recovered the spirit of the ancient republics. He was a Calvinist (he observed that most of Geneva's pastors actually resembled the Socinians against whom Calvin had fulminated: they dismissed the notion of the triune God and believed reason to be the sole and final authority in the interpretation of the scriptures), yet it was as a Catholic catechumen that he walked to Turin in 1724. His ideal was the Spartan hero, and yet the feminine element in his own nature was so strong he fulminated against it in print. 'The man should be strong and active; the woman should be weak and passive; the one must have both the power and the will; it is enough that the other should offer little resistance,' he wrote in *Emile, or On Education*; yet throughout his writing life he admits candidly to his longing for chastisement over the knees of an imperious governess. All his life he submitted to dominant, assertive females. His male friendships were curious too, to put it mildly. Having earlier made the acquaintance of

David Hume in Paris, he sought refuge from the French authorities in England: Hume gave him the use of his cottage, only for Rousseau to succumb to the delusion that *le bon David* was keeping tabs on him. The next moment, freed of his delusion, Mr Ross Hall, as he was later known to the locals at Wootton, another of the country houses offered to him during his English exile, embraced the bewildered philosopher with infantile protestations of affection. This most histrionic man hated the idea of theatre (burghers of Geneva who wished to see plays had to go to Carouge, now a part of the city but then a separate town owing allegiance to the Kingdom of Sardinia), despite his own attachment to writing dramatic works and, as he writes in a letter of 1754, his regard for 'that great man Molière'. Visiting a packed Drury Lane for a performance in which the famous Garrick specially played two characters for him, Garrick's wife wrote that he was 'so very anxious to display himself, and hung so forward over the box' that she had to hold onto the skirt of his coat to prevent him falling. The theatre was the place where a man could lose his own self: no prospect for a man who had grown up in Calvin's city could be more terrifying. Public festivals, open-air pageants and games (precursors of the happenings and open-air concerts of the 1960s) were much healthier. 'The only true joy is public joy.' Botany – which he called a 'lazy study' – brought him moments of intensely private joy too, especially when he lived in arcadian solitude on St Peter's Isle, on Lake Bienne in western Switzerland: every morning after breakfast he set out with a magnifying glass in his hand and Linnaeus' classifier under his arm in the hope of recording the peninsula's entire flora. His *Letters on the Elements of Botany Addressed to a Young Lady*, which was reprinted several times in translation in the 1790s, is still a useful guide to the herborium. His keenest sense of equality was reserved for festive occasions, when the social classes would meet in idyllic transport after the grape harvest. He immodestly described his *Confessions* as the first true autobiography ever written (he tells us, notoriously, about the remorse he felt all his life for the youthful lie told about a stolen ribbon that led to his fellow employee and friend, Marianne, losing her job and good name), though Rousseau was precisely the kind of man to tell a fib in order to conceal a greater lie. One thing was sure, even sacrosanct: 'I am commencing an undertaking, hitherto without precedent and which will never find an imitator. I desire to set before my fellows the likeness of a man in all the truth of nature, and that man myself. Myself alone! I know the feelings of my heart, and I know men. I am not like any of those I have seen; I venture to believe that I am not made like any of those who are in existence.' Sincerity was the one virtue that trumped the others. He took his own motives and nature to be entirely transparent, though it was David Hume's opinion 'that nobody knows himself less'. What counted was the full-hearted declaration, the self-exculpating tone of Protestant kitsch. Thomas Carlyle called him 'a morbid, excitable, spasmodic man'. But his protestations suggest that a person can sound sincere while being in bad faith, if sincerity is understood as not lying to others while good faith appendantly entails not lying to oneself. Literary instinct rather than detective work told William Blake he was a Pharisee: 'The Book written by Rousseau call'd his Confessions, is an apology & cloke for his sin & not a confession' (*Jerusalem*). Rousseau himself had said something similar about Montaigne, whom he accused of merely pretending to confess his faults, 'while taking good care to admit only likeable ones'. Unlike St Augustine, who addressed his confessions to God in fraught anticipation of salvation, Rousseau cast his blameless life before the reading public. His were the strange moral gymnastics of going about in sackcloth and ashes, the Voice of Him that cryeth in the Wilderness, with a sandwich board to advertise the fact. 'But in examining myself with greater care I was very surprised by the number of things which I had invented but which I remember saying as though they were true, at a time when, proud in myself of my love for the truth, I was sacrificing to it my security, my interests, and my own person with an impartiality of which I knew no other example among men.' Twentieth-century 'confessional' literature takes all its cues from

Rousseau, in its attempt to prove itself more neurotic than the neighbours. So, too, does the anti-literary philistinism that believes literature exists only to consolidate social relations, to uphold the values of citizenship, to blow the trumpet for fraternity. The idea of play as a release from the world of necessities and tasks was not at all congenial to Rousseau, though his conception of *mœurs* was more nuanced than Calvin's. Play was corrupting: Geneva had been so organised that men would never be idle, and therefore tempted to sin. Rousseau thought that people could live well only in self-sufficient villages – similar in size to Aristotle's ideal ancient city of a five thousand people able to hear the address of an orator – and it must have troubled him that for long periods he himself had no refuge anywhere, certainly not in Geneva. 'Cities,' he wrote, 'are the abyss of the human species.' Yet the great solitary was gripped by dreams of civic unity. What kind of mystic *polis* could Rousseau live in? Aristotle never mentions contracts when discussing his polity, whereas Rousseau, like all autarkic individualists, was an extreme contractarian (of the kind who thrives in a market society). Isaiah Berlin called him 'one of the most sinister and most formidable enemies of liberty in the whole history of modern thought,' and yet the procession that escorted his remains from their initial resting place at Ermenonville to the Pantheon was led by a captain of the United States Navy carrying the Stars and Stripes. Sociological realism might not have been Rousseau's forte, but here he stands disowned by his interpreters as the first apologist of unfreedom *and* an impossibly romantic anarchist. His personal tastes were frugal and he wrote more than once about the joys of a simple meal of fruit, cheese and bread. These were his communion articles for that melting of the inner self into the mystery of the great outdoors. And when the world threatens to disturb that repose, especially the social world, there is always the refuge of self-mastery. Many of his core beliefs were Stoic. His opera in the style of Pergolesi, *Le Devin du village* (The Village Soothsayer), portrayed the kind of simple and sincere culture that a later audience would see again through the eyes of Gretchen in

Goethe's *Faust*; a sophisticated court audience including Louis XV and Madame Pompadour lapped it up when it was first performed at Fontainebleau in 1752. Mozart was to borrow the plot for his *Bastien und Bastienne*. Rousseau slipped back to Paris rather than meet the King and have honours thrust upon him, for his conscience as a 'reformed man' made it clear to him that he could no longer be a person of integrity if he was in receipt of a pension. He was starting to be swayed by the arguments of his own books. The ostensible reason for avoiding the royal summons was his chronic bladder problem, probably some kind of urethral stricture, which plagued him in the latter part of his life. Rousseau abandoned the composition of music after the *querelle des bouffons* set off in 1753 by his polemic *Letter on French Music*, which claimed that French music (as represented by its spokesman Rameau) was corrupt. Rousseau came up with a new system of musical notation by means of which notes and pitch could be represented numerically: convention and tradition could – indeed ought to – be overthrown by the court of the individual sensibility, in this case his. Rousseau's system was never adopted, being plainly inadequate for the task which musical notation had *evolved* to deal with; but he couldn't leave unbroken the cake of custom. The English sense of modernity with its trust in the inherited wisdom of social institutions, that living record of the way in which past errors have been overcome, is utterly at odds with Rousseau's urge to reform our imperfect social arrangements. Because he comes across genuine authority not vested in any single person Rousseau seeks to challenge it. The only book he deems suitable for the education of Emile is the story of the shipwrecked Robinson Crusoe on his desert island: 'The surest way to raise him above prejudice and to found his judgements on the true relations of things, is to put him in the place of a solitary man, and to judge all things as they would be judged by such a man in relation to their own utility.' These are the outlines of the Cartesian effort to live every day as if it were the first. Legitimacy (which the eighteenth century regarded, almost unanimously, as deriving from nature) would be the key problem for any future participatory democracy; hence the endless search, more speculative than scientific, for origins. That was the presumption of the French Revolution, as Burke observed: it wanted to refound social institutions, not modify, like the English Revolution, existing historical experience. Politics gives us human understanding, not the other way around. For all its belief in progress, the nineteenth century fairly swarmed with thinkers who made valiant attempts to untangle the mystery of first things; and despite its keen anticipation of the future the twentieth proved to be the most retrospective century of them all. But that is what 'originality' originally meant. Just as the lowly Hebrews and not their Egyptian masters had come up with the first religion, so the amateur historian might devise the first modern anthropology. The pursuit of the archaic would be the next century's metaphor for its own modernity. Rousseau's comments on French music, its preference for the spatial properties of harmony over unison melody, which he saw as music's real driving force, was to lead him to make similarly unflattering comments about the French language in his *Essay on the Origin of Language*, published only after his death. It was an argument taken up by Herder and Goethe after they had been exposed to the thrilling tones of Shakespeare and Ossian: *Sturm und Drang* was launched in Strasburg in 1770 in explicit reaction to the 'lifelessness' of classicising French drama. 'O das verwünschte Wort: Classisch!...' as Herder lamented, in his fragment on the new German literature, blasting the idea of the classical as 'confounded'. The refusal to imitate: that was the clarion call of genius, astounded at its own originality. The locus of reality was moving inwards; and as it did, the old idea of the human soul warring with its sinful nature surrendered to a new but external dualism: between the blameless self and a corrupt society. Joseph Joubert wrote, after reading Rousseau: 'In his books we learn how to be discontented with everything outside of ourselves.' To the generations after Rousseau it seemed self-evident that what needed reforming was society, not the person: this is the *incipit* of modern politics, especially in its democratic and progressive forms. One day pious policy-makers would even get round, as they have at the start of the twenty-first century, to addressing God's scandalous error in allowing evil into the creation at all. Most contemporary Europeans, who remain firmly Augustinian in their understanding of international relations, recoil from politicians who promise to remove evil from the world in the name of the good. Being a born-again country, on the other hand, the United States goes down with the fever of recurrent innocence, and the continuing need to push ever further back the border between civilisation and the wild men of the undergrowth. But make no mistake – Europeans have explored the ruthlessness of sentiment, too. It took the Marquis de Sade to tell us, in *Philosophy in the Boudoir*, that benevolence is more obviously a vice of pride than a true virtue of the soul. Good deeds in the modern world are speculative, like all other actions. Rousseau is guilty of that modern delusion of seeing Christianity secularised solely in terms of its virtues, though he thought future men might turn to God again and beg for a clean slate: 'Give us back our innocence, ignorance and poverty, for that alone can make us happy and precious in Thy sight.' His anti-intellectualism disturbed his philosopher friends in Paris. They could go the distance with him in provocation, but they hesitated to embrace his taste for the dramatic in landscape: 'I must have torrents, rocks, pine trees, black forests, mountains, steep paths to climb and descend, precipices around all to make me feel fear.' The snow-covered mountains of the Valais rising south of Geneva were to form the natural cathedral for his residual deism. These mountain folk were considered dolts in Paris; Rousseau thought them the salt of the earth. On the whole he enjoyed being in Paris, but disapproved of it on principle. He once wrote to a Genevese friend: 'In Paris there is a certain purity of taste, a certain rightness of style that you will never find in the provinces.' According to himself he became more affable and good-natured in the countryside; his friends and patrons including Mme d'Epinay, who moved him into a little lodge near Montmorency (the Hermitage), claimed that solitude made him disagreeable. Diderot's quip in *The Natural Son* that 'only the bad man is alone' provoked a serious falling out with his best friend. Dressed in his now familiar Armenian robes and caftan, he told the young James Boswell when he visited him in his Swiss exile of Môtiers in 1772, that 'Mankind disgusts me... And my housekeeper tells me that I am in far better humour on the days when I have been alone than on those when I have been in company.' His eureka moment on the way to visit Diderot in Vincennes prison had revealed to him that liberty and authority could not be in conflict, being one and the same: good things must in the nature of things be in harmony (the dubious premiss of all eighteenth-century thinking). His concept of the general will would prove to be a Procrustean justification for forcing people to accept what they want *because* they don't know it, although something resembling the general will had long being active in history. Rousseau's hope, and the hope of all Romantic politics, was of obtaining an enlightened people which had learned to rule itself: it was the Enlightenment thinkers who preferred enlightened despots. Rousseau detested the very idea of revolution, but after his death his writings served as a rule-book for Robespierre, that man of 'profound sincerity' who ended up in the literal sense of the word a hypocrite, the leading player at the Festival of the Supreme Being of 8 June 1793 when he held a bouquet of flowers in one hand and an ear of wheat in the other. His understudy, Saint-Just, became a secular inquisitor who resolved to impose terror as the necessary path to the virtuous utopia sketched out by Rousseau. In the period from 1789 to 1800 a new printing of *The Social Contract* was being rushed off the presses roughly every four months. Jacobinism was Calvinism in the still plainer guise of rational morality: it was still a matter of the elect governing the reprobate. Sade wrote to his wife from his prison cell, on learning that he had been refused a volume of Rousseau: 'Rousseau is a salutary author for me. Jean-Jacques is to me what *The Imitations of Christ* is to you.' Rousseau had shown him that the 'real self' revealed by sincerity need not be bound by the kind of patrician civility required for a common political life; quite the reverse. Thus was born authenticity, and Lionel Trilling reminds us, in his ancestry of the word, what is habitually hidden behind, and at stake in, modern culture: '*Authenteo*: to have full power over; also, to commit a murder. *Authentes*: not only a master and a doer, but also a perpetrator, a murderer, even a self-murderer, a suicide.' Unshakeably convinced of his own goodness, Rousseau distrusted the princes and powers of this world, despising them for good measure too. But Rousseau was too worthy a citizen to detonate society in the name of violent self-expression. Ethics for him was coextensive with politics: like Machiavelli, he thought little of Christian otherworldliness, insisting that what linked the citizen to his *polis* was a genuine fiduciary bond whereas the union in Christ between the individual and humankind was a purely ideal relation. Yet Jean-Jacques' 'inner voice', the commandments of his spontaneous moral instinct, his sense of being unspotted by the world, were moved by the figure on the cross. The noble savage, too, was no longer just a personage to be admired or regretted, but a source of deep feelings. Only a few years after Rousseau's death we find the first explicit expression of this revolted sensibility (and the assumption that those afflicted with 'liberal guilt' ought to assuage it by speaking out on behalf of the wretched of the earth) when Chateaubriand visits Niagara, as reported in his *Essay on the Revolutions* (1797): snubbed by a young Indian brave who refuses his attempts to engage him in conversation, the French writer declares: 'How grateful I was to him for not liking me! I seemed to read in his heart the history of all the woes which the Europeans had brought upon his fatherland.' A new tone of self-reproach has entered a civilising discourse that does everything to disguise its own superiority: it will be Chateaubriand's culture and not that of the young American Indian which will give currency to the term 'ethnocentrism' (the concept was coined by Montaigne in his famous chapter on the cannibals) and create audiences to enjoy the art of the formerly despised. After all, the truly ethnocentric, those tribes who call themselves 'Man', are too naïvely self-absorbed to wonder how they stand in relation to others. Rousseau, we might agree, is the first sponsor of Third Worldism. In contrast to David Hume, who saw nothing very much to detain him in the Middle Ages (or, indeed, in the country of his birth), the Romantic school found something of value in every society: Walter Scott's novels alone are testimony to this intense nostalgia. Rousseau had discovered the absolute value of the modern concern for the victim: asymmetrical relations are illegitimate. The paradox was that in order to marshall that power he had to grovel in the dust for the greater glory of his victimhood. First fascinate the disinterested; then transform them into persecutors. 'God is just: he knows that I suffer and that I am innocent.' Entire populations have followed where Rousseau led: right-wingers used to castigate those who spoke Rousseau's language as whiners and losers but now even the most powerful country on earth portrays itself as a victim. And it doesn't stop there. Soon it may be possible to be a martyr simply by dint of having been born; though the crying truth is that if we are victims at all, it is of our overweening sense of entitlement. What Rousseau couldn't have anticipated is that the rush to adopt the victimary stance could in the long run become a greater threat to civilised order than victimisation itself, being itself a furtive form of victimising. Once the Master plays the victim all sense of history has been lost. It was therefore a great jest of history that the citizen of Geneva should have been alive at the same time as the *seigneur de Ferney*: Rousseau was insensible to the dart of Voltaire's mockery, except when it stung. He blurts it out, and Voltaire scorns him the more. His is the anti-satirical principle in French culture, its deadly earnest: he has nothing of the gaiety of Mirabeau's 'fond gaillard'. He was never able to laugh at himself, which is surely one of the supreme virtues introduced in the name of a higher conception of Christian folly by Erasmus and Rabelais. This innocence in contradiction, this saying *yes* and *no* with one breath, as Nietzsche wrote in *The Case of Wagner*: Rousseau was its initiator. Thoroughly familiar with the old and modern plans for utopia, he dropped all the mechanics for real-

A Critical Consciousness

Heinrich von Kleist

Heinrich von Kleist's life was 'rich in incidents of being unlike'. Born into a military family in 1777, he soldiered in his teens and left the army in 1799 as a second lieutenant. He engaged in a brief, intense period of study, principally of Kant and Rousseau, that was to provide him with much of the intellectual material he would mull over in his writing career – a bare nine years. It was a time of social unrest: Napoleonic levies went from one side of the continent to the other; in their wake went Kleist. A stay in Switzerland produced his early dramas, an event memorialised a hundred years later by Robert Walser in his story about the idyllic summer spent by Kleist on the Delosea Island in the River Aare near Thun where 'he wants to abandon himself to the entire catastrophe of being a poet'. Kleist considered fighting both for and against the French, and travelled to Boulogne in the hope of invading England in 1803; in the years that followed he was arrested more than once by the French on suspicion of spying. At the end of his life, despairing of that 'damned consul', he offered patriotic support to Prussia with his drama *The Prince of Homburg*. Venturing into journalism, he edited a literary journal called *Phöbus* with his friend Adam Müller; twelve issues appeared. His later attempt was one of the first daily newspapers to be produced in Germany, *Berliner Abendblätter*; it lasted six months. Both of these journals contained pieces in a variety of short forms, some of them never translated: geographical reports from Heligoland or news of Haydn's death, classical dialogues, verse like his bellicose and patriotic *Germania an ihre Kinder* or the weird anecdotes and snatches of casuistry that read like undeveloped notes for stories, one for instance from 1803 about a mother in St Omer who tried to save her children from attack by a rabid dog: she buries her children only to die from the disease herself a few days later. He even wrote a draft patent for a 'Bombenpost', and his startling one-page Hesiod redivivus, which upholds the Stoic belief in the world getting worse and worse (in flat contradiction to Kant's vision of rational progress), ends thus: 'These peoples [the Greeks and Romans] made a beginning with the heroic epoch which is undoubtedly the highest that can be attained; when heroes of humane or civic virtue died out, they created them in poetry; and when they could no longer create heroes in poetry, they devised the rules for it; and when they got tangled in the rules, they abstracted the philosophy of the wisdom of the world itself; and when they had done with that, they became evil.'

Shortly after the collapse of *Berliner Abendblätter*, Kleist, who had made a habit of buttonholing his friends and demanding whether they would die with him, formed a pact with Müller's former mistress, Henriette Vogel, who had been diagnosed a few months before as having incurable breast cancer. He shot her, and then himself, one November afternoon in 1811, on a hilltop near the Wannsee. It was his most fully accomplished action. 'For the noblest thing in life,' he had written to his sister Ulrike from Switzerland all those years before, 'is, after all, our ability nobly to discard it.' A day later, at the autopsy in Potsdam, things reverted to type: when the pathologists tried to open his cranium the blade of the fretsaw snapped.

Shortly before his suicide he had written a farewell note to Müller's sister. Its tone was one of ecstatic happiness: 'as our two souls like two cheerful balloonists rise over the world'. It is a phrase that has the emotional swoon of a Kleistian tale itself: feet that had a moment ago been on firm ground are, in a moment of distraction, trampling the thinnest air. Many of his characters, like Piachi, the father in *The Foundling*, are deeply confused about their motives; or do the right thing, like the honest horse-trader Kohlhaas – 'the very model of a good citizen' – in the famous novella *Michael Kohlhaas*, but immoderately. Since the world fails to uphold his 'inalienable' rights (two of his best horses and his stableman have been mishandled), Kohlhaas takes up arms to vindicate himself, and turns his private grievance into a public disaster. He possesses the two most admirable of the cardinal virtues, courage and justice; what he notably lacks is prudence, which, by being conspicuously absent from his actions, leads to disaster: even the personal intervention of Martin Luther is unable 'to press Kohlhaas back under the curb of human order'. His absolute sense of being in the right has something of the terrifying quality of Kant's insistence on telling the truth as 'an *unconditional duty* which holds in all circumstances' – without regard as to the possible consequences. Kohlhaas loses his head, figuratively speaking, and allows justice as an absolute to triumph over life itself; and then he loses it again, this time to the executioner's axe.

The innocent Littegarde in *The Duel*, by contrast, is so pressed by circumstantial evidence, and the outcome of a trial by combat, that she starts to believe she is guilty as charged, since 'God is truthful and never errs'. The problem is: she *knows* she is as innocent 'as the corpse of a nun who died in the vestry while taking the veil'. Kleist is fascinated by the arbitrary, by legality severed by the stroke of a pen. *The Earthquake in Chile* portrays a society in such duress that it refuses to accept contingency: desperate to make sense of natural evil (the earthquake) a mob kills a baby it believes to have been born of unholy union, preferring to be party to a form of evil it can at least acknowledge rather than accept the radical lack of meaning represented by the earthquake. Brilliant interrogation scenes show his talent for butting in, and asking awkward questions. His work reminds us that the director's 'Cut!' is a kind of syncope. Many films and television series have capitalised – unwittingly, I suppose – on the massive dramatic role he found for the Hand of Fate, which often intervenes, in a moment of desperate urgency and strain, as in *Michael Kohlhaas* or *The Marquise of O*, as a fainting attack. These losses of posture are not the swoon of melodrama. Things don't drop out of mind; mind asserts its prerogative, and floats free of intolerable reality. And if that doesn't happen, consciousness is unseated by the sting in the tail that so often serves as the closing gambit in *film noir*. At the end of *Amphitryon* Jupiter owns up to being the eponym's body-double, and restores Alcmene to her husband; but Kleist – unlike Molière, from whom he cribbed – puts Alcmene so prominently at centre-stage that the moral implications of her duped act of adultery loom larger than Jupiter's sublime announcement that she will bear a son (Hercules). One of his very few upbeat endings, at the end of *The Prince of Homburg*, a play about a dysfunctional son in a mili-tarised society, growls like Shakespeare's Bohemian bear returning to stage: 'in the dust with every enemy of Brandenburg'.

If ever a literary oeuvre seems like reason nodding off on the job, as in Goya's sinister *capricho*, and waking up to find itself menaced by all sorts of succubi bearing paternity claims, it is Kleist's. He was one of the first of a line of German writers whose inwardness was intense enough to dissolve the weak bonds of his society, while making his own existence untenable. Some of that inner turmoil must have derived from his reading of the epistemological short-comings Kant attempted to get into categorical shape in his *Critique of Pure Reason*: as Coleridge asked in a different but not unrelated context, if sense comes only through our senses how are we able to distinguish an ordinary day from a delirium? (Tricked out with a different vocabulary this question still taunts psychology.) Here is Kleist explaining his conviction that our faculties are not quite up to the job in a cataclysmic letter of March 1801 to Wilhelmine von Zenge, a general's daughter who had become his fiancée: 'If people all had green lenses instead of eyes they would be bound to think that the things they see through them *are* green – and they would never be able to decide whether the eye shows them things as they are or whether it isn't adding something to them belonging not to them but to the eye. It is the same with our minds. We cannot decide whether what we call truth is truly truth or whether it only seems so to us. If the latter then the truth we gather here is nothing after death – and all our striving to acquire something of our own that will go with us even into the grave, is in vain... Oh Wilhelmine, though your own heart may not be pierced by this thought do not think me ridiculous that I feel myself wounded deep in my innermost life by it. My highest and only goal has sunk and now I have none –'

Even as order and paternalism struggled to assert themselves in the private and public life of the nineteenth century, Kleist was introducing scenes of mob violence, cannibalism, and less than benevolent fathers. But he would be a less interesting author if he were merely an iconoclast. He tried to follow Enlightenment precepts; and his humanism is still lively enough to convince us that he subscribed, in part, to some of its ideals. (The motto tacked to Goya's etching actually reads in full: 'Imagination abandoned by reason produces impossible monsters: united with her, she is the mother of the arts and the source of her wonders.') Extremism was his nature: the letters to Wilhelmine von Zenge are moral exercises in the German schoolmasterly tradition distracted by flurries of enthusiasm. Years later, offering an excerpt of *Penthesilea* for his blessing to the Goethe who had already, and unsuccessfully, staged his comedy *The Broken Jug*, Kleist wrote to the older writer in terms both abject and provocative: 'on the "knees of my heart"'. Putting scare quotes around his gesture of meekness suggests Kleist knew in advance what Goethe's response would be. And if Goethe emerges from their encounter as cold and indifferent (after 1811, Goethe's name was taboo in the Kleist family), we have to remember that the older writer had committed himself to holding on a short rein what Kleist allowed himself to be dragged bodily behind. Kleist's tragedies were a threat to the tenuous emotional balance of Goethe's life in Weimar, so much so that Goethe could never see him as anything other than 'a Nordic phantom of acrimony and spleen'. Goethe turned his back on him, Nietzsche wrote, because of his sense of tragic sense of life – and there was no remedy for tragedy. '[Goethe] himself was conciliatory and curable.'

Kleist's stories demonstrate his attachment to a formal, rather legalistic language – the mould for Franz Kafka's urgent yet detached style. Perhaps the best description for them is *tableaux vivants.* They are not static, however: abrupt shifts of perspective and pace show how much Kleist learned from writing for the stage. And while his characters often seem in a trance, Kleist himself had a journalist's fascination for bare facts. These he reports on with a cool and clinical detachment, much like Gottfried Benn a century later, in the anecdotes and essays he published along with his major stage works. They amplify his fascination with modified states of consciousness, and suggest why his characters faint at dramatic junctures. In *Michael Kohlhaas*, it is not the protagonist who faints just before execution at what is the climax of the story, but the emissary from the Elector of Saxony with the blue and white plumed hat who expects him to reveal all: Kohlhaas takes the crucial manuscript – a paper ball of original knowledge – and swallows it in a final act of internalisation. 'Reflection', a bare page long, forestalls Auden's parvenu motto 'act from thought should quickly follow': 'the proper time for reflection, let me tell you,' writes Kleist, 'is not *before* you act, but *after.*' Live first, think after; for what a man takes to be the good is decided by how he acts (and not what determines that action). Heroes don't hesitate; not Kleist's at any rate. His exhortation suggests that an awareness of being unable to take acting for granted demeaned him in his own eyes. No premeditated act could be noble. It left a bad taste in the mouth. (It is not without pertinence that the Nazis, in a régime conspicuous for its cult of the Will, tried to shroud reflection in the animal spontaneity of what they called 'thinking with the blood'.) Nobody will be surprised to learn that Kleist was a stammerer; 'stammering' derives from the Latin verb that means 'to be in two minds'.

Kleist's best known work is his essay 'The Puppet Theatre', itself a string of anecdotes inside a fable about self-awareness as a performer's greatest disability. It has since been turned into a shibboleth by 'body theorists', though Kleist's wooden cyborg moves in a quite respectable intellectual tradition, Francis Bacon's notion of the Great Instauration: that the prelapsarian condition cannot be recovered except in the form of an inanimate object like the puppet ('something rather mindless') or through God's perfect consciousness. The very word *grace*, with its nice ambiguity, suggests as much: it is a rightness of physical coordination *and* a mark of divine favour. This idea has Pansophist credentials too, and probably came to Kleist from reading Leibniz: Adam possessed total knowledge but lost it at the time of the Fall, whereupon mankind was forced to set out on the present long slog through history to recoup what had been carelessly left hanging on the Tree of Knowledge. But isn't it in the nature of our experience, the sceptical reader might ask, that acquired knowledge provides new ethical problems to the solution of which it contributes almost nothing? If man succeeds in *infinitely* expanding his consciousness, Kleist's narrator says; for this will be the last chapter of the world's history. A few years before Kleist wrote his story the philosopher Lichtenberg penned a wonderful aphorism that goes in the opposite direction, ousting the expected adjective 'stupidest' with 'cleverest'. 'To err is *human* also in so far as animals seldom or never err – or at least only the cleverest of them do so.' Error enters proprioception, in which animals and God are infallible, by the agency of human or near-human reason; if we were truly aware of our own bodies we would never be able to walk, let alone dance. And what is dancing but a dare not to fall? Syncope is a term in music, as well as medicine. Kleist's bemused comment on self-consciousness and alienation, and his essay's register of astonishments served as a choreography for much of Rilke's *Duino Elegies*, especially the Fourth with its meditation on the blissful childish space readied for the coming of a pure event – 'between world and toy'.

Not unrelatedly, in 'On the Gradual Production of Thoughts Whilst Speaking', Kleist suggests that the text is always a little bit cleverer than its author: 'for it is not we who know things but preeminently a certain condition of ours which knows'. He is voicing the old idea of the writer as a vessel for the divine substance, and leading on to the individual-denying, will-evading thoughts of Schopenhauer's 'Sanskrit' philosophy (which has proved so appealing to contemporary cognitive neurologists); this may be compared to Milan Kundera's contrary (and naïve) assertion that the novelist should get another job if he isn't smarter than what he writes. It is in the nature of an utterance that it always potentially means *more* than its utterer intends.

While Kleist came to be hugely influential on the continent, not least for a generation of psychoanalysts, he has never been especially widely read in English. The industrious Carlyle wrote a first appreciation of the Tieck collected edition as early as 1827, but to Victorians his confidence in chaos would have seemed outlandishly histrionic and uncanny. Europe itself had to lose consciousness before Kleist made much sense. If 1914 was the vagus death of liberalism, it was only at the end of the 1950s that Kleist was properly 'rediscovered' in English, in Martin Greenberg's Penguin version. Now David Constantine, poet and Germanist, has taken pains to give us a literary Kleist, 'a writer we cannot do without'. One of his advantages of his omnibus collection is to reveal the parallels between different works. The theme of the Fall, for instance, links *The Puppet Theatre* and *The Broken Jug*, which is a brilliantly sustained verbal burlesque about a judge called Adam who tries to make the object of his cupidity, a girl called Eve, take the rap for his fall (out of her window, as it happens). Constantine is exceptionally faithful to the shape of Kleist's syntax, aiming for 'an English haunted and affected by the strangeness of the original'. This can result in a strained, slightly antiquarian feel: in the unfolding of the novella *Michael Kohlhaas*, Kleist's convolutions and suspensions occasionally make the going hard in English: 'the year was almost up before from Saxony even any response to the complaint he had lodged there let alone any resolution of it reached him'. The translator is right to opt for complexity, but while syntax may well be a figurative instance of how things hang together, image-making – 'the light from hell' – is just as tenaciously at work as a means of displacing causality, in which the 'truth' of syntax labours among a welter of metaphorical distortions: Elvire's fixation on the painting of the dead Colino in 'The Foundling' is a strikingly graphic example of this. Nothing is more typical of Kleist's writing than its ability to allow metaphor its head, to let his characters 'talk past one another' to a conclusion that is not necessarily the one sought. The volume concludes with a few of Kleist's 228 letters, mostly from his early period, which convey a strong impression of a young man struggling to balance the claims of reason with his own more radical doubts.

Although it omits 'Penthesilea', his bloodthirsty reinterpretation of the Amazon legend, this new translation of Kleist's stories and three key plays provides a compelling view of a misfit genius who, in one of his last notes, sounds almost expansive: 'the world is a strange set-up'.

Being Nice to Nietzsche

In April 1888, after years of stateless wandering across the continent, Friedrich Nietzsche stopped in Turin, a baroque urban planning project set out in its magnificent detail by the architect Guarino Guarini in the late seventeenth century. He took to it like no European city he had come across before. From the cheap lodgings he found with an Italian family in the historic centre of the city 'opposite the grand Palazzo Carignano of 1680, five paces from the great Portici and the Piazza Castello and the post office!,' he marvels in almost daily letters to his friends in the north about Turin's quiet, stately streets and the bracing wind, the theatre and the soft colours, the Galleria Subalpina orchestra striking up another overture. He can see beyond the city into the world of snow. The streets seem to run straight into the Alps. 'It is the *air* that does it – dry, exhilarating, happy.' He stands in awe of the Mole Antonelliana which, with its 165 metres of wrought iron on brick and granite, was the literal pinnacle of the great Piedmontese brick-building tradition: 'perhaps the most ingenious building ever constructed' reminded him 'of nothing so much as [his] *Zarathustra*'. He rediscovers the music of Bizet ('*tutto Torino carmenizzato!*') and Rossini's operas, deliciously light relief after Wagner. The restaurants and coffee houses are marvellous; the ice cream only thirty centimes a scoop; the streets clean and orderly; everything breathes an atmosphere of 'aristocratic tranquillity'. 'I find the inhabitants pleasant and I feel at home,' he tells his old friend Overbeck. It is where he writes his ultimate books, *Ecce Homo* (finished in three weeks), *Nietzsche contra Wagner* and the *Dithyrambs of Dionysus.* In a letter to his composer friend Peter Gast (Heinrich Köselitz) he describes it as 'the first place where I am *possible!*' A hundred and fifty years earlier, Jean-Jacques Rousseau had walked to Turin to consolidate his conversion to Catholicism, and had been similarly enchanted by the city: Mass at the Chapel Royal was effectively an orchestral concert. He, too, had thought the city would provide him with a stage on which he could indulge the 'hope of soon becoming a person worthy of [him]self'.

When Nietzsche returned to the city in September, after passing the summer in the mountains at Sils Maria, the elation had kiltered. Turin was now sanatorium and labyrinth, though bathed in a miracle of light: 'autumn here was a permanent Claude Lorraine – I often asked myself how such a thing could be possible on earth. Strange! For the misery of the summer up there, compensation did come. There we have it: the old God is still alive...' He gets a tailor to cut him a new suit, and revels in being received everywhere as a distinguished foreign visitor: the man facing him in the mirror has never looked better or younger. He dares to go walking without his glasses, and is gratified to observe young women turning to stare at him. He tells his former patron Malwida von Meysenbug – *verehrteste Freundin!* – that he has been 'suffering from a surfeit of righteousness'. He is waiting to reign in glory, 'the first and freest spirit of Europe', the philosopher whose writings 'will sunder the history of mankind'. He wants to shed a little light and terror as regards himself; the tone of his work, he tells Franz Overbeck, is 'one of gay detachment fraught with a sense of destiny'. Turin, he informs Meta von Salis, is not a place to leave. Nowhere else has he ever felt that the *nuances* were so well understood. He says Yes, he says it again and louder; nothing happens. Bismarck receives a copy of *Ecce Homo* in December and Nietzsche writes to Carl Fuchs that its publication should be accompanied by a declaration of war: 'the next few years will stand the world on its head: since the old God has abdicated, I shall from now on rule the world'. The world is stone-deaf: writing to his publisher in Leipzig in an attempt to buy back the rights to his books (he had never received any royalties), he tells him that he has the distinction 'of publishing the foremost human being of all millennia'. His mind parcels itself up into various personalities: Voltaire, Dionysus, Buddha, even two contemporary French criminals he had read about in the *Journal des Débats*. His last, disinhibited letter to his 'great teacher' Jacob Burckhardt accuses the old historian of 'private egoism' and cultivating an aesthetic detachment from the world (this was precisely what Nietzsche had tried to do with his famous adage about the world only being justifiable as an 'aesthetic phenomenon' – and here was evidence of its failure, this moral act of sacrifice!). He would have preferred, he tells Burckhardt, to have retained his professorship in Basle rather than play God – a god 'condemned to entertain the next eternity with bad jokes'. On 3 January 1889 he is reported to have embraced a mistreated cab-horse in the street, a theatrical gesture not unlike the dream of Raskolnikov, in which his younger self embraces an old mare which has been drunkenly battered to death by her peasant owner; bystanders promptly called the police. He was barely lucid. Years earlier he had written in his essay *Schopenhauer as Educator*: 'more profoundly feeling people have at all times felt sympathy for the animals'. Pity, Zarathustra once said, was his 'deepest abyss'.

Alerted by Burckhardt, his old friend Overbeck took the train a few days later from Basle, and found Nietzsche correcting proofs on the couch in his lodgings. Landlord and lady reported incessant piano-playing and nude dancing upstairs. With a dentist escort, they took the train back to Basle; Nietzsche sleepy with chloral tried to take off his clothes, talked to strangers and crooned the gondola song from *Nietzsche contra Wagner*. He was wearing his landlord's *papalina*, a nightcap with tassle. From Dr Wille's psychiatric clinic in Basle (a name no novelist would dare to invent) he was taken back to the asylum in Jena, his mother's house in the old ecclesiastical town of Naumburg where he had spent his youth, and the chalk landscapes near his old school. He had never entirely liberated himself emotionally from the stifling protestant atmosphere of Naumburg: now he was back within its actual walls. He lived on, a man who happened to bear his name, in a state of total incapacity. For another eleven etiolated years he was cared for by his mother and his sister Elisabeth who was to become not only the jealous administrator of his fame but the first of his vulgarisers. 'I don't like my mother,' he had written in 1883, 'and to hear my sister's voice is disagreeable to me; their company has always made me ill.' It might have been Friedrich who wrote the excerpts that were later published as *The Will to Power* but it was Elisabeth – 'the llama' as he nicknamed her – who counterfeited them as his last words in the biography that she saw through the presses between 1895 and 1904.

Nietzsche's act of 'self-criticism' in Turin is such a pathetically signal moment of modernity in crisis that Lesley Chamberlain must have had some doubts about addressing it all. His descent into personal Bedlam has been tackled by a large number of scholars, all of different ideological persuasions (something the contradictions in Nietzsche's unsystematic writings notoriously provide licence for), and several novelists have flogged to the bone that incident with the horse, but few English-speaking writers have tried to 'befriend' him in the passionate, committed way that Chamberlain has (she calls herself the 'lingering friend'). 'It is my fate to have to be the first *decent* human being,' Nietzsche wrote in the 'Why I am a Destiny' chapter of *Ecce Homo*; it is this humane version of the great browbeater that she develops. She is largely successful in doing so, despite an occasional tendency to yield to the novelistic – insinuating beyond the known facts, though it may well be all but true that Nietzsche never had an 'erotic friendship with a woman' – or to interpose such archly melodramatic phrases as 'I continue to live with Nietzsche then in that Dionysian spirit' or 'Yet, oh gods in heaven protect him, he still fell at Wagner's feet...'

Chamberlain quivers with the emotional needs which kept Nietzsche writing, even as his *Innerlichkeit* crushed him with despair – a man innocent of politics and social life, and in pursuit of the self-knowledge whose very lack was bound up with the institutional life he had turned his back on: if his former colleagues, the classical philologists, had really felt the realities of the world they studied they would have shrivelled in horror. (It didn't stop Nietzsche himself issuing calls for the resumption of human sacrifice.) His is, after all, a well-documented life: in reconstructing his last sane nine months she has been able to lean on the hugely detailed *Kritische Studienausgabe* and the Colli-Montinari edition of letters addressed to Nietzsche as well as his own bulletins to a wide circle of correspondents. Part of that context is, of course, Turin. With its veiled light sources and spatial harmony, the voluminously felt city – later to serve as a backdrop for Giorgio de Chirico and his *pittura metafisica*, Cesare Pavese and the level-headed Primo Levi (who didn't care at all for Nietzsche's shrill and hectoring tone) – is as much the book's subject as the philosopher. Turin was also home, when Nietzsche *was* there, to the criminologist Cesare Lombroso, though Chamberlain doesn't mention the rather ironic presence of the pioneering criminal anthropologist: Lombroso would surely have interested himself in a man plotting to overthrow the entire world order – had he heard of Nietzsche.

The 'royal residential city' also brings out a theme that runs through Nietzsche's creative years: how the Enlightenment project itself ultimately contributes to his credibility. Perhaps he felt that affinity himself when he called Turin a place that made him *possible*. Chamberlain registers the music of Nietzsche's German prose ('Before me one did not know what can be done with the German language'), his huge imaginative effort to get beyond strenuousness and 'sweaty' German values to 'a bold and exuberant intellectuality that runs *presto*'. The Greeks, he had written, were superficial out of profundity. In fact, his philosophy had to do a lot of sweating to aspire to the light, divine, mercurial thinking he valued so highly: Nietzsche is the Luther of the age of psychology. Thinking is what the body does – though as Martha Nussbaum has pointed out, for a philosopher who so conspicuously celebrates the body he appears wholly unconcerned with its material needs.

Heidegger, who talked a lot about the body too, can be accused of the same high-mindedness.

Together with the poignancy of Nietzsche's last few conscious months — and there can be little doubt that the *physical* basis of his dementia was tertiary syphilis — there is the uncanny way intellectual acuity continued to cohabit with a disintegrating psyche right up to the last few days. 'Sing a new song for me,' he wrote to Köselitz on 4 January, 'the world is transfigured and all the heavens rejoice.' He signed that thumbnail sketch of *The Birth of Tragedy* 'The Crucified One'. It was a tale of two men, and two cities. Overbeck, who came down from Basle — where it had all started when Nietzsche resigned his chair in 1879 — to rescue him in Turin on 8 January, comments in his memoirs that he could never quite resist the thought that his illness was simulated, and for several critics Nietzsche's behaviour suggests analogies to Hamlet's. There has hardly been a writer in the last two hundred years who hasn't felt Hamlet's predicament to be his own at some point, but none has fallen into the hands of the living God like Nietzsche, a fate which, as René Girard reminds us, is a dreadful one. Chamberlain cites his Burckhardt letter as a 'final plea for his worth as a Shakespearean fool to be considered', echoing Nietzsche's own description of buffoonery as a possible disguise for 'desperate, all-too-certain knowledge'. Why shouldn't we see Nietzsche as a fool for Christ? After feeling Dionysian for a while he tended to sign off as 'The Crucified'. The fool was unprotected. Nietzsche, in the end, was unequal to Zarathustra's call to overcome the spirit of revenge: his whole work is an accusation of an accusation. Only a poet might have avoided that bind; though the group of disciples who gathered around Stefan George and developed a 'party line' dedicated to 'the Master' brings even that supposition into question.

Nietzsche neglected to notice that his bright, clinical, hygienic deity Apollo had another face: as oppressor and flayer of Marsyas. And isn't there something of the Viennese doctor about Nietzsche? — forever diagnosing but short on therapy (schnapps was all they offered in the Vienna hospitals). Not that his philosophy took place under anything like clinically controlled conditions: the Superman went beyond good and evil, but as a populist demagogue of the most brutal kind. (A true Superman would be someone like Jesus, who, innocent of the need for Nietzsche's philosophy, would insist on telling others his kingdom was not of this world.) Nietzsche, like Dostoevsky, whose Grand Inquisitor turned up in Moscow in the 1930s, failed to foresee how explosively a moral-psychological grammar of catastrophe (and a heroics of self-overcoming empty of ethical content) would translate into practical politics. 'A dominant race will grow up only out of violent and terrible beginnings. Problem: *where are the barbarians of the twentieth century?*' Pascal, to whom Nietzsche owes much, could have told him that when men strive to be angels (supermen) they are just as likely to end up as beasts (submen). If some people can lift themselves above humanity, others can be safely excluded from its kind. Pascal could also have directed his attention to the fateful loss in his writings of the middle register, or as Chateaubriand called it: 'a moderation... without which everything is a lie'. Nietzsche's writings are so shrill with rhetorical one-upmanship as to be beyond what makes politics possible; and that, of course, is much of the problem. How could he call himself 'the last disciple of the philosopher Dionysus' when he must have known from his readings of Euripides that Dionysus, in his ability to accommodate all human passions, including the most ferocious homicidal frenzy, *is* the mob? Heraclitus, in one of his fragments (CXVI), even says that Hades (*aides* meant 'invisible' in the philosopher's Ionic dialect) and Dionysus are the same: what passes for enhanced vitality is, unbeknown to the bacchic celebrant, already psychic death.

Rigour – the kind of rigour which led Nietzsche to call Kant 'the Chinaman of Koenigsberg' – is a quality of mind that roused Nietzsche's suspicion: it seemed a mask of cowardice bound up with the need for certainty – but his suspicion itself is unthinkable without an altogether more positive and critical rigour. How could Nietzsche talk meaningfully about power without an intimate knowledge of the institutions set up to regulate it by appeal to a canon that determined its nature and scope? By what dint could he so consistently ridicule authority in others? Who, in what is an old problem of the German intellectual, constituted his public? (Nietzsche would surely be the last person to parrot Schiller, who, in 1784, declared 'the public is now everything to me – my preoccupation, my sovereign and my friend'.) Conversation, the supremely bourgeois value, seemed to Nietzsche the mark of an irremediable weakness. Only that 'damned soul' Max Stirner, psychopathic author of what is a grandiose parody of the subjective trend of Western individualism, *Der Einzige und sein Eigentum*, tried, in any similar way, to become a 'law unto himself'. Nietzsche's grand economy of self-preservation was built on a Schopenhauerian equation that self-evacuates, like the Cheshire cat from its smile: 'the species is everything, *one* is always none'. Similarly Nietzsche: music was the form in which we perceive 'the delight felt at the annihilation of the individual'. Is it this refusal of agency, even a most attenuated agency, that seems so suspect: Nietzsche took his own speculative freedom for granted, yet trying out ideas and their contraries, refashioning his life as a work of art could only have been possible within a liberal democracy (with the help of the University of Basle's modest pension plan). Even a century after the death of the master some of his French followers such as Gilles Deleuze and Michel Onfray still fail to appreciate just how important the market is in generating 'nomadic desire'. Indeed, it seems as if Nietzsche was foretelling not a struggle to the death between titanic ideas but the febrility of our present market society: 'become who you are' is the trademark slogan of the Prozac generation. No lifestyle choice can ever resemble an act of fate.

In the murk, which Goya had tried to paint at the other end of the nineteenth century, we find not Nietzsche's political programme, such as it was, but his *style*: radical negation that doesn't want to halt at No, disengagement from ordinary society, 'heroic' commitments. If Nietzsche's goad was a scripture, 'God shall vomit up the lukewarm', we need to ask why he called on Dionysus to bring back, rather than the weakened and internalised form of vengeance (*ressentiment*) he so detested, real carnage and slaughter. 'In times of painful tension and vulnerability, choose war: it hardens, it gives you muscles.' Had the terror of bloodshed become wholly unintelligible to the wealthy bourgeois civilisation of which Nietzsche was in so many respects a representative figure? If it had, the same can hardly be said of its twentieth-century extension. When democracy broke down in the 1930s it wasn't just the most cynical expression of the will-to-power (*der Wille zur Macht*) that flaunted itself, but a regressive tendency to put out the lights (*der Wille nur Nacht*) – the phrase comes from Ernst Weiss, Prague novelist and friend of Franz Kafka.

In the event, there was no haul back to lucidity for Nietzsche. His strategy for liberating the primitive sacred – G.K. Chesterton quipped that if God is great for Islam then Nietzsche merely upturns the formula and makes greatness his godhead – failed to bolster what often seems like a determination on his part to obliterate original sin, and in the century that he just lived into and described so unerringly well (having had a hand in writing it) walking along the mountain tops above the human fray has come to seem a pretty questionable aspiration. Nietzsche's primitivism was that eating from the Tree of Knowledge would make us conscious of our *innocence*, the ardent ability to be. It would be a state beyond guilt and sorrow, essentially a kind of unknowing. That, as Kleist wrote and Nietzsche surely took to heart, would be the last chapter of the history of the world, and is presumably why Chamberlain provides such a weighty subtitle to her book: the end of the future. But Nietzsche knew he couldn't escape his intensifications: Zarathustra had to step out as the *legislator* of freedom from the law. Victory didn't arrive, couldn't arrive, and madness arrived to wipe away doubt – and reason.

Harry Count Kessler, who helped finance the foundation run by Nietzsche's sister in Weimar, left a vivid description of the unmindful invalid recumbent in his sister's villa in Weimar: 'He was asleep on the sofa, his mighty head had sunk down and rightwards onto his chest, as if it were too heavy for his neck. His forehead was colossal; his great mane of hair is still dark-brown, like his shaggy, protruding moustache. Broad, dark brown lines beneath his eyes are cut deeply into his cheeks. One can still see in the lifeless, flaccid face a few deep folds cut there by his thought and will, but softened and getting smoothed out. His expression shows an infinite weariness. His hands are waxen, the veins a greenish violet, and a little swollen as they are on a corpse. The close air of a thunderstorm had tired him, and although his sister stroked him several times and fondly called him "darling, darling" he would not wake up. He did not resemble a patient or a lunatic, but rather a dead man.' Chamberlain is attempting in her book to do posthumously what so many young visitors to the benighted philosopher hoped to do while he was still alive: heal him by swaddling him in an adoring community. In so doing, she is actually subverting the signal insight of the philosopher who, somewhere in the thin pure air of Sils Maria, had grasped that being condemned to individuality was the worst pain of all. 'Life has proposed my duty to me,' he once wrote to a correspondent, 'with the terrible condition that I should fulfil that duty *in solitude.*'

It was his peculiar courage to endure this wound, done with a Swiss army knife in the Engadin high over the world: 'The last philosopher I call myself, for I am the last human being. No one speaks with me beside myself and my voice comes to me as the voice of one dying. With the beloved voice, with you the last remembered breath of human happiness, let me talk, even if only for another hour. Because of you, I delude myself as to my solitude and lie my way back to manifoldness and love, for my heart shies away from believing that love is dead. I cannot bear the icy shiver of solitude. It compels me to speak as though I were Two.'

That statement notwithstanding, empathy is not the right quality for approaching Nietzsche, who, in a letter of 1888, asked his future readers – 'monsters of curiosity' – not to side with him: 'a dose of curiosity, as if presented with some unfamiliar plant,

'excellent civil precepts and cautions', though aphorisms are often indifferent to civic virtues. Bacon called them a doctrine of scattered occasions. Yet most writers of aphorisms disclaim any overt preoccupation with the stylistic, with the *how* of what is said. That is the maxim, which is lapidary, at the service of society, and often pared down to a single phrase: the maxim has the force of law. That the maxim should have been popular in the age in which mathematics was held up as a model for cultivated expression is hardly a coincidence. François de la Rochefoucauld's disabused reflections are the achievement of a supreme stylist, and a man armed by the very elegance of his language: 'Self-love is the greatest of flatterers.' 'Nothing is rarer than true kindness; those who believe they possess it are usually only complacent or compliant.' 'We all have enough strength to endure the misfortunes of others.' 'Men wouldn't live long in society, if they didn't take each other in.' (The last gains an added dimension in English.) La Rochefoucauld was impervious to the acid of his own wit, while being recognisably one of those sociable men who, as Rousseau loudly complained, '[know] how to live only in the opinion of others'.

By the time the modern era comes along, the aphorism leaves natural history and enters literature: the aphorism has become self-conscious about language's own role in the shaping of its thought. The invention of that experimental form, the essay, by Montaigne ('come on, assay', Desdemona ill-advisedly urges Iago in Shakespeare's *Othello*) undoubtedly had something to do with this self-consciousness; and the novel idea that, once uncoupled from purpose, language could offer an apprenticeship in pleasure: the more written a culture the more philosophical its idea of play. Thoughts are nimble animals. 'I know nothing so contemptible as a mere paradox; a mere ingenious defence of the indefensible,' wrote G.K. Chesterton, who later defended Christianity as the religion which built its house not upon the rock, as recommended in Biblical parable, but upon paradox. The real father of paradox is not the Devil, but the Cretan liar: a phrase which calls itself into question is as human as it gets. 'An aphorism need not be true, but it should overtake truth,' wrote Karl Kraus, ' – it should get beyond it in one bound.' The word 'bound' in the original German, it is worth noting, is a beautifully apt but untranslatable pun, for it also means 'sentence'.

The aphorism turns on words: they are its Eros, pivot, illumination, and feral ambush.

It was another German writer, Friedrich Nietzsche, who took the aphorism to vertiginously new if oxygen-poor heights. He practised what he preached: if, as he insisted, the formal prolix pedantry of most philosophers was a camouflage for their passion, cunning and conceit, then the aphorism allowed him to turn his irony, reinforced by style, against the great system builders. 'We should neither conceal nor corrupt the actual way our thoughts come to us. The most profound and inexhaustible books will surely always have something of the aphoristic, abrupt quality of Pascal's *Pensées*.' Nietzsche had poor eyesight, and tended to recite to himself on his long walks, memorising what he would later write down. And he was deeply suspicious in any case of the allure of written language, for what was written gave readers an illusion of 'unity, identity, permanence, substance': he wanted words to be spoken 'in a loud voice: that is to say, with all the swellings, inflections and variations of key and changes in tempo, in which the ancient world took delight'. Yet the aphorism presents formidable difficulties, not least for a philosophical reading in an age of written texts; and as Walter Kaufmann has pointed out, Nietzsche's sketch of the style of decadence in *The Case of Wagner* may be the best critique of his own style: 'The word becomes sovereign and leaps out of the sentence, the sentence reaches out and obscures the meaning of the page, and the page comes to life at the expense of the whole – the whole is no longer a whole.' The truth of aphorisms does a lot of bounding and leaping: at some level we are still in the world of Pascal's wager.

On the mezzanine where I write in the hubbub of the family there is a small shelf set aside for collections of aphorisms; these books stand close to my writing desk because the aphorism is a form peculiarly and obviously suited to the second reading. Aphorisms are themselves a double look at language. If I can't write, I read aphorisms, hoping they will startle me unbidden into thought. 'Which is it?' asked Nietzsche; 'is man only God's mistake or God man's?' Elias Canetti abandoned the great Balzacian novel sequence he wanted to write in his youth (only Balzac could have written Balzac's novels) in favour of the miniaturism of the aphorism. One of his collections is called *The Agony of Flies*. He was working self-consciously in a German tradition that flowered most fantastically, because rationally, with Georg Christoph Lichtenberg. It was Lichtenberg, a careful observer of the apparent bizarreries of human conduct, who engendered the shortest aphorism ever written: 'the world of words'. It is pithier still in German: die Wörter-Welt. Lichtenberg was a supremely lucid writer, a thinker teeming with ideas. Canetti called him a 'flea with a human mind'. His epithet catches the essence of the aphorism, too: it is peremptory, hyperbolic, and quite often rude, not least about its own sense of what is proper. Perhaps it is the ideal form for the uncommitted, those who willingly court the risk, later in life, of turning into what Carlyle called a Professor of Things in General.

Karl Kraus, on the other hand, suggested aphorisms were like a long held breath – with the risk that the great dark looming condensation on the surface of the language might not let you up for air again. But nobody drowns in profundity: the aphorism is too little extended in time to allow the language to steal your breath. In the aphoristic mode you can actually dive down in one language and surface in another. It would be wrong to imagine, for instance, that this peculiar form of erudition is somehow almost exclusively German: my own favourites include the barbed French writer Jules Renard – 'His soul takes on a bit of girth', 'Irony is mankind's modesty', or even 'the peasant is perhaps the only kind of man who doesn't like the countryside and never looks at it' – and the acerbic Pole Stanislaw Jerzy Lec. Here are some of his sayings: 'Everything in the world has already been said but not everyone has said it.' 'What becomes of a devil who stops believing in God?' 'Puritans should wear two fig leaves: in front of their eyes.' 'It would have pleased me more if David had vanquished Goliath with his harp.' 'Do you hear that stammering? It's the choruses of the consonants after the extermination of the vowels.' One of the most provocative of all aphorists was Nicolas-Sébastien Roch de Chamfort (1741–94), who wrote, arguing the case against himself in a manner quite unlike that of La Rochefoucauld, 'If I am anything to go by, man is a foolish animal.'

Being succinct about their faults doesn't mean aphorists always have the last word, even though people actually used to memorise Oscar Wilde's sayings in an attempt to make an axiom out of a witticism. It was Mr Wilde's particular pleasure, of course, to help the axiomatically sincere to an understanding of why they were actually the worst kind of Philistines. The ferociously glum E. M. Cioran, who is something of a cult figure among European intellectuals, spent his entire adult life in Paris not conforming to anything at all (except his ideal of being a writer) and sent down aphorisms to posterity that toll like the Last Judgement: in a happier moment he wrote 'doctrines pass, anecdotes remain', which may well be true, though the philosopher would want to know *which* anecdotes remain, and *why*. Few aphorisms can afford to get quite as gossipy as the anecdote. Perhaps it's a matter of linguistic habits. Writers rarely stop to question whether they should write aphorisms; philosophers are obliged to, and then they lay theorems. In a newspaper article that came my way recently, the poet James Fenton insisted: 'Windbags can be right. Aphorists can be wrong. It's a tough world.' He was right, of course, but only aphoristically. Joseph Joubert, whose intermittences I recall for his mental picture of aphorisms as 'sneezes of the mind' (which blew mine), wrote in 1815: 'When we find what we've been looking for, we don't have time to say it. We must die.' The aphorism: as epitaph.

Scheherezade in Vienna

Joseph Roth's Nostalgia

The 1914–18 war was called a 'world' war, wrote Joseph Roth in one of his brilliant journalist forays, 'not because the entire world had conducted it but because, owing to it, we all lost a world, our world'. The world he was referring to was the Austro-Hungarian Dual Monarchy, one of the unlikeliest forces ever to hold sway over European politics. It was the Holy Roman Empire reinstated as carnival; a cartographic familiar of stamp-collecting children. When Joseph Roth was born in 1894 in the small Galician town of Brody, one of the Monarchy's eastern outposts, it had long been threatening to collapse if given a push.

Austrian policy at the beginning of the twentieth century, as many contemporary visitors noted, was a continual struggle to save face. Such was the logic of its situation in the centre of Europe, and so potentially fissiparous its empire, that it had settled for an easy-going, rather slovenly style of *Schlamperei und Schweinerei* – a philosophy of putting off decisions and muddling through. Not for nothing was its insignia an ironic, double-headed eagle. The struggle to save face marked many of its institutions and was especially characteristic of the army, which was full of gloriously outfitted aristocrats on little pay and with rusty equipment – until reality finally obtruded on the eastern front in 1914. After the war Austria lost nearly everything, including its monarchy, being reduced to a rump of its original territory. Instead of reforming the empire and preserving the balance of power, the Treaty of Versailles replaced the multi-ethnic Habsburg-Danubian order with weak nation-states and allowed the Germans to think of themselves as victims: those same weak nation-states, which were almost as ethnically complex as the old Empire, were easy pickings for the Nazis twenty years later. Yet this unwieldy empire that stretched to the Mediterranean, with its fifteen official languages and deeply conservative Catholicism, with its Jewish and Moslem subjects, left a mark on the twentieth century like no other. Out of Vienna, its vaunted capital, in those golden years before the war, came signal achievements in the arts and philosophy, the word-ethics of Karl Kraus ('even the noises of a Viennese rush hour are directed from a cosmic point'), Freud's mind-reading, Adolf Loos's anti-ornamental architecture, Arthur Schnitzler's tales of what the bourgeois did with their private parts, Alban Berg's disgust at 'operetta and farces', Robert Musil's essayism, F. A. Hayek's attempt to explain to the British the nature of their century-old freedoms, Felix Salten's *Bambi*, and of course Adolf Hitler's prose and programme.

After serving as a soldier in the Austrian Army, probably at a desk job rather than in the more glorious roles he was in the habit of inventing for himself, Roth became a correspondent in the 1920s for a number of leading German newspapers. It should be remembered too, since his writing pretends otherwise, that Berlin – in those days the newspaper capital of the world – was his base, not Vienna. Initially sympathetic to the Soviet cause in the Polish-Russian war fought around his home town (the Russian writer Isaac Babel has several stories set around Brody in his terse collection *Red Cavalry*), Roth began a ten-year association in 1923 with the *Frankfurter Zeitung*, a newspaper renowned for its exacting literary standards. He was sent to every part of the continent: brilliant dispatches followed from fascist Italy, the Harz mountains, Paris, Red Square on the ninth anniversary of the October Revolution, Mussolini's Italy. Walter Benjamin and Ernst Bloch were also on the staff of the paper, in some function or other, but Roth went out of his way to avoid intellectuals. There were some people he just didn't care to know.

He preferred to hit the road; it allowed him to be an agitator of sorts. None of it would have been possible without the newspapers, which in those days always had column space for the unclassifiable. His articles were widely read, and brought him handsome fees; some were collected in a book called *Wandering Jews* (1927), an account of the hard life of eastern Jews on the move, scapegraces for just about everybody including the assimilated western Jews of Vienna – those who've moved up in a highly conceptualised, rule-bound society have no burning desire to be reminded of their own previously stigmatised and oversocialised origins. This book reads like a leavetaking of his own origins, for the wandering is mostly Roth's. Despite its fierce partisanship, it exposes one of Roth's limitations as a writer: his blindness to intellectual currents leads him to overlook the revival of interest already under way among the 'citified' into precisely these traditions. He never mentions figures like Buber and Rosenzweig. But 1927 seems to have been a year of acute existential crisis for Roth: the words that he puts in the mind of Lieutenant Tunda, returned from Siberia to a Europe he can barely credit, in one of his other great novels *Flight without End*, suggests Roth knew there was no home-coming – not for any of us. 'It seems to me that there can no longer be any choice between enduring the torment of reality, of false categories, soulless concepts, amorphous schemata, and the pleasure of living in a fully accepted unreality.' Yet he was perfectly capable of writing, when rejecting the Zionist idea of a Jewish homeland, 'wandering is not a malediction, but a benediction'.

Viennese free-thinkers and liberals were among the staunchest supporters of this 'apostolic' empire that had been thrown together from rickety feudal fiefs and sealed with a baroquely absolutist lacquer. Roth, strictly in terms of his origins, might have been expected to be in sympathy with those on the ethnic fringes of the empire who pored over their Herder and stood opposed to rootless cosmopolitanism. In *Job, The Story of a Simple Man*, Mendel Singer is a man who trusts in God even while allowing himself to be dazzled by the Big Smoke. Roth's mature style betrays something of this division of allegiance too: he upholds a kind of Café Central individualism while being quite explicit about his loathing of the 'general state of mind of our modern world, this religious nihilism, the inheritance of long-forgotten élites, which had now become the property of the masses'. His statement makes perfect sense in terms of how liberal values were generated in the empire, though its sense could only come in retrospect. It was the seemingly inexorable rise of Hitler (mentioned as early as 1923 in Roth's novel *The Spider's Web*), a man without nostalgia for the old Vienna which had shaped his politics, that gave a quality of desperation to Roth's search for a way out of unbelief. He eschewed the self-protective ironic distance of someone like Robert Musil – whose witty toilet term for the former K & K empire, Kakania, didn't go down at all well with Roth – for the less guarded emotions of someone buffeted by history itself.

Over three thousand pages of laconic, impressionistic, meticulously phrased reportage can be found in the collected German edition of his works, and his colleague Soma Morgenstern was later to claim, somewhat disingenuously in view of the seamlessness of Roth's two activities (many of his novels were serialised in newspapers), that his journalism was in fact his greater accomplishment. Serialisation imposed a style, and its saccadic shorthand offers a parallel, from the perspective of German writing of that period, with Hemingway's very influential adoption of the deadpan. Morgenstern had, however, put his finger on a tendency which is sometimes apparent in Roth the novelist, though it may have come from Roth the journalist's acceptance of the given: he can be facile. At their best, his novellas are as achingly memorable as those of his friend Stefan Zweig, whose novel *Beware of Pity* (1938) reworked the plot of Roth's *The Radetsky March* (1932), cautioned against the glib sentimentality of that very condition, 'which is really no more than the heart's impatience to be rid as quickly as possible of the painful emotion aroused by the sight of another's unhappiness'.

When Hitler came to power in 1933, Roth severed all ties with Germany. He went to live in Paris on the fame of *The Radetsky March*, wrote for émigré publications, and already a drinker, drank harder than ever. He wrote much as he always had, sitting at the Hôtel-Café de la Poste near the Luxembourg Gardens, glass at hand. By then he had become an active monarchist, addressing Otto, the exiled son of the last Habsburg Emperor, as 'Your Majesty'. Roth's sincere patriotism was a source of amusement and irritation to his fellow exiles. It probably had more to do with a fear of what the future would do to the past than escapism from the present. He continued writing to the end, never losing his power to express what faith and simple verities meant to him: the destitute, poor man's Paris described in Roth's last novel *The Legend of the Holy Drinker* is softened by its being told like a fable. Roth called this the 'grace of misery'; he had converted to Catholicism. Around him, the world was about to give itself over to violence on the grand scale. Despite a lifeline to the United States, Roth gave up living in May 1939: his admission to hospital for pneumonia probably led to his death from the effects of acute alcohol withdrawal: delirium tremens. He was forty-four. There was no help for Joseph Roth on earth: the phrase he quoted to his friend Ceza von Cziffra – one first formulated by Kleist in his suicide letter to his sister in 1811 – was not carved as an epitaph on his tomb. He left a threadbare suit, an overcoat and his manuscripts; and was interred on 30 May, 1939, in the cimetière Thiais, a desolate place among the breeze-blocks of Vitry and Choisy in outer Paris. Paul Celan, a later emigrant to France from old Austria, is also buried there.

The Tale of the 1002nd Night, which was originally published by the Dutch house De Gemeenschap in 1938 – when Austria had actually ceased to exist at all – commemorates Vienna, the city recalled from a time when 'the world was deeply and frivolously at peace'. It is a novel redolent of Vienna's streets and smells, its social rankings and architecture, and the whole contraption of administration that made empire possible. It title hints at a level of artificiality unusual for Roth: Michael Hofmann calls it a 'fairy story that has swallowed a novel'. It exaggerates, in fact, what Settembrini in *The*

Magic Mountain disparages as Vienna's 'Asiatic principle' (and we ought to remember that the Nazis used the terms 'Oriental' and 'Asiatic' to vilify those aspects of German culture they regarded as alien). Based on an actual visit by the Shah of Persia to Europe in 1873, it finds the 'Shah-in-Shah' sejourning in the city the Ottomans failed to take by storm in the seventeenth century. Not satisfied with his 365 wives, the Shah wishes to sleep with a beautiful countess espied at a ball in his honour.

It falls to the Captain of Horse, Baron Taittinger, a character singularly lacking in insight, but with a certain savvy in practical matters, to fix the assignment. He replaces the countess, married and unobtainable, with his ex-mistress, Mizzi Schinagl, an ordinary Viennese girl who happens to resemble her. It is, he says, an 'approximation': Mizzi works in a closed house. The Shah remains oblivious to the deception practised on him, and afterwards sends Mizzi a string of pearls. The pearls must give off a subtle poison, since the lives of all who come in contact with them get botched; only the pearls remain unaltered, increasing fourfold in value in the course of the book.

As the story unfolds, social distinctions lose meaning, and money becomes a corrupting agent of exchange: having brought a Shah to a brothel, it brings the establishment's madam, Frau Matzner, to live in a respectable part of town; Mizzi, who sells the pearls for a fabulous sum, to prison for selling fake Brussels lace; and the gutter-journalist Lazik to write a penny-dreadful of Taittinger's role as pimp. Shamed out of the army, and burdened by Mizzi and their illegitimate son, Taittinger ends up purchasing his mistress, once she gets out of prison, a garish waxworks on the Prater – the new World Bioscope Theater – with money he hardly has. Like everyone else around him, he has suspended his critical faculties and invested in a dream.

The supernumerary Arabian Night, the 1002nd, returns to haunt the fairy tale like a scandal: the Shah returns to Vienna, farcically recapitulating his original visit. By now the novel has swallowed its own tail. Mizzi, the original double appears, to

Taittinger's chagrin, as a variety act in his waxwork show, in a tableau of the story of the pearls. Unable to return to the army (the Shah's visit has frozen all official business), Taittinger shoots himself, his life as waxy as the panopticon dummies he now owns. And in this piling up of simulacra and doubles, Roth concludes with a chilling little cameo from the World Bioscope waxworker himself: 'I might be capable of making figures that have heart, conscience, passion, emotion, and decency. But there's no call for that at all in the world. All the world wants are curiosities; it wants monsters, really. Monsters are what they want!'

World wants, world gets.

In the novel, Roth's sad adoration of his vanished Austro-Hungary is most apparent in his listing of the nationalities, as when Taittinger returns to his estate in the Carpathians: 'The Mayor – Wenk – was a German, one of a scattering of Saxon colonists who lived in the area. The steward was from Moravia, the peasants were Carpathian Russians, the now-deaf footman was a Hungarian, who had completely forgotten where he had come from, and when and why... The forester was a Ruthenian from Galicia; the Police Sergeant came from Bratislava.' That fantastic, splendid, unlikely and *unspecialised* empire was Roth's bulwark against moral indifference in the modern world. One thinks of today's Europe, faced with a similar profusion of rival nations which can't bear the smell of each other but are terribly susceptible to the myrrh and not-so-frank-incense of a geographically reinstated Christendom.

It is hardly surprising that Roth described himself in terms of the same profusion of allegiances: he was 'a Frenchman from the east, a humanist, a rationalist with religious faith, a Catholic with a Jewish brain, a true revolutionary'. It is probably more exact to say that he was a man in search of his father, of the paternal authority that bestows, as he wrote in *Rebellion*, one of his 1920s novels, the authority to live, and yet, at the same time, has to be faced up to and even gainsaid. At his burial, the presence of a priest prevented his friend and the Talmud scholar Gottfarstein from reading the Kaddish. Roth's real faith being the Empire, an imperial aide-de-camp then stepped forward and laid a black and yellow wreath bearing the simple legend 'Otto'. It was a token of recognition from the Habsburgs to one of their most faithful subjects. The aide-de-camp recalled Roth warmly as 'a true fighter for the Monarchy,' whereupon consternation broke out among Roth's socialist friends, all of whom tried to shout the speaker down.

Nostalgia can make of history itself a pathetic fallacy. Today the Austrian capital looks as if had been put in aspic since Franz Josef's glory days; Roth himself is not immune to the charge of high kitsch. But there is pathos in his last days in Paris. The memorialist from the marches had come to the end of his tether. He *couldn't* go anywhere else. If ever a cause was lost it was then: Roth wouldn't have survived the unfettered cynicism of the Greater Germany, where the Fairy Prince with the liquorice moustache was telling his people all the wicked spirits were about to be banished from the land. Only those seduced by these wicked spirits, the Fairy Prince bellowed into the radio (where fairy tales worked best by conjuring up images), would henceforth think them human. Illusion isn't something put over on people, it is something they want to dress themselves in. In the articles he wrote in the thirties Roth identified Hitler as the Antichrist. Europe had capitulated – 'out of weakness, out of laziness, out of indifference, out of ignorance (it will be the task of the future to identify the reasons for this shameful surrender)'.

Long before he went into exile Roth had jotted down in *The Radetsky March*: 'The world worth living in was doomed. The world that would follow it deserved no decent inhabitants.'

Berlin Diary

20 November 1989

5 a.m. I waken to the reverberations of the first S-Bahn of the day screeching to a halt at the Savignyplatz station a hundred metres from my window. So much for the double-glazing. A dull light dribbles in through the bay windows; the reverberations get louder. The overhead S-Bahn line to Wannsee on the outskirts of the city also happens to be the main line west to Hanover; for years sealed trains have trundled along these tracks from what used to be a bit of the British crown in Germany, passengers clutching the transit visa that permitted them, in best bureaucratic German, to cross the *Hoheitsgebiet* (sovereign territory) of the GDR. Now the trains are thundering past every ten minutes.

Bleibtreustrasse – it cuts between two of the great thoroughfares of Berlin: Kantstrasse and the Kurfürstendamm. I make a mental note to look up Herr Bleibtreu in my father-in-law's Brockhaus encyclopaedia when I get back to Munich. Walter Benjamin describes the area in his memoir of his childhood *A Berlin Chronicle*; on the other side of the train line was his old school parish. Keep practising if you want to get lost in a city, look as if you're taking nothing in. So the myopic Benjamin. Underneath my digs, on the first floor, is a brothel called Dr Frühling; it's discreetly lit from outside to resemble a dentist's surgery, though I don't think anyone would make the mistake of going there to have tartar taken off his teeth. Perhaps I'm sleeping too soundly to hear anything, but business seems to be very discreet. My brother-in-law, who's a lawyer, assures me it's a going concern. He's their lawyer. I half expect during my stay to meet a wanton out of Otto Dix, encrusted with cheap jewels (more likely a rubber fetishist), but I don't. Across the road is a row of cafés, a small cinema, a clothes shop; all shuttered at this early hour, since nothing much happens in Berlin – at least in this part of the city – in the early morning. Certainly not true of the rest of Germany.

The sky over Berlin (the original title of Wim Wenders' film *Wings of Desire* in which an angel falls – literally of course – in love, and loses his wings in a deterritorialised Berlin of vacant lots and barrack-like houses) is mostly grey, the weather like today, cold and clammy. In winter the air is so thick it can be tasted. West Berlin has more heavy industry than the whole of Ireland; the smog of thousands of Trabants and the brown coal fires of East Berlin have long made a travesty of borders.

Like something melodramatically dropped from a *billet doux*, the name of the street keeps repeating itself inanely in my mind. Who was Bleibtreu? What should the hopeful, perhaps ironic appeal of his name to posterity mean to me? All day long I puzzle over its familiarity.

At long last the answer comes to me. In *Ulysses*, Joyce drops little hints to the reader of Leopold Bloom's impending status as cuckold. Soon enough I find the passage: Bleibtreustrasse is the address of one Agendath Netaim, proposer of methods for the 'reclamation of funams of waste arenary soil', for the 'cultivation of orange plantations and melonfields and reafforestation'.

Serendipity, I thought – the vision of a blooming desert.

A little more than a week after the breakthrough, the East Germans in the streets of West Berlin stop cheering the buses that bundle past with ads on their sides for the authentic spirit of the times. The spirit is a vodka called Gorbatschow.

New arrivals disembark from the S-Bahn stop at Berlin Zoo and gawk at the neon, the efflorescence of plastic, the glass façades. For a moment, modernity is a chasm opening down the street. Commodities are everywhere, quietly self-replicating. After escape comes escapism; an easy exhibitionist high. In the Europa Center and down the Kurfürstendamm the supermarkets make a pre-Christmas killing: huge stockpiles of coffee and chocolate, made-in-China toys, ghettoblasters and blank cassettes are surrounded by crowds of eager buyers and bemused onlookers. The banana is king. There are piles of discarded bottles and crates awaiting collection, bin bags torn and spilled in the gutter, not a scene I've ever seen anywhere else in Germany. And in the next street, outside the Beate Uhse sex-shop, there's a patient, unembarrassed queue of couples waiting to pass beyond the tacky purple drape and enter the sanctum.

The euphoria of last week seems to be evaporating, but there's still a sense of expectation in the air. Berlin has been living from this sense of drama, on itself in effect, for years. In the daytime hours the city is rentier, shabby-respectable, full of post-prandial office workers; come nightfall it turns hedonistic and camp, and stalks home at four on amphetamines and raucous laughter.

The Ku'damm isn't much more than a century old; the heroine of Fontane's *Irrungen Wirrungen* walked it for miles, but it was all fields then. Less than a decade after Fontane published his novel, the fields were being cut for the laying of a broad new avenue which, it was hoped, would outdo the Champs-Elysées. The showpiece of imperial Berlin is a symbol of Bismarck's *Zug nach den Westen* – the westward drive of the Reich after its defeat of France in 1870. Berlin became imperial capital after the acquisition of a large swathe of French territory, and the seizure of two French cities, Strassburg and Metz. War reparations from France helped to build it. Today, like any of the great boulevards of Europe, it's a vitrine for triumphant capital. Rebuilt after the war, it hasn't got much of its former *weltglanz*, and these days its detractors seem to be more vocal than its admirers. De Beauvoir and Sartre, chronicling the continent between the wars, came here in its 'brown years'; Nabokov, not often thought of as a Berlin writer, lived for thirteen years in the city where his father was assassinated, though he makes only the briefest of passing references to it in *Speak, Memory*, recalling the shop windows bedecked with photographs of Hindenburg and Hitler the year his son was born; a year later, in 1935, Thomas Wolfe thought he had found the Twenties living on virtually intact in the street he called 'Europe's biggest café'.

In those days, the Ufa-cinema along from the Romanische Café (Benjamin says it was better known to its inmates as Café Megalomania, perhaps because of its famously bad-tempered hunchback waiter, Richard) was screening Leni Riefenstahl's *Triumph of the Will* and final preparations were being made for one of the few ceremonies at which the Nazi flag took a subordinate place to another: the Olympic Games. It was the end of the cinema which had steered Christopher Isherwood so directly to his 'I am a camera' technique. He had lived near a different overhead railway station, the Nollendorfplatz, for much of the early 1930s, brought there by Auden who had proclaimed himself the 'king of Berlin' when he arrived in October 1928. Auden worked on his charade *Paid on Both Sides* in Berlin, kept a journal (mostly unpublished) and had innumerable brief affairs.

The Nazis loathed Scandal Avenue, and kept up a steady tirade against its frivolity and decadence, its evident attractions for pleasure-seekers and *flâneurs*. In addition to Café Megalomania, there was also the West End, Viktoria and the Princess, where Benjamin sat 'long evenings next to the jazz band, discreetly consulting sheets and scraps of paper, writing my *Origin of German Tragic Drama*'. Despite the fact that Goebbels had spent a good deal of the Weimar era in just such a milieu, the Nazis considered it a display of everything *unecht* and foreign, hot provocative wails in the key of sex. Not surprisingly a number of their 'clean-ups' started here; it was the obvious place with all that plate glass in view.

Grumblingly compliant rather than vociferously antagonistic, present-day Germans put up with Berlin's assumptions of difference, its laziness and subsidised commitment to pleasure. About half the budget for running the city is allocated by central government in Bonn, the village-capital by the Rhine. Berlin stands defiantly outside the squeaky-clean consensus. Unlike most

German cities, where the guilt of having too much followed with almost indecent haste on the shame of not having enough, it seems less stifled by affluence. Life in other German cities is sometimes a bit like living in very plushly upholstered cells. Less cosmopolitan than it was in its heyday, Berlin still offers a Babylonian solidity to the outside world. Berlin is the only plausible capital Germany has ever had, people tell me, and shrug their shoulders when I mention that its seventy-five years as German capital only ever brought fifteen years of democracy. Now it seems to be witnessing the Fifties all over again; restoration of its missing half, the capital of the other Germany that refused to call itself *East* Berlin, has all the embarrassment and fumbling good will of a couple of relatives meeting after three decades of living apart.

Barely six months ago Egon Krenz – a toothy *apparatchik* – could be seen on the East German news programme Aktuelle Kamera lending his support to the heroic reinstatement of law and order by his brother socialists in Tienanmen square. After his takeover of power from Erich Honecker ('Honni') four weeks' ago, odds are being laid on how long he's going to stay in the saddle. The sophisticated read his opening of the Wall as a shrewd, rather than despairing, move – calling Bonn's bluff in effect, forcing it to shore his régime up in order to prevent a massive feet-voting efflux of East Germans into the Federal Republic. It looks as if he'll survive the Communist Party Congress next month (though whether his party could survive a countrywide multiparty election is another matter). The German Democratic Republic may have to answer for the first time for the lying epithet in its official title (no genuinely democratic state would have to sport such a monicker – it's like calling yourself a 'scientific mathematician'). What's being heard is something quite different from the usual fudge: we are the people and this is what we can do. This is the distinguishing feature of the past week's revolution, what Martin Walser calls *die sanfte Revolution*; a peaceful grass-roots revolution without obvious leaders. Vox pop is calling the tune.

Only two weeks ago, the largest spontaneous assembly since the end of the First World War amassed on the Alexanderplatz in East Berlin. Christa Wolf, literary *eminence grise* of a grey country, suggested to the crowd that henceforth, on May Day, the leadership should march past the people. Stefan Heym, one of several writers who returned to the GDR in the Fifties (from the United States of the McCarthy era) and the best known of all the literary 'non-persons', was quoted as saying: 'It's as if someone had pushed open a window after years of spiritual, economic and political stagnation, after rot and fug, language-washing, bureaucratic whims and blindness.' The posters were at least as heroic. 'After years in the wilderness we don't believe in the old prophets any more.' Not a single placard at that assembly could be seen pleading for reunification.

A bare week later, in the early evening of Thursday, Günter Schabowski, a Politburo member, announced almost under his breath at a press conference that private travel outside the GDR no longer required any of the hitherto applicable list of bureaucratic justifications. His statement was so unexpected he was asked to repeat it, and still nobody knew how to interpret it: the staid ARD, West Germany's main TV channel, decided not to alter any of the evening's scheduled programmes. Ten thousand people in Leipzig, unaware of the sensational news from Berlin, proceeded silently through the streets, remembering the Jewish victims of the Night-of-Broken-Glass pogrom of 1938.

The next day, having run out of meaningful by-words, the Bundestag in Bonn broke into a rendition of the national anthem. Soon the message caught fire. A mere identity card was enough to cross what had been for the lifetime of any German my age, a solid fixture – ugly, bulky and not to be thought away. Most people were lost for words, for the very means to express their emotions, after thirty years of probing words before they left their mouths. *Wahnsinnig* was the term of approval I heard most often. Crazy. Far out. Unbelievable.

Sections of the Wall are already being dismantled by souvenir hunters and impatient punks, hands poking through gaps in the concrete torn with pick-axes. Today I put my own hand into the mouth of the beast. East German border guards on the other side are learning to use their facial muscles after years of atrophy. Television reports show long stacks of Trabants and Wartburgs at the checkpoints and large plumes of exhaust trailing behind them. Many people are perched on motorbikes as old as the GDR itself (the waiting time for a car is ten years). And others are standing in the rain outside the banks, waiting to claim the 100 DM *Begrüssungsgeld*, the annual sum of friendly money which the West German treasury sets aside for the visitor from the GDR. Last year the treasury forked out 270 million; that amount must have been withdrawn over the second weekend in November alone.

Celebrations go on into the nights of Saturday and Sunday, but Chancellor Kohl has gone to Silesia — odd timing, it would seem — to visit the minority German population in what was once the territory of the old Prussian knights. Though he went out of his way not to offend his host, the Polish premier Mazowiecki, the German-speakers there welcomed him with a good deal more cheer than the crowd outside the Berlin Town Hall on the historic Friday. Sharing the platform along with Willi Brandt, former Bürgermeister of Berlin in the years when the Wall was actually built, Kohl had been whistled and booed into inaudibility.

And he only wanted to say the word on his lips was reconciliation, not reunification.

In her diaries, Simone de Beauvoir mentions walking several times the length of the Kurfürstendamm and through the Brandenburg Gate to the Alexanderplatz. Nobody, of course, has been able to do that in three decades.

Since the gridlock extended for a couple of kilometres, I got out of the car, skirted the gilt Angel of Victory pointing the way to Sedan and triumph over the French in 1870 and walked down

Strasse des 17. Juni, the date of the suppressed workers' uprising of 1953 to which Brecht had appended his famous *bon mot*, suggesting it would be easier for the government to dissolve the people and elect another. Over one of the signposts someone has draped a new legend in cardboard to cover the original date: now it read *Strasse des 9. November*.

The Brandenburg Gate is clogged with spectators. A small tribune has been constructed, stage left, to house the world's TV cameras. Nobody's expecting anything to happen soon, since the stands are empty. A hot dog salesman covers everyone with the stench of burning fat. Free-lovers distribute pamphlets urging us to tap into this release of positive world-energy, trying to reclaim one more lost cause from the Sixties. A tinny hammering noise carried in the air; souvenir hunters and enterprising small boys are working away on the Wall with hammers, attempting to prise off loose handsized chunks of entirely unremarkable bench-grade concrete. They're called *Mauerspechte* – wall peckers. The débris looks as if it's changing hands fairly rapidly since the intrepid demolition men are surrounded by a gaggle of Japanese tourists. The Wall itself looks like a hangover from a Sixties happening, festooned from top to bottom with ironic or merely despairing graffiti: Vive de Gaulle, Freedom for Lithuania, No Ego(n)ism, Christ is coming. Many of the more recent slogans involve untranslatable wordplay on the near-homophony between Egon Krenz's surname and the word Grenze (border). Some wit has even daubed a Scottish Saltire alongside the Joseph Beuys and Keith Haring exhibits: no lost cause lost enough, it would seem.

Further along towards the Spree, a wire fence under the ponderous shadow of the former Reichstag bears the names of the more than a hundred would-be escapees killed in the twenty-eight years of the Wall's existence. Some of their attempts – like flying over the *Grenzgebiet* in a homemade glider – were ingenious, others just plain desperate. The names are all male. The freshest, still decked with faded lilies, is that of Winfried Freudenberg. He died, attempting to sail over in a hot-air balloon, in March this year.

In the other direction a passage has been made in the 'anti-fascist protection barrier' at Potsdamer Platz, almost directly over Hitler's old bunker, in the old centre of the city. This void had once been the hub of the city: in Wenders' film an old man wanders across the western part of it muttering, 'It's got to be here somewhere.' A steady stream of Trabis passes through under the benevolent gaze of well-wishers and sight-seers after the most cursory of inspections from the border police. The Trabant: a sewing machine on wheels. *Le Monde*'s correspondent calls it *pétaradante*, a probably unimprovable term for the nervous salvos of carbon monoxide it backfires under duress. *Die Zeit* magazine, making a none too subtle swipe at the German obsession with the internal combustion engine, goes so far as to award it the ironic title 'Car of the Year': the day after publication a Trabant is stolen in Hamburg, the first ever to be pinched in the West. *Objekt der Begierde.* A strange item to covet, this crankhandle parody of the turbodriven; perhaps, as *die Zeit* wetly implies, it's a case of the tortoise imposing itself on Achilles at long last.

Five minutes' walk from the Potsdamer Platz is the well-known Polish market, well-known to Berliners at any rate. It's an abject street market; the whole thing enclosed by wire fencing, rows of vendors guarding pathetic arrays of items. Stacks of trinkets, dolls, pots of jams, gherkins; most bought in East Berlin at subsidised prices and sold to anyone who'll buy them, anything to touch the almighty Mark. It's a sad, shabby congregation, a scene from the war's end long after the film has ended.

This triangular contraband trade doesn't interest the boys in green (the Federal Police) but apparently it's of major concern to the East Berliners. So widespread has it become that passports have to be shown at the entrances to supermarkets. It's not just the Poles who make a bob from this capitalist paradigm: even at the derisory current exchange rate, East Germans smuggle over their Ost-marks to change them in the West, along with the kind of antiquated household items which are more likely to get a patronising laugh than a buyer on the other side, though there may well be the odd bit of family silver among the dross. There's no shortage of printed money in the GDR: it's an inflationary problem which has the government peddling faster and faster just to keep still, since with an economy only forty per cent as productive as the West (and a GNP four times less) the problem is attracting enough foreign currency to tide over interest payments on the current debt.

The West Germans' bogey seems to be an ingress of illicit cheap labour, but it seems a bogey their economy can say boo to. The country is already the dominant trading partner of all the eastern European countries; the same weekend, the closing prices on the Frankfurt stock market indicate a twenty per cent rise in the share price for construction firms, consumer goods suppliers and machine-based industries.

It may be easy this week for East Berliners to enter the West, but for visitors in the opposite direction it's pretty much business as usual – the time-honoured rigmarole of having to obtain a one-day visa at Checkpoint Charley or the Friedrichstrasse U-Bahn station and exchange a fixed sum of 25 D-marks at the fantasy rate of parity. (The black market rate today is 30 to 1 and falling.)

With its 1930s architecture and red-liveried wooden-slatted coaches the S-Bahn system feels like a slip in back in time; the line into East Berlin snakes through the Tiergarten and past a couple of bricked-up and long-abandoned stations, the Reichstag looming bleakly through the fog on one side, and on the other the famous Charité Hospital where Benn worked as a house-physician and Brecht died. They are book-ends to the entire range of German poetry in this troubled century: Benn the self-proclaimed 'superni-hilist' and Nietzsche acolyte, the scientist-observer who said aesthetics had nothing to do with politics yet put his intellect at the service of men out to destroy the mind when he briefly supported the Nazis in 1933 – Brecht the cynical populist and theatre propagandist who wrote for Soviet cause yet at the same time wrote page on page of poignant but irredeemably 'bourgeois' love-poems.

The disembarkment point lead down through stairwells and jerrybuilt passages to a shabby customs shed, a row of cubicles with metallic flaps on either side. Formalities were brief. I now possess a slip a paper in officialese instructing me to return through the same entry point before midnight. A crowd of us are funnelled towards a cashier who exchanges the obligatory 25 D-marks for 25 of the other kind. *Drübriges Geld*: money from over there.

A few steps from the doors of the station is Under den Linden itself, the most monumental of the avenues that hive off around the Brandenburg Gate. Here are the opera, cathedral, the Pergamon museum and the Staatsbibliothek, the latter still bearing pockmarks from the last days of the war. Two motionless, severe-looking guards are on duty outside the shrine to the East German state. Inside, a gas-fed flame flutters in its prism; the plinth to the unknown soldier is flanked by an identical plinth to the unknown resistance fighter. The revolutionary German tradition clearly has a selective memory. On the street outside, Frederick the Great straddles an enormous bronze steed. He's peering eastwards: Spartan habits, Roman ambitions, Junker blood – waiting for a quite different Messiah to call history to judgement.

Closer to the Brandenburg Gate are a number of embassies. In the window of the British Embassy there's a small illustrated exhibition to – of all people – the life and works of Graham Greene. Despite all of his fugitive antipathy to the continent and Germany, it seems an unintentionally inspired choice. A quote from *Journey without Maps*, displayed in the window and written in West Africa in 1934, catches my eye: 'even the seediness of civilisation has a deep appeal... It seems to justify the sense of nostalgia for something lost. My journey represented a distrust of any future based on what we are.' Sure enough: I'm standing in Greeneland.

Apparently Greene initially wanted to set *Our Man in Havana* in Tallinn, the capital of Estonia. That Liberian 'seediness' would describe the capitals of Eastern Europe equally well, shabby genteel hearts of stone surrounded by bidonvilles, row on row of Stalin baroque housing programmes, chimney stacks leaving a fine toxic nimbus in the air. Monumental eclectic tenements yielding to orbital gigantism: flaky stucco, mildewed concrete, jerry-built shacks. Not poverty, the way it is in Africa, something more conforming. The further from the seat of power, the seedier. But to imagine seediness appealing to those living it, or in it, is a massive condescension: one of the deep resentments in the GDR has been the siphoning of funds from the provinces to pay for the fortieth anniversary whoop-up in the capital.

A few nights ago East Germans saw how much more equal conditions were for the *nomenklatura* living in their mansions in Wandlitz: a television team had been allowed to roam through the exclusive quarter, hitherto more securely guarded than Bel Air. Krenz, astutely enough, tried to forestall any criticism that he had benefited from his assumption of power – within days he has moved his own family out of their luxury villa to a more representative flat in the suburb of Pankow. Having a social conscience and showing it suddenly becomes indispensable. An official spokesman announces that Wandlitz with its swimming pools and luxury stores is to become a residential area for old people. They haven't heard of market forces yet.

I walk though little lanes and back streets, past bare linden trees on the edge of fouled-up wasteland, tenement blocks with their sides ripped off, streets going nowhere. I'm struck by how much this monochrome landscape with its rather bleary sun reminds me of parts of Glasgow, my home city.

Before leaving East Berlin I decide to visit Brecht's house in the Chauseestrasse, now a small industry churning out posters and memorabilia. Lots of eager high-school kids crowd in around me. Behind the shop is the apartment where he lived with Helene Weigel until his death in 1956. Inside the house his Noh masks and the famous scroll of the Doubter are still in place, along with the furniture and library. The view from the window perches directly over the old Huguenot cemetery where they are buried in adjacent tombs.

Brecht, the artful dodger, always had an anomalous position in his fledgling corporative state. None of his successors ever acquired his equipoise, his sly ability to navigate between fellow travellers and propagandists. Or knew of his Swiss bank account and Austrian passport until well after his death. He lent the state his prestige, in return for retaining his freedom to make sceptical remarks about its leaders. His response to current events might have been what he wrote forty years ago in Bad Times: 'Praise be to those who forget the unworkable plan.' Praise be indeed.

Even Brecht's crafty dialectic would have been one step behind in this revolution.

After forty years of stasis, events are moving faster than words. Now that a mood of change in Czechoslovakia is following hard on that from East Germany, Mitteleuropa has ceased to be merely a literary concept, a junked demonology or a pass-word. In the years of its ideological division, Günter Grass always insisted that Berlin was the true capital of the continent. Claudio Magris's *Danube* confirms that supposition: one story of the Danube is that of peacefully spreading German mercantilism in eastern Europe long before the dreams of thunder wrecked everything.

A hundred years forwards; a hundred years back. The Soviet gendarme withdraws, the continent shifts eastwards. Of all the anniversaries that have fallen this year, the one which still seems to possess power simply by virtue of its having happened is that of the French Revolution. Question is: who can tell a nationalist from a patriot?

The Wall is toppling, but the rhetoric of state-sanctified socialism will take a lot longer to go. A redundant frontier will soon mean a redundant vocabulary. Addressing the Volkskammer, Erich Mielke, head of the detested Stasi, the state police organisation, points out that his organisation represents the interests of the workers. 'We have extraordinarily close contact with the workers…' 'Außerordentliche hohe Kontakte' is pure socialist cant, and it brought a gale of laughter at the idea that the Stasi should seek to further its links with the workers. Some estimates suggest that several million East Germans (in a population of seventeen million) already have extraordinarily close contacts with the state apparatus. The German language's propensity to put on petty official garb and intone vacuous and sometimes malign drivel is no secret, and a mistrust people share in both Germanys, the one of mercantile triumphalism, the other of shabby political oppression; quick-setting concrete being the stuff and symbol of the Wall itself, perhaps the German language has become *einbe-toniert* too.

I can't detach myself from the impression that Europe has a pre-1914 feel to it; hardly *belle époque*, but nostalgic for the time when a passport wasn't necessary to cross borders, and Balkanisation was a new term in the political diaries. Almost obscured by what is happening in Berlin, I read that representatives of Italy, Austria, Yugoslavia and Hungary – the old territories of Karl Kraus's *Kakania* – have been meeting this week in Budapest to improve relations. A faint echo of Kossuth's grandiose plans for a Danube confederation? Or is it just that these grandiose ideas get taken off the shelf and dusted down whenever the cultural commissars have got nothing better to do? And what does Mrs Thatcher's handbag have to do with it all?

Truth is: the straightforward Cold War story of Europe is losing its thread and the labyrinth is likely to get more convoluted. To take a term from Lukacs, but not as he would have relished it: this is a time of the 'weakening of reality'. As he feared, Nietzsche is perhaps about to win the battle of the titans over Marx, whose clarion-call of 1843, after all, was '[practise] the ruthless criticism of all that exists' – the battle for custody of our historical souls, for culture as spectacle. Perhaps, despite appearances, we're going back to the nineteenth century.

Looking at my copy of Ulysses I check my memories of my first visit to Berlin against Bloom's genealogy: 'Bloom, only born male transsubstantial heir of Rudolf Virag (subsequently Rudolph Bloom) of Szombathély, Vienna, Budapest, Milan, London and

A Jolly Good Show

How the British Saw Their Empire

Well known for his trenchant views on the monarchy in its years of decline, David Cannadine, in his new book *Ornamentalism*, extends some of his earlier work on class in Britain to the janissary cosmopolis that was once the British Empire. Now that it has ended up as pap for televisual nostalgia, where it is often portrayed as a Retreat for Gracious Living (which it surely was for some: mansions with the Queen's portrait can still be found perched among the tea plantations of Sri Lanka and may even still straddle the very exclusive crest of Victoria Peak on Hong Kong Island), Cannadine seeks to give us a view from the inside – a view of the Empire as a social entity rather than a political construct, even though that is pre-eminently what it was. What attitudes kept the Empire on the stage of world history until the last scene of its last act in 1950, the year the author was born? One influential view holds that it was a ramshackle edifice acquired by men who knew not what they did (and who lost it with similar nonchalance); Cannadine attempts to show that, as an imagined community, it was a good deal more robustly self-deceiving than that. Though what the ordinary mass of people thought of it will, of course, probably remain for ever beyond the historian's reach.

While many famous continental thinkers and writers – including a certain Captain Korzeniowski, who elected to become English under the name Joseph Conrad, and another Sigmund Freud, who, when forced to, told H.G. Wells he had actually nourished the fantasy of becoming English all his life – thought the British successful empire-builders because they were 'naturally' individualistic (every man his own Crusoe), Cannadine lends weight to the static. Ornamentalism, as he defines it, leaning on Edward Said's influential if very partial notion of orientalism, was 'hierarchy made visible, immanent and actual'. The British went out to rule the world, and they had their own way of ordering it. The most desolate, parched, wind-tormented landscapes were domesticated to the damp green smell of the Home Counties: I can remember my bemusement, the year I lived in the Australian outback, on being told by Flying Doctor colleagues that the miles and miles of parched scrub they visited weekly on the border between New South Wales and Queensland were called Durham Downs. I shouldn't have been so surprised. From the deism of the Whigs to the Edwardianism of Rupert Brooke, 'England' was the surrogate heaven thrown up by the British Empire. England was the garden at the heart of the world. And atavism embraced more than territory in the dominions. 'Natives' were perceived as the equivalent of the 'lower orders' back home (for whom Empire held almost no interest), and a Sultan or Pasha was honorary royalty. Those in the ruling upper-middle-class élite mixed with local chiefs; the aspiring middle-classes were much too earnest and ambitious. The freemasonry of rank trumped that of race. Cannadine cites the words of the wife of a Governor of Fiji in her defence of the high-born locals: 'Nurse can't understand it all, she looks down on them as an inferior race. I don't like to tell her that these ladies are my equals, which she is not!'

Status was everything in the business of being British. Indeed, the more horizontally mobile Empire became, especially after 1857, the more encrusted, rigid, layered and Burkean its hierarchy. New money could always be found to maintain old style. It was a class act all the way: an elephant's back offered a prime view on what was going on at street level. Tocqueville asked himself why – unlike the Americans – the English abroad failed to greet one another, and surmised that the security conferred by being high-born had given way to moneyed birth and 'the immediate result is an unspoken warfare between all the citizens... Aristocratic pride still being a very strong force with the English and the boundaries of the aristocracy having become doubtful each man is constantly afraid lest advantage be taken of his familiarity'. Mind you, once the elephant had vanished the whole thing looked pretty silly. Being theatrical about life's worst experiences, as in the 12,000 kilometres of First World War trenches which served to bury the dream of Empire alive, came about only partly through long steeping in Shakespeare: an unforced ability to play roles, stiffen the upper lip, and not take modernity very seriously until the coming of a certain Mrs Thatcher (who thought, by a sublime ruse of reason, that she was reclaiming precisely those virtues under the banner of nationalism) would not have been possible without an almost feudal sense of station and due. 'Good show!', as they said in Empire days, is a term of approval to be heard nowadays only on the stickiest of Home County wickets.

India, of course, played a key role in high ornamentalism, especially after Disraeli passed the Imperial Titles Act in 1876 that made Queen Victoria an empress. This produced an obsession with style, of which the most grandiose manifestations were the durbars. India may have been Europeanised by 1900, as Claude Lévi-Strauss noted in *Tristes Tropiques*, but the turn of the century was also the west's 'Hindu period': 'it was marked by great displays of wealth, indifference to poverty, a liking for languid and over-elaborate shapes, sensuality, a love of flowers and perfumes, and even by tapering moustaches, curls, frills and furbelows'. After 1911, New Delhi was the grandest city in the British Empire; and the imported Indo-Saracenic style set the architectural tone for many cities in the UK: Glasgow, where I grew up, is still heavy with it. India's was a caste system more rigid than Britain's own. Nehru once commented on the irony that the ruling members of the west's most dynamic nation always sought to ally themselves not with Calcutta intellectuals but with the most reactionary elements of Indian society. There was a logic to it, of course, and it wasn't so different from what the Habsburgs, another conservative dynastic empire, did in their patchwork central European empire:

indirect rule allowed sheikhs, emirs, sultans, maharajahs, roas, khans, nizams, ranas, jams and nawabs (India alone had more than 500 of these local dignitaries) a degree of local autonomy while drastically curtailing their wider powers. They got to live in florid pomp, but were really jacks of the union. It could be argued that, in the long run, allowing themselves to be seduced by the mystique of India forced the British, against their earlier free-trade intentions, into the protectionism and colony-bagging that was typical of the last frantic Imperial Preference phase of the nineteenth century.

Then again, the British Empire wasn't just a case of having one's cake as a capitalist entrepreneur, and wanting to eat it collectively (with a toast to the Great White Queen). If an empire was to be run on the cheap, local élites *had* to be recruited to the cause. Cannadine details the 'unprecedented honorific inventiveness' of the late nineteenth century when, under Disraeli, the honours system swelled, and even minor bureaucrats could expect their CMG (Call Me God). Baubles proved to be a potent way of bringing proconsuls and nabobs together; their swagger portraits ornament the book from cover to cover. Cannadine calls them 'walking Christmas trees of stars and collars, medals and sashes, ermine robes and coronets'. Indeed, as the monarch became more imperial, so the Empire became more royal; after Victoria's jubilee it was the done thing to make the pilgrimage to London for state events. Progress was made to serve chivalry. Though Victoria's name was scattered unto the dominions, the once deferential colonies became with time more like America: egalitarian, meritocratic and even a bit uppity.

Now that Empire is over, it is easy enough to identify 'a pantaloon in a prelate, a satyr in a judge, a porker in a cleric, an ostrich in a crown minister and a goose in his under-secretary', as Diderot once put it. But Cannadine makes a serious gaffe with his intellectual history. Enlightenment thinkers believed there would be a direct transition from a traditional closed world to a universal human society founded on reason; they certainly did not believe in 'the intrinsic inferiority of dark-skinned people'. They were universalists; though it was their universalism which paradoxically opened up the prospect of a fully rationalised humanity achieved to different degrees by different peoples. Enlightenment despair at the daunting task of educating the masses may have fed a certain snobbish disdain, but the idea of race, which was first mooted by the Manchester doctor Charles White in 1799 (*An Account of the Regular Graduations in Man*), gained ground as a concept only in the 1850s, as a *reaction* to mobility, anonymity, and the egalitarianism that had, I would suggest, already entered deeply into accepted ways of thinking about the nature of society. Conquest had been its own justification, insofar as force of arms proved the superiority of culture. Europeans now assumed that military superiority somehow equated with intellectual and even biological superiority. A sub-rational notion had been found to explain why the same species differed so much. Results were taken for causes. Racism became a full-blown form of explanation in the writings of Robert Knox, Scottish anatomist, and Thomas Huxley, scientist and true Empire man: they thought both race and class were traits which matched the hierarchy found in nature itself. The stigmata of skin colour could be recruited in the attempt to square the automatism of progress with what seemed to be 'natural' distinctions in the rate at which different people – and peoples – moved towards the hypothetical enlightened unity: accent could be used to rank the 'lower orders' as readily as skin colour. Some – Englishmen like Huxley – were clearly destined to travel faster on the progress road; Galton, for instance, devised a scheme with 24 gradations from A to X to explain why. 'Perpetual inferiors' were bound to follow the adult white male, though at a slower pace and perhaps only so far. Herbert Spencer, on the other hand, thought true philanthropy meant helping the inferior races to die out. If Christian conscience was a pathological denial of aggression and Enlightenment reason an illusion, clearly racism was poised to become more than just the objection to someone's smell that Orwell, honest as ever, struggled with when gathering material for *Wigan Pier*. He, like the Governor of Fiji's wife, was put out less by his Burmese manservant than by the malodorous kitchens of the English working class.

In an age of unprecedented horizontal mobility and techno-logical novelty, the common unvoiced fear was of chaos. Dickens's books provide scores of scenes attesting to all three. It took roughly another hundred years till the educated members of those previously compliant middle-classes attacked the colonisers with their own intellectual weaponry, and agitated for the overthrow of colonialism. Mahatma Gandhi, Michael Manley and Lee Kuan Yew had mastered the master's ways so thoroughly they were able to undo then (though passing from being a colonial protectorate to assuming the full burden of nationhood in a merciless interna-tional market proved to be another kind of undoing for some). The hitherto unknown phenomenon of 'white guilt' played a huge part in moulding the shape of the world after 1945; and it is still with us, even if the guilt attaches not to the whiteness of skin but the blankness of semiotics. One of the traditional pretensions of – and excuses for – imperialism of the British sort was that it extended liberty: there was therefore some logic in Britain's rati-fication of the European Convention on Human Rights in 1951 even though it ran against the grain of the island's legal history and parliamentary tradition. Brought up on honour and fair play, the colonisers had to accept that the imbalance between them and the colonised was repugnant, and did the decent thing by leaving on the next boat. The salt march of the saintly Gandhi was partic-ularly shaming; and it is not generally recalled that no less than three million colonial subjects perished in the Bengal famine of 1943–4, thus sullying the British reputation for being – at least – decent administrators. But those who left could console them-selves, hypocritically, with the thought that other European empires were brought to bloodier ends.

From 1783 until 1920, the British amassed a catalogue of about 200 colonies, and imposed their rule at one time or another on about a quarter of the globe. At the time of the Anglo-German naval dispute in 1913 that led to war, Churchill, ever the romantic imperialist, made a frank declaration: 'We have got all we want in territory, and our claim to be left in unmolested enjoyment of vast and splendid possessions, mainly acquired by violence, largely maintained by force, often seems less reasonable to others than to us.' Even then, the British never overruled the market: the Gold Standard continued to regulate the amount of credit in the world economy, like a kind of monetary Super-Ego. Globalisation was probably more advanced in 1914 than it is now; and some people may possibly have assumed that money had been made eternal. What we have now is something else, and it probably began at the Battle of Omdurman when the Maxim-Nordenfeldt gun, at absurdly minimal loss, routed a superior Dervish army: Churchill, who was present on horseback and compared the moments before the battle to 'a race luncheon before the Derby', expressed his admiration for the enemy, gallant in the utter hopelessness of its cause. 'It had all ended very happily,' as Lytton Strachey wrote at the close of his debunking book *Eminent Victorians*, 'in a glorious slaughter of twenty thousand Arabs'. Killing at a distance was all the art. It is a far cry from ornamentalism. Churchill might have been frank enough to admit that violence was part of the colonial enterprise, but he wasn't modern enough to recognise that over-whelming technological superiority could provide its own reasons for killing: that lesson would only arrive on the Somme.

Away from the horror that underwrites the ornamentalism, the historian Arnold Toynbee perhaps captures that last phase of Empire best when recalling Victoria's jubilee in his memoirs. 'I remember the atmosphere. It was: well here we are on the top of the world, and we have arrived at this peak to stay there – for ever! There is of course a thing called history, but history is something unpleasant that happens to other people.' Theirs was the Empire; ours is the aftermath. Modern Britain is an offspring of Empire, just like its one-time colonies: the political culture of the mother country may dominate its Empire, but it has itself been changed by the cultures once brought under the umbrella.

Cannadine's final chapter is a more personal essay about his childhood, when Britannia was called in. Now even the royal yacht of the same name is defunct; and if the history of empire and Britain itself are one, then Robinson will soon be missing Friday. The law of unintended consequences is a powerful one in human affairs, and it may well be that another option has come into play: now that politics no longer seems so important in Europe, it appears that we have been colonised by our own utopia. Colonised, in fact, by the post-imperial Empire that pretends not to be one at all. If 'a fit of absence of mind' was how the British acquired their Empire (after the piratical start-up phase), then deep denial marks American hegemony, in which the rhetoric of freedom conceals unparalleled economic, cultural and military clout: let us not forget the network of more than 700 military bases across the globe. The United States is sustained by a powerful creation myth of its self-orphaning into agrarian liberty from a disciplinarian Tory father, which somehow overlooks the fact that Britain was the liberal paragon for the entire eighteenth-century world. (Amazing as it sounds, some Americans really did just want to enjoy the rights of Englishmen, not restart history in the manner of St Just.) There are some frankly utopian aspects to consider, however. Consider the general disbelief in the rest of the world accompanying the increasing number of attempts by the US Patent Office to put plant, animal and human tissue under private ownership as 'intellectual property'. That disbelief is hardly different in kind from the incredulity of the Massasoit, American Indians who, when confronted by the land-grabbing colonists of the seventeenth century, talked not about fathers but about their idea of mother, which encompassed just about everything: 'the land is our mother, nourishing all her children, beasts, birds, fish, and all men. The woods, the streams, everything on it belongs to everybody and is for the use of all. How can one man say it belongs to him?' The last person to talk like that in Europe was Meister Eckhart, landlocked in the fourteenth century.

Overwhelmed by Aura

ATGET'S PARIS

There is a famous profile portrait of him, gaunt-cheeked, old and slightly gibbous, the face luminously pale above the black coat and trousers, the monumental line of which is broken only by the soft blur of the hand. It is an ash-and-clinker picture, as weighty and dark as Whistler's famous painting of his mother. It dates from the last year of his life, 1927, when he was known to every self-respecting surrealist, if not to the public: the picture was taken by the young American photographer Berenice Abbott in her studio on the rue du Bac; her boyfriend, Man Ray, had been neighbour to the photographer in his little *trois-pièces* at 17 bis rue Campagne-Première, a spartan, utile studio-apartment which turns up in many of his prints. Atget was in the retail trade. The sign on his door read simply: 'Documents pour artistes.'

His first biographer had problems finding out anything at all about the earlier life of Eugène Atget. Born in modest circumstances at Libourne in Gascony in 1857, he was brought up in Bordeaux. He roamed France as a touring player, met and married his considerably older wife Valentine while doing the round of provincial theatres, and was then paid off at the age of 30. His strong south-west accent had led to him being typecast as a stage Gascon too. He painted, in Paris, for a decade; also without success. It was only towards 1897, having made a modest niche for himself as a producer of photographic images for artists, that he started doing the documentary work that would eventually make his name. Like many contemporary institutions, the heritage industry actually goes back to the nineteenth century, when the

Committee for Old Paris was set up to document everyday life in the French capital. As a voracious reader of Victor Hugo, Atget would have remembered the exiled writer lamenting the disappearance of the old Paris: what he was photographing was the modern city that had been created in the middle of the century on the orders of the Préfet de la Seine known to his compatriots as The Ripper ('l'Eventreur'). The poets gave Haussmann such a bad name as Napoleon III's wrecker that his reputation has never quite recovered: many modern Parisians still think of him with distaste, as if he had laid waste to the city, rather than created a modern imperial capital. Hausmann 'aerated' the smelly slums of the old medieval city, put in large parks at either end (the Bois de Boulogne and the Parc de Vincennes), laid down proper plumbing and sewers for the new quartiers and planned what is still one of the best urban transport systems in the world. His boulevards of solid six-storey apartment blocks were lined with the plane-trees that Rabelais had introduced to France in the sixteenth century. Paris had to wear a new architectural style. But thirty years later it was a classic style: the city had become the model for urban planners from Cairo to Buenos Aires.

Atget started on two series, making a distinction between animate life and the architectural sublime. The first series, 'Paris pittoresque', reproduced street scenes and markets, including the poultry racks and fish counters at the old Halles, the famous 'belly of Paris'; the second, 'Le Vieux Paris', documented the city's parks, squares and buildings. In 1900, he was to spend months seeking out less noticed features of the city, photographing balconies, stairwells, street signs and other decorative paraphernalia, before doing a series of topographical studies after a commission from the librarians of the Bibliothèque historique de la Ville de Paris. It was only in 1910 that he went back to his 'Paris pittoresque' series, with a renewed sense of purpose: this time he recorded the bars and stores of Paris, as well as the ordinary people who moved about in them: the *bouqainistes* with their stalls along the Seine, the poor people of St Merry, the blistered endwalls with their posters and advertisements, legions of costermongers, barrowmen and hawkers. Paris is a warren of urban hamlets from which the suburbs of the Zone are about to mushroom. The war years obliged him to take stock: Atget found himself in possession of one of the most complete visual records of the city. He wrote to the minister Paul Léon, offering his plates to the nation. So began a process that was completed only after his death in August 1927: the attribution of thousands of his glass negatives and prints to museums and institutions across the world from the Museum of Modern Art in New York to the Bibliothèque Nationale in Paris.

Atget, as Emmanuel Songez has written, 'never realised that he was Atget'. That is patronising: he never considered himself an artist. Atget was an artisan, a tradesman who happened to own a camera. He expected no more than the traditional respect for a job well done. What he was producing were true likenesses that required no artistic formalisation beyond the framing of a scene. He even pleaded with Man Ray not to attribute to him the photographs reproduced in issues 7 and 8 of *La Révolution surréaliste*.

His working life was arduous. Atget carried his equipment everywhere with him: an 18 × 24 cm plate and bellows camera, a wooden tripod, and the glass plates that allowed him to make his albumin prints. All in all it weighed about twenty kilograms, a fact which rebuffs Susan Sontag's supposition that the photographer is an 'armed version of the solitary walker'. Atget's day was a labour of Hercules. He travelled everywhere by Métro and bus. His photos indicate that they were taken from a low height, presumably with him sitting on his box of plates. Often he photographed in the light of early morning, which meant getting up before the first streaks of Baudelaire's *crépuscule de l'aube*. There are no vehicles in his Le Vieux Paris series, and the city seems weirdly chaste: the streets are empty, the cobblestones glossy in the rain, the glass fronts impenetrable. Twenty years later, Paris would be a byword for traffic-jams. The surrealist painter Giorgio de Chirico, another artist who lived on the rue Campagne-Première, was fascinated by

Atget's contours and textures. They give his buildings a brooding solidity and density, and impart an atmosphere of desolation. This is made even more mysterious by the blurred figures of onlookers moving through the camera's field of vision as the picture was being taken, as in the famous picture of the waiter with his burly moustache at the door of L'Homme Armé, rue des Archives, 1901, or the phantomic customers of Au Tambour, quai de la Tournelle, 1908. People flit out of focus, or seem ghosts of their own time. Baudelaire had a political explanation for the power of black and white: 'And observe that the black frock-coat and the tail-coat may boast not only their political beauty, which is the expression of universal equality, but also their poetic beauty, which is the expression of the public soul.' In his eyes, democracy had brought about the death of genuine individuality, and following that death, democratic life could only be 'an immense procession of undertakers' mutes, political mutes, mutes in love, bourgeois mutes'.

It is doubtful whether Atget was visited by such sombre thoughts. He was a kind of prosaic primitivist who refused to adapt to the soft-focus pictorialist aesthetic of his time, which used gum bichromate to allow retouching and added 'artistic' effects. Even when paper became readily available he stayed loyal to his heavy glass plates. Atget's images were nearly all albumen prints developed in silver nitrate, then dried and toned with a gold salt. They are 'clean' in a way that anticipates the disinfected functionalism that was to spread out of Weimar after the war, *die neue Sachlichkeit*. Their lack of contrivances and distortions made them irresistible to the Surrealists; his scene of a shop-front display 'Vitrine, fête du Trône (le géant et le nain)', 1925, is stranger than a Magritte painting. As Karl Marx wrote, commodities are queer things, 'abounding in metaphysical subtleties and theological niceties'. If Atget was 'a master of the realm of dreams' it was because he still had the ability to be startled by the city he lived in. Paris was all his theatre. Here is the Quai de Jemappes where the cars still have to wait for the lockbridge to close on the intermittent barges, and next to it the Hôtel du Nord, now a protected public monument even though Marcel Carné's film of the same name was entirely shot in a studio location. I've even found earlier incarnations of my own temporary residences in Paris recorded years before my passage by Atget: a view along the rue St Sulpice to the happy summer I spent above the *bondieuserie* shops in a tiny book-lined apartment that resounded to the matutinal bells; the corner apartment with a view of the old burial ground of Place des Innocents and, downstairs, Le Petit Ramoneur, one of the last working-class restaurants in the rue St Denis to dish up *boeuf gros sel*; or my address for a year in the hanging street of old Paris, rue de l'Arbre Sec, which turns up somewhere in La Fontaine. Atget's view of the street shows two tilted carts in front of a furrier's shop 'Fourrures Confectionnées' and next door, a haberdashery that was to become the Caveau François Villon, a restaurant with a noose for a sign.

Walter Benjamin thought Atget's photographs resembled those of the scene of a crime. The corpse must have been spirited away, unless Benjamin thought that the city itself was the culprit. It is the general lack of passers-by which lends Atget's views of Paris their uncanniness. Unlike the work of the photographers who came after him, especially Doisneau and Brassaï, Atget's city is very nearly unpeopled. What is noticable is the jagged geography of roof-top Paris, the chimney-pots stuck on in mad rows seemingly as an afterthought, the streets seen from the rooftops as a river of bitumen at the bottom of a chasm, the blaze of the cafés on streets that had seen the atrocities of the Commune. Photographs are not transcendent: they are the unique traces of a historical reality that is no longer available to us as experience but which technology has turned into a historical index. Benjamin thought that they take the 'aura' out of reality; if anything, these relics of lost time have more aura than a mind can absorb.

Which is why having seen gallery upon gallery of them, I feel compelled to walk from the Marais along the rue St Honoré again, something I haven't done in ages, and skirt what used to be not just Paris's belly but its underbelly (although, as Georges Brassens

Politics and Aesthetics

*I consider politics, political action, all forms of politics,
as inferior values and inferior activities of the mind.*

Paul Valéry

THE RED COUNT: HARRY GRAF KESSLER

It is 28 December 1918, just over a month since German capitula-
tion and the end of fighting in the Great War. Kaiser Wilhelm II
has abdicated and fled to the Netherlands, bringing to an end five
hundred years of Prussian domination by the Hohenzollern
dynasty. In Kiel the German navy mutinies, and the black, red and
gold flag of the republic flutters over the Reichstag. Karl
Liebknecht calls for a socialist revolution. The Berlin Dada Club
invents the dada two-step, as a preamble to world revolution.
Western values are collapsing. On the way to lunch, Count Harry
Kessler pays a visit to the Kaiser's private apartments; there, in the
Imperial Palace, among the shattered glass, looted furniture and
broken swagger-sticks, the whole tawdriness of the atmosphere
out of which war had come weighs on him. 'In this rubbishy,
trivial, unreal microcosm, furnished with nothing but false values
which deceived him and others, he made his judgements, plans,
and decisions. Morbid taste and a pathologically excitable character in charge of an all too well-oiled machine of state. Now the
symbols of his futile animating spirit lie strewn around here in the
shape of doltish odds and ends. I feel no sympathy, only aversion
and complicity when I reflect that this world was not done away
with long ago…'

Bad aesthetics, bad ethics. Kessler's verdict on the Kaiser takes
a leaf from the book of his contemporary, the great Viennese
satirist Karl Kraus, who, at the end of his colossal montage drama

The Last Days of Mankind, had no less a character than God echo the Kaiser's famous statement: 'This was not my will.' The buck stops here – the Kaiser had less excuse than God for not knowing what he was doing. Harry Kessler's critical sense was sharpened by two facts: he himself was by birth a member of this old order. Not only that, but his mother, a famous beauty, was reputed to have been the old Kaiser's last mistress, and wags even bandied it about that Kessler was 'cousin' to Wilhelm II (he wasn't). But it lends his judgement piquancy, and we are left to guess what his allegiance to the Weimar Republic must have cost him in terms of his standing among his upper-class contemporaries. He reports Richard Strauss's wife accusing him, in 1926, of being a class traitor: 'People do say, and Pauline [Strauss] bends forward to whisper it stealthily, that Count Kessler has become quite a Red. Oh no, I answer, I am just a simple democrat. Pauline: A democrat, you, who are a Count? In that case you are fouling your own nest.'

A democrat Kessler might have been, but colour-scheme-simple he wasn't. Allied insistence on Article 231, which attributed all guilt for the war to the Germans, must have made life difficult for a representative of a nation that, rightly or wrongly, believed surrender had been an 'offering' to Wilson's 14 Points. Excluded from the club of nations after the Paris Conference of 1919, in disregard of historical precedent (France had been brought back into the fold after Metternich's Vienna), Germany was left to the Reds. It went brown instead. Nest-fouling was what the European powers had done in the belief that each was acting in its own interest. Chivalry was dead. 'This is the age of little men,' Kessler tells us, in a passage in which he extols his 'submarine sailor friend', one of those rugged working-class types who were such a draw for Auden and Isherwood in 1930: like many of his class, he tends to idealise workers while spoofing the pretensions of his bourgeois Social Democrat colleagues. How can we account for Kessler's commitment? As a rather fastidious aesthete, he would seem a perfect candidate for the circle of homosexual acolytes around his exact contemporary, the poet Stefan George, who made out of the adage 'art for art's sake' a code for living. In politicised times, it was an inadequate pose. Before 1914, the orchid in the buttonhole of any number of German writers had been a badge for jingoism and war fervour; after 1918, retreat into the ivory tower and disdain for the 'little men' was a gift to the Nazis. Hannah Arendt once wrote a blistering essay about the Weimar intellectuals' self-serving aloofness from politics: Kessler could hardly be said to be one of them. He is humane and phlegmatic, no gourmet of catastrophes. Perhaps he would have argued that the true aesthete is a moralist, since he cares about the beauty of his soul. But Kessler could do little to save the ramshackle liberal constitution which had come into being after the war: he hears its death-knell when the leading social democrat Gustav Stresemann died (of natural causes) in 1929. Things couldn't go on. When the Great Depression reached its nadir in 1931, and unemployment bottomed out in Germany at 5,615,000, they didn't. Numbers were about to exact a terrible revenge.

Born in 1868 to a German banker and an artistic Irish mother called Alice Harriet Blosse-Lynch, Kessler went to prep school at Ascot and trained as a lawyer before devoting his energies – and money – to the arts. He was a discriminating Maecenas. He introduced impressionism to Germany, supported poets and artists including Rilke and Munch, developed the Weimar seminars which were later to become influential and more widely known as the Bauhaus, and under his own imprint The Cranach Press produced some classic fine books, notably a superb edition of *Hamlet* with woodcuts by Edward Gordon Craig which is now a collector's item. He briefly served as a reserve officer in the early months of the war, worked as a cultural attaché in Bern, and was the first German diplomat in Warsaw after cessation of hostilities. He attended the fateful Genoa Conference of 1922 that dismantled one of the pillars of the liberal world order, the metallic convertibility of currency based on gold, and made possible the great credit boom and ensuing Great Depression. Until 1924, he was constantly on the move across Europe to arrange new terms for the payment of German war reparations, making proposals to incorporate Germany in the new League of Nations through the auspices of his own initiative the New Fatherland League, and witnessing, at first hand, the political unrest after the imposition of the Versailles Treaty. In Germany it was an age of assassinations, and Kessler was probably lucky not to have been shot himself. When the distinguished foreign minister Walter Rathenau, who served as the model for the industrialist Paul Armheim in Musil's novel *The Man without Qualities* (and whose biography would later be written by Kessler), was murdered by right-wingers in June 1922, he notes that more than 500 left-wing politicians had been killed since war's end.

The title of his diaries in English, *Berlin in Lights*, comes from a squib of verse by Kurt Weill, and is presumably meant to lend the book a touch of cabaret naughtiness. Apart from the odd passing mention of 'voluptuaries' and all-night bars, Kessler is remarkably chaste about Babylon-on-the-Spree. His is an account of the early days of that chimera the United States of Europe – single currency and customs union and all – reminding us that it was on diplomats' lips long before the moral disaster which is conventionally thought to be its raison d'être. Then as now, it was primarily a French-German affair. Kessler's cultured Europe is a lost continent though. Despite the craze in the 1920s for all things American, not least jazz, it is evident from his descriptions that Paris and Berlin were still dazzled by their own *weltglanz*: it is hard to imagine French audiences today flocking to view a German film *(Mädchen in Uniform)* for weeks on end as they did in 1932. Kessler suggests why: 'Germany is (alas!) once more the international star whose antics the masses watch, in the papers and in the cinema, with a mixture of fright, incomprehension, and reluctant admiration laced with quite an amount of glee at the trouble we are in.'

What distinguishes his diary (which he apparently started in 1880, making this book merely its latter third), is Kessler's tone, which is elegant, fastidious, *distanziert*. This man who brought his gifts of mind to bear on the tragic carnival of his era was a very distinguished prose-writer. Needless to say his aestheticism is a pole apart from the political philosophy he acted out: his brilliantly unflattering thumbnail sketches of some of his fellow politicians make that all too clear. Many entries have an aphoristic force: 'Bolshevism demands the staff-college touch [events in the post-war period bear him out in ways he couldn't have predicted], cowardice is the subtlest and most tragic of human qualities' or, in an intriguing, Rousseau-like aside from a man as exquisitely 'denatured' by culture as he happened to be: 'All education is violence of a sort, just as every state is. Education, society, and the state exist simply to sublimate the cruder forms of force into more refined ones. That amounts to a difference in manner and degree, not of principle.' About the private man we learn almost nothing, other than the names of his now obscure high-society friends, Baby Goldschmidt-Rothschild being one that trips off the tongue. At a dinner in her luxurious Pariser Platz apartment in Berlin, Kessler sees red: 'After the meal thirty van Gogh letters, in an excessively ornate, ugly binding, were handed round with cigarettes and coffee. Poor van Gogh!' He is a Proust with a social conscience, forthright about his dislikes – Ernst Toller's play *Maschinenstürmer* is 'untalented rubbish', the poet Else Lasker-Schüler 'this beastly person'. At first hand, he witnesses George Grosz's attempts to become the German Hogarth, noting that 'he is reactionary and revolutionary in one, a symbol of the times'. He supplies Hugo von Hofmannsthal with the story which the latter works up into *der Rosenkavelier*, and observes a vital quality evacuating from his own life when Hofmannsthal dies on his way to attend the funeral of his suicided elder son Franz – 'a part of my world has died with him'.

Repeated visits to the Nietzsche Archive in Weimar (which he supported financially in its early days) convince him that its guardian, Nietzsche's infamous sister Elisabeth Foerster, is 'a flapper at heart'. She in turn insists on calling him her 'oldest friend', even though he ridicules her right-wing leanings and the strong dollar, to non-conformist life in Paris between the wars. Most famously, he edited *transition*, the little magazine that ran for eleven years between 1927 and 1938 and in which *Finnegans Wake* first appeared as 'Work in Progress' (Jolas was the first of Joyce's friends to guess the title Joyce had reserved for the work); other contributions included Gottfried Benn's essays, the very first translations of Kafka (by Jolas himself), squibs from the Dadaists and Surrealists, Gertrude Stein's 'esoteric stutterings' (Jolas was not a fan) and work by the young Dylan Thomas. Anglo-American literature of the time under the influence of Imagism aspired to be any art other than verbal, preferably a *hard* one like sculpture, but Jolas reintroduced it to the 'Word', fostered experimentalism, and promoted what might loosely and collectively be called continental antirealism.

Interesting as the *transition* saga is, and no chapter is more convincingly written than 'Ananke Strikes the Poet', Jolas's richly anecdotal reminiscence of the Joyce who so exasperated Monsieur Noël, *transition*'s printer in St-Dizier ('St Dizzier') with last-minute manuscript changes that he used his name as an objurgation – 'Joyce, *alors!*' – ; but there is a great deal else in Jolas's autobiography, which is published for the first time in an edited version almost fifty years after his death in 1952. *Man from Babel* is the intellectual history of a poet, in this rather particular case Jolas the trilingual poet, in which his wife Maria and two daughters are rather shadowy presences, as well as a retrospective of his singular career as a journalist and translator – his version of Döblin's *Berlin Alexanderplatz* is still in print.

Born in New Jersey in 1894, and brought back to Europe as an infant by his French-German parents, Jolas grew up in the Lorraine town of Forbach, then part of the German Reich, a frontier-zone subject to the competing claims of French and German, with the local patois as escape route, shibboleth or recipe for calling down a plague on both houses. In 1909, Jolas returned alone to New York 'as a liberty-hungry, America-dreaming youngster'. He did odd jobs, learning English on the street, before moving from alien journalism (as the foreign-language press was then called in the States) to being a 'tab' reporter in New York. Then as now, the newspaper trade was cut-throat, although reporters appeared to be more inventive, vying with each other to invent words and even encouraging their readers in the use of this 'slanguage'. Though he rapidly made his name as a journalist, Jolas continued to read Novalis in his mother-tongue, wrote romantic poems, and dreamed of going back to Europe. 'Flight meant taking a train for the unknown, it meant geographical dislocations, it meant mirac-ulous possibilities,' he writes at a time when he was jobbing as a crime reporter in Savannah. He was never able to resist the siren call of that phrase, and it landed him at various times of his life on one side of the Atlantic, only for him to hear it boom out from the other.

He duly returned to Forbach, in time to cycle down to Strasburg to befriend René Schickele and meet the l'Arc group of writers: the connection stood him in good stead a few years later when recruiting French Surrealists for *transition*. In the mid-1920s he returned again to France, this time as a literary journalist, filing reports for the *Chicago Tribune* on the Paris scene (his column was called 'Rambles through Literary Paris'); the finances for the 27 issues of *transition* were largely bled from his salary. For much of the 1920s the magazine was actually edited from the Jolas's family house in Colombey-les-Deux-Eglises until it was sold in 1929 to a certain French colonel called de Gaulle. In New England during the war years he provided support and succour to a group of French artists and writers including Masson and Breton (and pushed the vanguard on to James Laughlin's *New Directions*). In 1944 he was sent as a press officer with the US Office of War Information to help set up a free press in Germany: he launched the *Aachener Nachrichten* as its first post-war democratic paper. He was later editor-in-chief of the Deutsche Allgemeine Nachrichten-Agentur (DANA). His brief was to root out suspect journalists, replace the feuilletonistic, flabby *Plakat* style so characteristic of German newspapers with American 'hard-fact' journalism ('who, when, where, why, how?...') and skewer terms and concepts corrupted by the Nazis: these were published in a glossary called *Wörterbuch des Unmenchen*. He also set up a 'think paper', *Die Wandlung*, which was one of the first intellectual journals to examine the question of German war guilt. Several times he mentions his dismay at the 'pathological self-pity' of German writers, observing that the speakers at the Point Zero congress after the war were 'pompous, hollow and full of resentment'; and his account of his brief period in 1950 as news editor of the army-accredited Munich paper *Neue Zeitung* frankly portrays it as the 'last redoubt of Nazi journalism.'

Not having envisaged a link between mid-century politics and German romanticism, least of all that of his own 'gentle Novalis', Jolas admits to a 'sense of betrayal'. There had been essays on Novalis in the *Völkische Beobachter*, as Jean Améry once wrote (and how much more pained and insightful his writing is than Jolas's), 'and at times they were not at all that stupid'. The later chapters of *Man from Babel* sag under the shock of having to register – after its imposition – the menace in Benn's 1932 phrase that 'the new man's chief characteristic will be revolt against the intellect'. The shock is one of self-recognition, too. There is a striking disjunction between Gene the hard-headed newspaperman who preferred the 'lobster-shift' and writing under pressure, and the 'genial young poetriarch Euge' as Joyce called him in a limerick. In that, he resembles the expressionist poet he so admired in the *transition* years: in his journalism Gottfried Benn displays exactly the same blend of clinical toughness and aesthetic self-reliance as Jolas. Another revealing moment occurs when Jolas the metaphysician, appalled by what he has seen in the rubbleland – as he calls it – writes in a purple manner he would hardly have tolerated as an editor: 'Yes, I am an American press officer. I think and write in German like a mythical "culture-bearer" to a people who have just passed through the Hitlerian night and who are still sick in heart and mind. I am engaged in a supreme adventure, in a Gutenbergian rite, that is rooted in the magical forces of language.' As for the alleged flabbiness of the German press under the Nazis, it is not without interest that Victor Klemperer, in his close philological study of Nazi jargon and usage, *LTI*, takes a more discriminating view: by beefing up headlines and omitting articles before nouns the Nazi press had actually shown, in its mastery of the hard sell, just how much it had learned from America – 'compounding the strict concision favoured by the military, sport and business'.

Man from Babel can hardly be read as anything other than the record of a disappointment, the failure of Jolas's Revolution of the Word proclamation (item 12: 'the plain reader be damned'), and of the language of 'millions of words' which he hoped would be a guarantor of racial and ethnic equality. Today's Euro-English, for instance, is a stunted thing by comparison, if words alone are all that counts, and even the heat under the American melting-pot is no longer as intense as it was. His own style, in effect, throws into relief the great issue of his life. For more than anything else his autobiography is a love affair with words, individual words. They are his most vivid memories: crucible expressions from the American Army in the First World War, patois relished by the country folk near Forbach, and the maimed creatures caught on the wing by the reporter-warrior when they 'crashed, blasted, strafed, pounded, shelled, roared, wept and shrieked in my inner ear, now in French, now in English, now in German'. His attitude to them recalls Dylan Thomas's despairing self-indictment that he was a 'word-freak'; it is essentially a mystical, incantatory attitude which divests syntax of its civic and organising functions. Perhaps it's just that his words aren't *thick* enough. His own macaronic poems, which are interspersed throughout *Man from Babel*, suggest how remote a 'super-tongue for intercontinental expression' really is – 'intercontinental' being a word reserved for grand hotels and ballistic missiles. Despite his trilingualism (often within the same poem) Jolas wrote poems that snag the eye rather than catch the ear; their deep structure is all distracted surface. His words have 'amerigated', as he put it. He envied the author of *Ulysses*, feeling that his English allowed him to do things his more conservative

French and German idioms would not permit, although he failed to see that in his 'abnihilation of the ethym' Joyce, rather than enriching English, was slyly sabotaging it with dud taxonomies. Arch-modernist he might have been, but Joyce was also a Thomist who never forgot mother Ireland; it is revealing of his genial enthusiast Jolas – whose declaration 'I also suffered language' is the one constant in his autobiography – that almost the only piece of plain wisdom he brings along from his frontier-zone is the folk-refrain of *Hans im Schnokeloch*, who has everything he needs – 'but what he's got he doesn't want, and what he wants he hasn't got'.

THE USUAL BUSINESS: WOLFGANG KOEPPEN

'You ought to realise,' a young British officer tells a startled Stephen Spender in *European Witness*, an account of his mission to find out what was left of intellectual life on the continent in the autumn of 1945 and a book which ought to be still in print, 'that the Christian Democrat Party is a large scale Catholic racket in Cologne. The whole administration is corrupt.' The only other party, the Social Democrats, he avers, 'are too honest to get anywhere'.

Keetenheuve, the politician hero of Wolfgang Koeppen's *The Hothouse*, a masterpiece of German fiction first published in 1953, is one of these social democrat Honest Joes, way too honest to be an effective member of the Bundestag. Oppressed by institutional life, the ghastly afterlife of Nazi jargon and the opposition – the paraphernalia of what some Germans liked to call *Demokratur* (elective dictatorship under the tutelage of Chancellor Adenauer), he keeps reminding himself that he is really a 'reader and devotee of contemporary poetry'. Having weathered the war years in England, he has come back to the Germany of gutted cities and displaced persons: 'The end of the war had made him somewhat optimistic, and he thought it was right that he should now devote himself to a cause, having been a marginal figure for so long.' It soon becomes clear that had it not been for the doings of Hitler's killer battal-ions, and his own unimpeachable anti-Nazi record, Keetenheuve would be nowhere near the corridors of power at all. No sooner does he stand up to speak than he is dumbfounded by the point-lessness of what he is saying. When he sits in committee he can't follow the language any more. 'What were they speaking in? Chinese? It was committee German. It was a language he knew!' He lacks the equivocation and vanity of party-spirit, feeling himself to be a 'grain of salt, the germ of unrest in their bland and sluggish porridge of a party, a man of conscience and thereby an irritant'. Lieber Herr Keutenheuve is a belated man.

The hothouse is Bonn, the Rhineland city that served as Germany's capital for nearly fifty years; it is the novel's other protagonist, with its 'parliamentary ghetto', press ship, wine bars, executive offices and bridge over the sluggish Rhine. 'Distant hills arced up out of the early morning haze. Keetenheuve breathed in the mild air and straightaway felt sad. Chambers of commerce and tour operators described the area as the Rhine Riviera. A hothouse climate flourished in the basin between the hills; the air stagnated over the river and its banks. Villas stood beside the water, roses were bred, prosperity strode through the parkland wielding hedge clippers, gravel crunched crisply under the pensioners' lightweight footwear, Keetenheuve would never join their ranks, never own a home here, never trim or breed roses, the *nobiles*, *Rosa indica*, which put him in mind of *Erysipelas traumaticum*, faith healers were at work here, Germany was one large public hothouse, Keetenheuve took in rare flora, greedy, curious plants, giant phalluses like chimney stacks full of billowing smoke, blue-green, red-yellow, toxic, but it was a fertility without youth and sap, it was all putrid, all ancient, the growths swelled, but it was all *Elephantiasis arabum*.'

Imposed on the nation by Adenauer, leader of the Christian Democrat majority in the new house and the Federal Republic's first chancellor, Bonn was, as one early critic of the book observed, the most arbitrarily designated capital in Europe. 'Even the storms seemed to be manmade here, an artificial entertainment in the restoration business of Fatherland & Sons, Inc.' Keetenheuve's colleagues – Mergentheim, an ex-Nazi fellow-traveller, Korodin, a prophecy-scouring Christian in the CDU ranks, and Knurrewahn, his party boss, 'who dreamed of becoming the man of reunification (a common enough dream)' – play the courtiers to his Hamlet. (It is of more than passing historical interest that Shakespeare was a fully-integrated part of the Nazi propaganda machine: some of his plays – the buccaneering ones especially – were performed more often during the Third Reich than the German classics. The twenty-thousand Hitler-adoring newsreel faces – '*Do you want total war? Yeah yeah yeah*' – watched by Keetenheuve with a kind of detached revulsion one afternoon in the cinema just happens to be the strength of the army Hamlet sees annihilated for 'a fantasy and a trick of fame'.) Not surprisingly, party headquarters wants to move him on and out. An ambassador's post to Guatemala – Malcolm Lowry territory – is offered as bait. 'It might be his salvation, the chance to grow old.' But he doesn't take it: boredom has left him, like Hamlet, beleaguered. He addresses the chamber, knowing the stenographers who type his speech won't recall a word of it should he meet them strolling down beside the Rhine. They probably wouldn't recognise him anyway. In a nightmarish closing sequence he has a weird tryst in the rubble of a bombed-out house with a Salvation Army girl called Lena, while her friend sings 'the song of the heavenly bridegroom'. It dawns on him that 'there was no guilt, no love, just a grave. It was the grave in him.' He walks past the sign still pointing to an air-raid shelter to the bridge over the turgid Rhine: 'The delegate was utterly useless, he was a burden to himself, and a leap from the bridge set him free.'

Koeppen's novel stands right at the beginning of the economic miracle, a few years after the newly sovereign Federal Republic had been incorporated into the Coal and Steel Community, the forerunner of today's European Union. In 1952, Ludwig Erhard, Adenauer's finance minister, introduced the social market economy, a blend of paternalism and economic growthmanship. The highest good was to be goods, lots and lots of them. Wooden language was the tribute; most thought it worth paying. Germany needed economic diversity to generate its boom, and it needed social and political pluralism to counteract the inevitable push towards bureaucratic command and control. Koeppen's novel was written in the gap between setting up the former, and working out how to conceal the latter. Above all, the postwar order required a pliable human substrate, and a sociology that had freed itself of the now unthinkable assumption of biologically-ordained racial superiority. Ecce Homo Unesco! Humans are plastic. Culture now explained what race once had: the constant element was the anthropological certainty that humanity could and ought to be *shaped*, assembly-line-style. Behind the cynicism about knowledge and power was an urgent need to defuse human aggression, to hoop all under the rule of law, to 'mollify' as Keetenheuve says. Even God could be called down for special bonding purposes. (Having just told Spender in *European Witness* about his plans for reconstruction, Adenauer, then mayor of Cologne, terminates the interview with a phrase that could have come from Dostoevsky's Grand Inquisitor: 'The imagination has to be provided for.')

The ideal Keetenheuve clings to, on the other hand, is individual freedom; it is not altogether compatible with his job description. Politics is a menial profession, like taking away household refuse: Keetenheuve internalises the disgust felt for those who do society's dirty work while failing to enjoy the fringe benefits. He wants people to step forward as subjects; his job demands he manipulate them as objects – all equal. Other things trouble him too. The much-vaunted 'consensus' society seems absolutist in spirit since it credits itself with total rectitude. Shouldn't politicians think of themselves as citizens too? And what about the unspoken continuities with the past? 'If you looked at the blueprints, it was the Nazi idiom they were still building in, and if you looked at the names of the architects, it was the Nazi architects who were still working...' Figures bear out Keetenheuve's claim – 34 per cent of

Foreign Ministry posts were occupied by former Nazis, though Adenauer claimed that the country would be ungovernable if they were barred from the administration: one of his wily *realpolitik* manoeuvres in the early days of the republic was to absorb the potentially disruptive nationalistic Refugee Party within his own CDU ranks. As this reconstituted West Germany set out in the polarised atmosphere of the Cold War to dazzle the rest of the world with its democratic credentials, *The Hothouse* staged a one-man protest against its ability to obscure its links with the past.

Koeppen's act of provocation – and *The Hothouse* is a furious piece of writing – earned him some sharp comments in the press. 'Not to be touched with a bargepole,' read one review in 1953. *The Hothouse* was decidedly not *Entspannungsliteratur*, a innovative term for a book to relax with over a stiff drink, something the new Germans were starting to feel they were entitled to after a long day at the office. It was only fifteen years later, when the Federal Republic was more secure in its democracy, and a lot more affluent, that Koeppen's arguments resurfaced: it was the leisured offspring of the post-war generation which challenged the legitimacy of that order in 1968, making way for the extra-parliamentary opposition and the New Left. Hans Magnus Enzensberger's influential essays on the technocracy of repression can be read as a cooler version of Keetenheuve's hamletry. But then, by a ghastly dialectic of history, those on the left, who, like Koeppen, considered themselves 'objects, perhaps even victims of politics', had to experience how, in opposing the imperialist West, they had become imitators of the hated Nazis themselves.

Perhaps because of its stops and starts (not all of his own making), Koeppen's career failed to consolidate into that of a novelist of the first rank. Its stops and starts are remarkable. A journalist for left-wing papers in Weimar Berlin, he left the country when the Nazis came to power in 1933: unlike his hero, Koeppen went to the Netherlands. Unaccountably, he returned to Berlin in 1939, and spent the war years writing scripts for the Universum-Film AG, better known as Ufa. Ufa was the German film production company which groomed Ernst Lubitsch and produced some of the most brilliant films of the 1920s and 1930s, including Fritz Lang's *Metropolis*. Koeppen once said that his scripts were just good enough to keep him in a job, but not good enough to get made, which wasn't quite true: one or two did. Apart from two novels before the war, a Holocaust memoir which he 'quarried' from an original manuscript by a survivor (*Jakob Littners Aufzeichningen aus einem Erdloch*, a book which caused controversy when Koeppen republished it as a novel under his own name in 1992), it is essentially for his Fifties trilogy that Koeppen will be remembered, the last book of which *Death in Rome* (1954) has already been translated into English. Siegfried Unseld, Koeppen's generous publisher, maintained him on a pension for the last forty years of his life (he died aged ninety in 1996), but he never came up with the great follow-up novel everybody had been waiting for. There may be things we simply do not know about Koeppen: his seems at some level an implausible life.

The technique that propels *The Hothouse* is essentially cinematic. It is an example of what Nietzsche called monologic art – a rejection of naturalism and mimetic effects. Its jittery, headlong style derives as much from a poem like Gottfried Benn's *Monolog* (1948) as from any novel of the time: this is heard to good effect when the wheels of Keetenheuve's train ('the Nibelungen Express') farcically stotter over the Rhine Maidens' 'Wagalaweia'. Italic script is interpolated into the flicker of consciousness like the captions in silent movies, underscoring the division between Keetenheuve's cool observations of his careerist colleagues, and his sense of personal failure. (Indeed, having a politician hero who translates Baudelaire in his office time suggests Koeppen is enacting his own predicament a bit too nakedly: the artist alienated from society goes a long way back in German literature.) Filmic scenes of German towns with their neatly stacked rubble abruptly shift to a close-up of his wife, Elke, the Gauleiter's daughter, who dies as the novel opens. Keetenheuve moves in a circle of Purgatory and his punishment is unreality. Perhaps his 'sin' is to have fallen victim

to the democratic piety that there can be such a thing as government by the people: the many have always been governed by the
few — politics, unfortunately, has to be based on policy. And if
few good works of literature ever get written about politicians,
Spender's friend W.H. Auden once suggested why: a poem in the
image of a political democracy would be 'formless, windy, banal
and utterly boring'. (Conversely, the Thousand Year Reich did
everything to pretend that an essentially stagey sense of German
nationhood, runes and bearskins and folkish roots and all, was
really, deeply, organically *authentic*.) Lucidity and old-fashioned
decency condemn Keetenheuve to isolation in a social order that
displays all the claustrophobic traits once associated with the
natural, yet, like everyone else, he is hopelessly dependent upon it
— he may indeed be even *more* dependent because of his lack of
will.

Overwhelmed by the impersonality of politics, refusing the
consolations of what Heinrich Böll called 'keeping your superiority feeling fresh in a refrigerator of irony', his final act snaps shut
as neatly as an aphorism in Theodor Adorno's book of minimal
morality, a book published fifty years ago too: rebuilding a culture
already implies its negation.

'You Must Change Your Life'

A Letter from Kakania

Does memory have a colour? If it does, it must lie somewhere in the palette between sepia and mahogany. A beautiful word the latter, even if I hear it these days as the spaced-out syllables of Brecht's decadent city, Mahagonny. *Ma-ha-gon-ny.* Mahagonny was the prototypic American city dreamed up in Europe. A city redolent of stiff-backed Biedermeier furniture, sepia daguerreotypes, Havana cigars, Worcestershire sauce, cocoa and the little lumps of dehydrated meat extract Nietzsche used to live on. When I was a boy they were called Oxo cubes.

And the more I look around, the more my observation receives official imprimatur. Memory *is* brown. Drive down the super-efficient tollways after the Channel Tunnel, those long concrete snakes cut around the contoured hills and ideological carcases of *la bonne vieille France*, and you can hardly miss them, deep ochre panels pointing out one architectural marvel after another, one battlefield after the next, the great arks bearing a generation's collective undertakings and understanding into the next. Cut off from the landscape by your car's metal cocoon the brown signs whiz past, pointers to what you almost slid through, at high speed, unawares. These are your didactic lessons for the day, visual lozenges of the continent's history. And by the time you turn east of Paris to travel the four hundred odd kilometres to the flatland of the Rhine Valley – *Verdun, le grès rose des Vosges, Strasbourg et sa cathédrale* – and Germany takes over – *schwäbische Alb, Ulmer Dom, Naturpark Augsburg, Stadt Dachau* – you've realised it at last: Europe is one enormous museum. A Bloomuselam. Perhaps you'll stop in

94

Strasburg to visit the cathedral that so impressed the young Goethe in the 1770s when liking Gothic wasn't the done thing. Gothic cathedrals are great improvisations, the work of hundreds of hands. No wonder their builders proudly insisted they were descended from the men who built King Solomon's temple. Next to you, a guide is pointing out that on account of its soft red sandstone blocks which need replacing every few hundred years it will one day, like Otto Neurath's shipshape definition of knowledge, be a resplendently new millennial vessel just like the old one. But will it still *be* the old one? That is a question which goes back to Plutarch, and the Athenians who preserved Theseus' thirty-oared galley down to the time of Demetrius of Phalerum (317–307 BC). It is surely one you will want to ponder in the café opposite the cathedral as you sip a demitasse of dark brown espresso.

Display your discernment, but don't stop too long. Europe's on the move – backwards, to get a better view of its cathedrals.

And once you've driven down the Rhine Valley, where a strange woodcutter of a philosopher proclaimed that not only had we forgotten what Being is, but that we had forgotten our forgetting, you can just about make out the peaks of the Alps far off in the distance, those magic mountains that Thomas Mann made so famous with his novel of sanatoria and big ideas, in which the volatile colonial subject Naphta, who has aligned himself entirely with the Jesuit order that once persecuted his Jewish father, and the doctrinaire liberal Settembrini battle it out in Davos. For what? The virgin soul of the man in the middle, the middling Hans Castorp, 'the plastic youth' who yields his body, in 'one riotously sweet hour' between exposing his lungs to the chill air of the mountain that also accommodates an abyss, to the beguilements of the seductive Clavdia Chauchat, the woman with the Kirghiz eyes. Myth has been banished from the world, but there are ample sexual signs to take its place. *The Magic Mountain* is a novel not just about illness and initiation, adventures of the spirit, the inability to live in the 'low country'; it is also about how, under a bombardment of Röntgen rays, a young man becomes, in the very broadest sense, 'media-conscious'. Among the grandiose ruminations on humanism and high tech, the patients have evidently not been told not to eat chocolate before dinner: 'Everybody's mouth was stained brown, and the Berghof kitchen offered its most elaborate delicacies to captious and indifferent diners who had lost their appetites to *Milka-Nut*, *Chocolat à la crème d'amandes*, *Marquis-napoli-tains*, and gold-besprinkled cats' tongues.'

Davos was the place where, in 1929, Martin Heidegger and Ernst Cassirer met for a legendary debate: the existential woodcutter was asked straight out by the neo-Kantian whether he wished to destroy the only rampart that gave some kind of order to the radical contingency of human life. Individuals, retorted Heidegger, unabashed, had to return to 'the hardness of fate'.

Snow turns to slush: Castorp planned to stay in the sanatorium for three weeks and spent seven years there, waiting for her to return while endeavouring to understand what it meant to be a fully-fledged individual in 'a capitalistic economy that was still functioning well and normally', as Mann himself wrote: he goes to some lengths to tell us Hans' income, the cost of a month's lodging at the Berghof, the interest on his capital investment, and so on. If he had waited seventy instead of seven, he would surely have wandered into one of the annual meetings of the World Economic Forum in the same place, and discovered that there's only one agenda after all, and it doesn't have very much to do with Europe.

Deeper into the mountains (for now your journey is starting to resemble the classic Orient Express) is the hydrocephalic capital of that other Alp-bound country that once commanded an empire. After Kurt Waldheim, it has to play down the significance of a bronze-faced ski instructor who has been posing lately as a politician: his grasp of reality is so feeble he doesn't realise Austria will have to quadruple the number of immigrants to the country over the next half-century if it wants to stay as wealthy as it now is. As Karl Kraus once said: 'through her political scandals, Austria has succeeded in drawing the larger world's attention to herself – and at last is no longer confused with Australia'. The export trade keeps product recognition at a high level: between the wars the same drastically reduced mountain nation generously sent Britain five or six brilliant philosophers (the philosophical work which has had more influence than any other on the main current of English-speaking philosophy since the war, Wittgenstein's *Philosophical Investigations*, opens with a line from the classic Viennese comedy-writer Nestroy one of whose sayings once impressed me enough to enter my notebook: 'Resignation is the best nation').

It also gave us that greatest unfinished novel of the twentieth century, one which describes the break-up of a farflung empire called Kakania. Kakania was Musil's very rude soubriquet – Joseph Roth, who actually *believed* in the monarchy, didn't like it one bit – for the domain from Switzerland to Russia ruled over by the Habsburg monarch, whose title starts off 'Emperor of Austria, King of Hungary, of Bohemia, of Dalmatia, Croatia, Slavonia, Galicia, Lodomeria, and Illyria; King of Jerusalem, etc.; Archduke of Austria, Grand Duke of Tuscany and Cracow; Duke of Lothringia, of Salzburg, Styria, Carinthia, Carniola, and Bukinowa; Grand Duke of Transylvania, Margrave of Moravia; Duke of Upper and Lower Silesia, of Modena, Parma, Piacenza, and Guastella, of Auschwitz and Sator, of Teschen, Friaul, Ragusa and Zara; Princely Count of Habsburg and Tyrol, of Kyburg, Görz, and Gradiska; Duke of Trent and Brizen; Margrave of Upper and Lower Lausitz and in Istria; Count of Hohenembs, Feldkirch, Bregenz, Sonnenburg, etc.; Lord of Trieste, of Cattaro, and above the Windisch Mark; Great Voyvod of the Voyvodina, Servia... etc.' The royal palace in Vienna had an elegant and far shorter manner of doing the rounds: it bore the vowels AEIOU on the keystone of its gate: Austriacorum Est Imperare Orbi Universo.

Musil, a man of many qualities, could have been describing the break-up of Ukania, our Untied Kingdom. (Substitute 'England' for Musil's Austria and 'Scotland' for Hungary and you get this observation: 'Britain,' he nearly wrote, 'did not consist of an

English part and a Scottish part that... combined to form a unity, but of a whole and a part: namely, of a Scottish and a British sense of nationhood, and the latter was at home in England, whereby the English sense of nationhood actually became homeless.' But not for much longer, it seems.) Musil fled the Nazis for neutral Geneva and died doing his press-ups one morning in 1942 with, as his wife said, a smirk on his face. Arthur Koestler managed to find refuge in London, and thought Britain 'a kind of Davos for internally bruised veterans of the totalitarian age'. There's one good thing about the Alps though. On a clear day they offer a splendid vantage point for espying what Paul Valéry called the 'immense sort of terrace of Elsinor that stretches from Basel to Cologne, fringed by the sands of Nieuport, the marshes of the Somme, the limestone of Champagne, the granites of Alsace'. A dead waste for any Hamlet to keep watch upon, gazing bleary-eyed on the millions of dead after the First War. Would he recognise what the colour of memory is doing to his continent? Valéry's list anticipates it – geography is even now taking its dundrab revenge on history.

Yet that cloud of unknowing – *l'air du temps, Zeitgeist* – pouring down the mountains has an unmistakable scent to it. It's not springtime for Europe: it's Naphta's namesake you can smell, a crystalline sublimate of bitumen and asphalt. After all, *The Magic Mountain* was actually a farewell to the era that believed in ideas: when Settembrini and Naphta fight it out their duel has nothing to do with what they took two hundred pages to discuss. Now you can smell the latter's old Jesuitical spirit in the pungent odour of mothballs, naphthalene. And you've twigged it at last: this is museum Europe. Imagine how proud our ancestors must have been to know they'd one day end up being us. But what does a museum do – what's it *for*?

Once museums were asylums for art works. Now they're built to upstage the art they hold. Masterpieces arranged in scores all shouting 'Look at me!' lose a little bit of their masterliness. Surely no one can imagine visiting the Louvre and being smitten with an aura like that other Austrian, Rainer Maria Rilke, who in 1906 saw an early fifth-century BC torso of a youth from Miletus and wrote a poem — about the Word made not so much flesh as work of art — in which he instructed the reader: 'You must change your life.' Or imagine attending, a few years later, an archaeology lecture at the University of Freiburg during which the classical archaeologist Ernst Bluchor recited that very poem at the end of his lecture and then burst into tears. Musil said monuments are public works whose essential function is to be overlooked; nobody overlooks a museum, which is a place of devout lies where people go to admire what they think they ought to admire. In one of his diaries the exiled Polish writer Witold Gombrowicz noted that if we could scrutinise viewers' reactions more empirically we'd find an absolute falseness that would bring the Parthenon crashing down and explode the Sistine Chapel for shame. Perhaps only monuments irreconcilably at odds with their surroundings have any kind of force — like Alfred Hrdlicka's 'Street-washing Jew', an old man on all fours scrubbing the pavement outside the Sacher Café in Vienna, or the 'stumble-stones' which have been inserted into the pavement of Berlin streets to mark a former Jewish dwelling. Most museums are monuments to nostalgia, in spite of what the backward glance did to Lot's wife: we have Biblical authority for the modern tactic of *fuite à l'avance*. But build a museum and in no time memory takes on the petrified façade of the heritage industry — *la patrimoine*.

What we're worrying over is authenticity, that ominous word that only a civilisation anxious about its legitimacy could find so engaging. Authenticity is a word that has escaped from the zoo (another kind of museum) and gone on rampage.

But aren't there other, more mobile species of memory? Individuals secrete a kind of memory, as volatile and subtle as body heat. People go to sleep, not to rest but to forget; and while they sleep the sweats of the spirit burn. And that's the problem for memorialists, because experience can't be relived. The harder we try to, the tackier it looks. Memory begins in Homer with

Odysseus who, when asked who he is, describes his home land of Ithaca: 'a rough land, but it nurtures fine men. And I know of no sweeter sight for a man's eyes than his own country.' He wasn't a theme-park operator selling Ithaca but a man making a claim about the distinctiveness of his own identity. It may be a rough land, Ithaca, but it's his. He knows its eucalyptus trees, the colour of the hills in autumn, the pungency of the earth underfoot in high summer. For twenty years Odysseus took his bags with him round the Aegean, and if it weren't for his example – as perpetuated by Leopold Bloom's dad – the only idea of memory we'd have would be the lex of the Holy Roman Empire, even though Voltaire pointed out a long time ago that it was neither holy, nor Roman, nor an empire. Outsiders take their identity from place to place, until further notice. They travel memory. 'It is even part of my good fortune not to be a house owner,' wrote Nietzsche. But that no-fixed-abode notion of Europe is unsettling, a provocation to those who believe, like Burke, that nothing is more dangerous to ordered society than the energy of ability without property. From Neolithic times, nomads have always attracted the hate of the sedentary. They riled the self-appointed cleaners of Augean stables too. Odd, while on the subject, that people so dedicated to racial purity and cinematic Alpine white-outs as the Nazis should choose brown as their party colour.

Museums don't make anything. Or do they? Mnemosyne, the Greek goddess of memory was latinised as Moneta, another name for Juno, in whose temple the Roman mint was to be found. Hence the English word *money*. Queen Money, as Robert Burton called her, to whom we daily offer sacrifice. Museums help to make this rich European colour of brown. They make age. And then some – which is called *hors d'âge*, like a good XO cognac, so old it can't get any older. But juggle a few letters and Europe's museums start to resemble mausoleums, its musealisation mummification. America feeds on amnesia, data lives for ever in Cyberia, but mummies come from Egypt. Actually, the word mummy (*mumiyah*) came from Persia, once *the* fashionably exotic culture as defined by Montesquieu: mummy is the Parsi term for asphalt resin. Bitumen of Judea dissolved in oil of lavender: that was the mixture applied to a tin plate and used by the pioneering photographer Nicéphore Niepce to obtain an image of his window in 1826. Pitch and body parts – 'somewhat acrid and bitterish', *Pharmacopoiea Universalis*, London, 1747 – marked the beginning of the pharmaceutical industry, now globally dedicated to helping us outlive ourselves. 'After eighty,' a patient once said to me, 'you lose interest in your self, though you'd still like to know how it turns out with the world.' He was rid of the fear that shrinks people from the inside, until they dry up: Egyptianism. But the faith that built cathedrals has gone – though their vaults still hang suspended like airy cages from their convictions – and there's no way to get it back, not even faith in the beauty that stole into them by the side-door, as it were, to soften the uncanny feeling that overcame worshippers adjacent to the divine presence, the dread of such places being, as Nietzsche once said, their presupposition. And faith in Europe? See under: *Gesamtkunstwerk*.

Cathedrals, as Marcel says, thrusting his head through the prose of *In Search of Lost Time*, should be venerated until the day when, in order to save them, one would have to renounce the truths they teach. He is condemning art as idolatry, which is to say himself.

Not that my being blue is any obstacle to the collecting. The exhibits pile up under cupolas and in hushed corridors – cartons and pochettes, crates with stickers on them, great wooden bazaars. Colporters bring in more and more. In the great hydrocarbon cities of Mahagonny everything is turning slowly brown. Don't you smell it? And that stifled reverential coughing – can it be Anubis barking? It certainly isn't Argos.

Now the guardians are coming to tell us not to touch the exhibits. And I don't need to tell you the colour of their uniforms.

Bile with Style

'How do you tell a true patriot?' asked the cabarettist Helmut Qualtinger a few years ago. 'He's ashamed of his countrymen.' The remark goes further than Austria, but Thomas Bernhard's writings, slabs of lyophilised bile from his first mature work *Verstörung* (1967) through the numerous novels and plays and six volumes of autobiography, are characteristic of a pronounced strain in Austrian literature: the writer as malcontent and whinger. It is a love-hate relationship which precedes this century, it can be found simmering away in Grillparzer and Nestroy, for example; the age of the great coffee houses and newspapers refined it to exquisite parody, and Austria's ignominious collapse in the First War envenomed it. Karl Kraus, something of a scold himself, even inserted a grumbling character called 'Der Nörgler' in his docudrama, *The Last Days of Mankind*. After the terrible disclosures of the Second War, it was left to Bernhard to add his own withering definitions of 'Austrian brainlessness, in all its subtle shades'.

This kind of invective follows its own dynamic, of course: the Austro-Bavarian adjective for it is *grantig* and nearly all of Bernhard's prolific writings can be seen as various kinds of qualitative variations on its noun-form *Grant* – a uniquely middle European blend of melancholic dissatisfaction and choleric tetchiness. In his theatrepiece *Heldenplatz* he suggests 'the Austrian is unhappy by nature'; rubbing salt in the wound, his writing represents the quintessence of a creative attitude which needs as subject what it can hardly bear to live with. It justifies itself as a kind of hyperbole and licensed clowning, although it surely takes querulousness of a perversely metaphysical order to sustain the high flight of Bernhard's wrath: its fluency is inversely proportional to any real or continuing friction in the writer's social situation or standing.

Scandal accompanied Bernhard through his writing career, but nothing catered for quite such scandal as his death in 1989. Anticipating the vulture-like habits of the keepers of the culture – Austria is home to that other odd tradition, the splendid cadaver (*die schöne Leiche*) – Bernhard stipulated in his will that none of his works, 'published in his lifetime or posthumously, in any form whatsoever, written or edited, shall for the duration of its legal copyright be performed, published or recited within the Austrian state'. He thereby proved himself to be a major strategist of *Grant*: by drastically smothering the expectation that once he was dead, he would return to his public, he set off a rumpus that had his German publisher in Frankfurt accusing Austrian journalists of posthumous defamation and the director of the Vienna Burgtheater bemoaning the fact that, for two generations, there will be no opportunity to present on stage the work of one of the few Austrian writers of international rank.

Grouchiness in writers is not that rare, usually something of a highly developed mannerism or tic; but it often diverts attention from the substance of the work at hand. In Bernhard's case the grumbling is what he advances with. Style was his mask, a severely elegant and demanding one which bore the imprints of philosophical writers like Pascal and Schopenhauer, and one which he used repeatedly to test the self-proclaimed tolerance and beneficence of those in power. Terse descriptiveness, stylised indirect speech and cursory characterisations – with not so much as a paragraph ending in sight – are the techniques he uses to propel his fictions. His declaration in *Extinction* that 'to think is to fail' brings him, as many commentators have observed, close to Samuel Beckett.

Although he was actually born in the Netherlands, in 1931, Bernhard had a representatively miserable boyhood during the

Nazi period; illegitimate and a chronic bed-wetter, he was humiliated at school and by the local Hitler youth group, and ended up at a correction camp in Thuringia. Life between the red and the brown, and the torment of spending much of his eighteenth year in a TB sanatorium looking at the same view of mountains seems to have instilled a fierce determination in him to become a writer. Like all his novels, *Extinction* returns seamlessly to the single story Bernhard insisted every genuine artist was always refining; like many, it presents a character who has just inherited an estate: the dilemma of what to do with this estate, corrupted at different levels of its existence, forms the novel's initiating event.

In so much as the novel has a plot it can be summed up in a few lines. Franz-Josef Murau, disaffected intellectual and family blacksheep has recently returned from the marriage of his sister Caecilia on the family estate of Wolfsegg in Upper Austria to his self-imposed exile in Rome, where he is tutor to a young Italian, Gambetti. He receives a telegram informing him that his parents and elder brother Johannes have been killed in a car crash. His musings on his earlier life, growing up in the gloomy family demesne of Wolfsegg, form the first half of the book, entitled 'The Telegram'.

Wolfsegg is presented as a stifling place dominated by an awful mother who, he suggests, has been carrying on a longtime tryst with the papal archbishop Spandolini. A colonel during the war, the opportunist father is portrayed as a Nazi fellow-traveller. Afterwards, he shelters SS on the run while vaunting his Catholicism and his title (this seems a special term of abuse) as Master of the Hunt. Denazification is a hollow joke: 'the National Socialists are the people they look up to and secretly acknowledge as their leaders'. The children regularly persecute and inform on each other. The only family member to show an interest in nurturing the young boy is his Uncle Georg (very much like the maternal grandfather in Bernhard's autobiography), who opens up the five libraries in Wolfsegg for Franz-Josef.

The second half of the book 'The Will', details Murau's return

...am on an individual act of migration, the Hegira; and the
...ebrews made of the Exodus not only a means to preserve their
...tional identity but the very ethical principle that would allow
...odern egalitarian societies to emerge from the hierarchy of
...pire. No wonder its epic solemnising appealed to Gandhi and
...ao. The long walk burns the way for nearly all revolutionary
...roes.

...Thoreau's rather more lenient walkers set out in hope rather
...n the expectation of arriving, their gaze fixed on what the poet
...allace Stevens would later call 'the palm at the end of the mind'.
...e journey becomes the horizon, the life an errance. This is close
... Lao-Tzu's philosophy of 'tao', which in Chinese script is
...tten 'head' upon 'road' – the life of the mind on the open road.
... if saunterers are to feel at home everywhere, as Thoreau says,
...y have to be fully embodied: the walker takes his time, refusing
...et time impose itself on him.

...rimitivism is a modern consciousness gone walkabout only
...iscover that it is barely 'modern' at all: our lunging forwards
... freedom is a function of the bipedal instability of the
...nnah hominids. The Fall is a more literal threat than we might
...pose.

...he peripatetic Greek philosophers had already established a
... between walking and the good life, with the preference of the
...ics for *physis* (what they couldn't do without) over *nomos* (what
...r people told them to do) and the lawless tramping that took
...n beyond the walls of the city; but it was Jean-Jacques
...sseau who made the 'solitary walker' into an instantly recog-
...le figure on the cultural landscape, and the early Romantics
...invested walking with value, just before the primary mode of
...an propulsion began to be threatened by the view from the
...ay carriage window. If a gentleman had sought exercise in the
...eenth century he would be seen to go riding; walking was for
... who had no horse. Rousseau was to turn his afternoon walk
...enty kilometres into a new kind of devotion.

...horeau's piece is written in Rousseau's shadow. For Rousseau,

---

to the family property and preparations for the funeral in the
Orangery, 'the unmistakable smell of bodies lying in state'. But
once returned to oversee the funeral, the black mystery of
Wolfsegg dissolves and the only point of tension comes from
Murau's barely suppressible desire to lift the lid off his mother's
sealed coffin and look at her face, which had been disfigured in
the fatal car accident. His detailed description of the catafalque
and the burial under the presiding presence of Spandolini point
toward his realisation that the moral prevarications of his parents,
and the hypocrisy, blight and ugliness he sees as inextricably linked
to most people who have anything to do with the estate, are part
of his own condition too. More than three hundred pages of
relentless pillory and unflagging monologue come to rest on the
final page when he decides to turn Wolfsegg, and everything
belonging to it, over to the Jewish community in Vienna.

Bernhard's tirades still display all his reckless and sometimes
exhilarating *ex cathedra* finality. 'This state [Austria] is unspeakable.'
'Belgian doctors are notorious as the most stupid in Europe.'
Bruch's violin concerto and the Brucknerhaus by the Danube join
familiar targets such as the Austrian press, dirndls, 'Catholic histrionics' and post-war socialism. A whole page ridicules the
idolisation of Goethe – 'the classifier of stones, the stargazer, the
philosophical thumb-sucker of the Germans, who ladled their
spiritual jam into household canning jars, to be consumed at any
time and for any purpose'. Some of the kicking against the pricks
is funny and inspired, such as his exposition on the role of three-
ring binders in the development of 'bureaucratic' German
literature. Only Kafka (actual working bureaucrat in his daytime
life), escapes the general sweeping-out: 'anyone who writes so
much as a postcard nowadays calls himself a writer'.

Referring to himself during the book as an 'expert in extinction', and announcing his intention, like so many Bernhard
protagonists, of writing the great work, a book called *Extinction*,
Murau suggests that his own death will follow swiftly from the
dissolution of the estate. On the first page of the novel he relates

to the family property and preparations for the funeral in the Orangery, 'the unmistakable smell of bodies lying in state'. But once returned to oversee the funeral, the black mystery of Wolfsegg dissolves and the only point of tension comes from Murau's barely suppressible desire to lift the lid off his mother's sealed coffin and look at her face, which had been disfigured in the fatal car accident. His detailed description of the catafalque and the burial under the presiding presence of Spandolini point toward his realisation that the moral prevarications of his parents, and the hypocrisy, blight and ugliness he sees as inextricably linked to most people who have anything to do with the estate, are part of his own condition too. More than three hundred pages of relentless pillory and unflagging monologue come to rest on the final page when he decides to turn Wolfsegg, and everything belonging to it, over to the Jewish community in Vienna.

Bernhard's tirades still display all his reckless and sometimes exhilarating *ex cathedra* finality. 'This state [Austria] is unspeakable.' 'Belgian doctors are notorious as the most stupid in Europe.' Bruch's violin concerto and the Brucknerhaus by the Danube join familiar targets such as the Austrian press, dirndls, 'Catholic histrionics' and post-war socialism. A whole page ridicules the idolisation of Goethe – 'the classifier of stones, the stargazer, the philosophical thumb-sucker of the Germans, who ladled their spiritual jam into household canning jars, to be consumed at any time and for any purpose'. Some of the kicking against the pricks is funny and inspired, such as his exposition on the role of three-ring binders in the development of 'bureaucratic' German literature. Only Kafka (actual working bureaucrat in his daytime life), escapes the general sweeping-out: 'anyone who writes so much as a postcard nowadays calls himself a writer'.

Referring to himself during the book as an 'expert in extinction', and announcing his intention, like so many Bernhard protagonists, of writing the great work, a book called *Extinction*, Murau suggests that his own death will follow swiftly from the dissolution of the estate. On the first page of the novel he relates that he has given his pupil Gambetti five classic books in German to read including one by 'Thomas Bernhard'. This commingling and subtlising of reality and personal identity is typical of the author: it got one of his previous novels *Holzfällen* (1984) banned in Austria as libellous. But it also suggests that the failure of the inner life to mesh with outer reality is Bernhard's driving force; it gives his work its tragi-comic note of moral and linguistic urgency and suggests why he found Nietzsche's prescription for 'exaggerated honesty' the great organising principle he needed – in the intense sense of *duty* he brings to being a writer: 'those who are most successful at tiding themselves over existence have always been the great exaggerators'. That neatly organic phrase conveys much of the productive rage and stylistic verve of Bernhard's *via negativa*. Otherwise we might as well accept the Austrian version of Murphy's Law: nothing much need happen in the world before we have to bury it.

The Future of the Walk

'I have met with but one or two persons in the course of my life who understood the art of Walking, that is, of taking walks, who had a genius, so to speak, for sauntering; which word is beautifully derived "from idle people who roved about the country, in the middle ages, and asked charity, under pretence of going à la Sainte Terre" — to the holy land, till the children exclaimed, "There goes a Sainte-Terrer," a saunterer — a holy-lander. They who never go to the holy land in their walks, as they pretend, are indeed mere idlers and vagabonds, but they who do go there are saunterers in the good sense, such as I mean. Some, however, would derive the word from sans terre, without land or a home, which, therefore, in the good sense, will mean, having no particular home, but equally at home everywhere. For this is the secret of successful sauntering.'

The jaunty opening of Henry David Thoreau's essay 'Walking' (1843) confects two spurious but compelling etymologies for the word 'sauntering' (the OED entry simply says 'origin obscure'). A saunter is the best way to walk, a slow stately progress in the manner of the camel which, Thoreau observes, is the only beast able at the same time to ruminate and ambulate.

Walking, that alternating movement of pedestal and pendulum, is perhaps the intentional act closest to the unwilled rhythms of the body itself. That must be why pilgrimage is almost universally embodied in culture as a movement towards spiritual discovery, and the travail associated with horizontal displacement recognised as an essentially *transcendental* aspiration. Mohammed founded

Islam on an individual act of migration, the Hegira; and the Hebrews made of the Exodus not only a means to preserve their national identity but the very ethical principle that would allow modern egalitarian societies to emerge from the hierarchy of empire. No wonder its epic solemnising appealed to Gandhi and Mao. The long walk burns the way for nearly all revolutionary heroes.

Thoreau's rather more lenient walkers set out in hope rather than the expectation of arriving, their gaze fixed on what the poet Wallace Stevens would later call 'the palm at the end of the mind'. The journey becomes the horizon, the life an errance. This is close to Lao-Tzu's philosophy of 'tao', which in Chinese script is written 'head' upon 'road' – the life of the mind on the open road. But if saunterers are to feel at home everywhere, as Thoreau says, they have to be fully embodied: the walker takes his time, refusing to let time impose itself on him.

Primitivism is a modern consciousness gone walkabout only to discover that it is barely 'modern' at all: our lunging forwards into freedom is a function of the bipedal instability of the savannah hominids. The Fall is a more literal threat than we might suppose.

The peripatetic Greek philosophers had already established a link between walking and the good life, with the preference of the Cynics for *physis* (what they couldn't do without) over *nomos* (what other people told them to do) and the lawless tramping that took them beyond the walls of the city; but it was Jean-Jacques Rousseau who made the 'solitary walker' into an instantly recognisable figure on the cultural landscape, and the early Romantics who invested walking with value, just before the primary mode of human propulsion began to be threatened by the view from the railway carriage window. If a gentleman had sought exercise in the eighteenth century he would be seen to go riding; walking was for those who had no horse. Rousseau was to turn his afternoon walk of twenty kilometres into a new kind of devotion.

Thoreau's piece is written in Rousseau's shadow. For Rousseau, the *promenade pédestre* was joy itself: 'walking does something which animates and stimulates my ideas; I can hardly think when I am still; my body must be in motion for my mind to work.' His pedestrian discovery wasn't news. In his *Brief Lives*, John Aubrey tells us that Thomas Hobbes wrote his philosophical works on his 'delicious walkes': the philosopher was in the habit of contemplating a problem for a week or more while he walked, 'and he had in the head of his Staffe a pen and inke-horne, carried always a Notebook in his pocket, and as soon as a notion darted, he presently entered it into his Booke'. The Russian poet and essayist Osip Mandelstam wondered how many oxhide soles Dante wore out writing his *Divine Comedy* on the goat-paths of Italy: 'the step, linked with breathing and saturated with thought, Dante understood as the beginning of prosody'.

Because it liberates thought, engaging with the body at a proto-linguistic level, a walk is mental as well as physical; it has deep and perhaps surprising affinities with mnemonics and architecture. Architecture is a *gesture*, as Wittgenstein wrote. It is easy to imagine Bach anticipating the great contrapuntal structures he would hear when Dietrich Buxtehude played the organ in Lübeck: he took a month off from his duties in Arnstadt to walk the two hundred miles there and back. Freud knew, too, what he was hinting at when he likened his monumental *The Interpretation of Dreams* to 'an imaginary walk'. Every geographical feature of aboriginal Australia, every billabong and ridge and trail, is conceptualised as a songline. Walking is part of what R.L. Stevenson, leading his donkey Modestine over the Cevennes, called the great theorem of the liveableness of life.

With the 'trailside god' Wordsworth and his sister Dorothy, walking acquired a radical edge in Britain, one perpetuated in the image of an earlier tradition from Bunyan, in which walking was a literal mode of progress. Wordsworth made walking democratic, and opened up the studious mind to the ever-changing scenes of nature. The pace his chubby friend Coleridge managed to maintain in 1803 – covering the poor highland roads from Arrochar to Edinburgh 'in eight days' – was by no means untypical. One of the most famous men of the day was the explorer Walking (John) Stewart, who did all his journeys on foot: the composer Michael Kelly met him in Vienna in 1784 on his way from Calais to Constantinople.

It was a more earnest strand of the Romantic tradition that sermonised about walking, pandering to the rising middle-class religion of nature which made walking 'good for you': a prescription. But a more radical sense of walking has persisted in Britain, where the civic disobedience movements Right to Roam and Reclaim the Streets have promoted trespassing as a mass movement in order to uphold the ancient rights of common access to the countryside. Walking is an expression, and extension, of civil liberties: it was the splendid Thoreau who first used the term 'civil disobedience'.

'Back over the old roads again... Let's go! The walk, the burden, the wilderness, the tedium, the anger.' That was Arthur Rimbaud, the teenage '*promeneur*', walking home to Charleville from Paris in 1873 in the conviction that his literary career was at an end. When he got back after a week on the road, he burned all his manuscripts. He walked from the Ardennes to Marseille in 1877, and from the Ardennes to Genoa the following year, before walking himself right out of Europe. His journey had taken him into the experience of distance itself. In fact, Rimbaud kept walking through Africa until he developed a terrible pain in his right knee in 1891: it was the first manifestation of the sarcoma that would kill him.

Earlier poets thought nothing of walking from one end of the continent to the other: Hölderlin walked from Bordeaux back to the Neckar, and Goethe's friend, the poet Jakob Michael Reinhold Lenz, wandered in a trance all over Europe from the Alps to the North Sea until the bottle claimed him in a freezing Moscow street in 1792. And Nietzsche loved to bestride the belvedere that separates northern from southern Europe: walking was his minimal form of dancing, the rise and fall of his feet echoing his heart-beat and breathing until the twentieth century that he helped to bring about married the syncopated energy of African dance to the four-square regularity of European folk music: light feet, Nietzsche wrote, are perhaps inseparable from the notion of God, an observation which might have come from the mouth of a Sufi.

Every nation seems to have its cultural stereotype of the walker. The twee rambler in Britain has never cut quite as resolute a figure as the metaphysical Wanderer looking down on a mountain range from above the clouds. On the other hand, *trek* has entered the English language from Afrikaans as a very special kind of walk – away from the British soldiery. The French make a nice distinction between a genteel *promenade* and a longer *randonnée*, and tend to tog up for the latter in absurdly over-elaborate gear. In the United States, John Muir's thousand-mile walk from Indianapolis to the Florida Keys established a bond between walking and the politics of environmental awareness. Nowadays in suburbanised America, of course, walking is a kind of deviancy, an activity reserved for hobos and the slightly unhinged, like the character Travis in Wim Wenders' film *Paris, Texas*.

Stravaigin is a lovely Scots word for a kind of aimless wandering. It is not the kind of walking encouraged by politicians, who like to promote the symbolic power of the virtuous walk: a rather obscure European subcommittee (European Committee of Cultural Itineraries) produces material on some of the famous pilgrimage and trade routes that straddled the continent in the heyday of Christendom. The numerous pilgrims tramping the thickly signposted trail to Santiago de Compostela might be surprised to learn that their trademark accoutrements, a knapsack and stock, actually hark back to those ancient Cynics.

A few years ago the cultural historian Ian Hacking wrote an intriguing book about mad travellers, the pathological walkers first described by alienists (early psychiatrists) in the 1880s, when travel journalism was entering its golden age (Stevenson and Twain) and

Thomas Cook developing what would later become the seasonal migration patterns of mass tourism.

It was a diagnosis that had found a niche in the rapidly organising societies of modern Europe; the codification of psychiatry along organic lines and the growing power of the press bruited and just as quickly smothered it: for a while, though, a transient illness of the mind had found a way to give itself legs. Reports on the first case of oneiric fugue or dromomania, a young man in a psychiatric hospital in Bordeaux who had made trips to 'calm his headaches' to Algiers, Moscow and Constantinople without papers and not much sense of fixed identity either, set off an epidemic of cases throughout Europe. Most of the trip seemed to be made in a complete absence of mind.

After a lull, oneiric fugue returned with a vengeance during the trench warfare of the First World War, when many British soldiers were found wandering in or around the main Channel port of Boulogne. Some received treatment; others were shot as deserters. The diagnosis of 'shellshock' had created its own symptoms. Long after the war, thousands of desperate families still hoped that their loved ones, reported as 'missing in action', were alive and wandering either the trenches or the corridors of a hospital.

Fact is, these days we're all *fugueurs*, though few of us flee on foot or get committed to asylums. 'Psychiatry's fugues are literature's flights,' as Karl Miller has written; and the great madcap novelist Nikolai Gogol was once described by his countryman Vladimir Nabokov as never being at ease 'except in flight, including from his subject'.

The word *distance* only daunts those too poor to surmount it; space has become a function of economics. Now that modern transport has rendered the act of walking in order to get somewhere seem a kind of wilful contortionism, walking looks frankly absurd. If we do go walking it is not to go somewhere: we want to discover the friction of 'slow time'. Joseph Roth commented on this phenomenon in its early years, in one of his feuilletons: 'Western Europeans set out into nature as if to a costume party.

They have a sort of loden-jacket relationship with nature. I saw hikers who were accountants in civilian life. What did they need their walking sticks for? The ground is so flat and smooth that a fountain pen would have served them just as well. But the man doesn't see the flat and smooth ground. He sees "nature"' (*Going for a Walk*, 1921).

Reviewing the loden-jacket trend after the war, Theodor Adorno, in one of the short essays collected in his *Minima Moralia*, was even more dismissive: 'The body's habituation to walking as normal stems from the good old days. It was the bourgeois form of locomotion: physical demythologisation, free of the spell of heiratic pacing, roofless wandering, breathless flight. Human dignity insisted on the right to walk, a rhythm not extorted from the body by command or terror. The walk, the stroll, were private ways of passing time, the heritage of the feudal promenade in the nineteenth century. With the liberal era walking is dying out, even where people do not go by car. The Youth Movement, sensing these tendencies with infallible masochism, challenged the parental Sunday excursions and replaced them by voluntary forced marches, naming them, in medieval fashion, Fahrt [journey, drive] when the Model Ford was about to become available for such purposes.'

The Swiss writer Robert Walser, a man of truly infallible masochism, paid no attention at all to Adorno's withering dismissal of old-style perambulation. Walser grew up at the foot of the mountain-girded Bieler See (Lac de Bienne), the place where the indefatigable Rousseau found his arcadia, as described in the Fifth Walk of *Reveries d'un Promeneur Solitaire*; and he was to return there when he was no longer able to eke out a living selling his essays and stories to the Berlin newspapers after the Great War.

Walser was a literary chamois, shy but surefooted on the sheer slopes of his own writing. The narrator of his novella *The Walk* (1917) launches into a rapture of description as he contemplates the inner nature of his experience: 'Indeed it is heavenly and a simplicity most ancient and proper to walk on foot, provided of course that shoes and boots are in good condition.' It is a phrase both metaphysical and practical: the Infinite comes to the world with bare feet, as a Dadaist poet put it, but it damn well makes sure it has hobnailed boots. Ominously enough, *The Walk* mentions the hapless Lenz who, 'having fallen into madness and despair, learned how to make shoes and indeed made them'; in 1932 Walser committed himself to a mental institution.

A decade earlier – at the same time as his countryman Paul Klee was taking lines on a walk, in the interests of theoretical instruction at the Bauhaus – Walser had suffered an episode of writer's block. The psychosomatic cramps that afflicted his writing hand were, he decided, related to his inability to transfer the bodily rhythm of walking into calligraphy. His solution: to adopt what he called his 'pencil method' – all his late works are written in a microscript that allowed his thoughts-turned-heroes to 'saunter' across the page in a reverie both striding and sidestepping.

There are many reasons why a writer might choose one writing instrument over another, but the fluidity and lack of finality of a pencilled script has a surprisingly close filiation to the walking mind. It was none other than Henry David Thoreau who, while experimenting in his father's Concord workshop in the 1830s, came up with a method of mixing clay and powdered graphite to produce the shaft of 'lead' encased in a cylinder of cedar. So began the production of cheap and efficient writing instruments: the Thoreau family business was one of the first successful manufacturers of the graded lead pencil.

Although most cities have been refashioned not by sweat and leather but by the rubber and metal of the Model T Ford and its successors, some retain a strong connection with walking. Walt Whitman, unlike most writers before him, found the jostle and tumult of the busy street exciting, a call to merge with the oceanic swell of democracy: the modern urban crowd was his longitudinal waterfall. 'Multitudes' was his chosen term for the nascent American people, those he contained within himself, never 'masses'. Baudelaire took Whitman's longing to his favourite Paris café: it was the revelation of seeing desire in a stranger's gaze, the simultaneous arousal and resignation of 'love at last sight'.

Paris is still the capital of *flâneurs*; I've spent many a Saturday walking the length of the old city, from the Bois de Vincennes to the Pont de Neuilly: it is the route followed underground by Métro Ligne 1. 'Paris *should* be walked,' wrote Richard Cobb, 'because much of it, the most secret, the most modest, the most bizarre, the tiniest, is only discoverable by the pedestrian who is prepared to push behind the boulevards and the long straight streets of the Second Empire and the early confident years of the Third Republic.'

City walking is the freedom of anonymity, the moment when, as Virginia Woolf wrote in her essay 'Street Haunting', we can 'shed the self our friends know us by' and set out in the dusk, as she did, to buy a pencil. Fleshier kinds of solace can be had too. Until Woolf's time no respectable woman would be seen walking unaccompanied, for the only kind of promenade allowed the single woman was for the purposes of sexual commerce: street-walking. In any event, dress fashion and tailoring, until the early years of the twentieth century, barely allowed a woman to walk: it was only in the 1920s that a woman's legs and feet became operative.

Woolf was self-consciously and rebelliously following in the steps of the opium-eating Thomas de Quincey, who discovered veritable *terrae incognitae* in the back streets of London: 'such knotty problems of alleys, such enigmatical entries, and such sphinx's riddles of streets without thoroughfares'. Yet the most haunting tale of a woman on the streets, for reader as well as writer, is the one De Quincey tells in *Confessions of an English Opium-Eater* about Ann, the sixteen-year-old destitute 'female peripatetic' who revived him with a glass of port when he collapsed, at the end of his tether, on the steps of a house in Soho Square: knowing only her first name he was unable, despite his frantic later efforts, to find out where she lived. She had been swallowed up by the labyrinth of London.

Dream-walkers like Louis Aragon who wrote *Le Paysan de Paris* with his feet have to learn how to surrender to the flow of the street. In his essay on the surrealists Walter Benjamin called *flânerie* 'botanizing on the asphalt' (the streets being less dangerous for urban botanists then), and Guy Debord, leader of the International Situationist movement that flourished in the 1960s, developed his rather fanciful notion of 'psychogeography' from a phrase about discovering the urban North-West passage in the same essay by De Quincey.

Psychogeography is a kind of dyslexic trespass mythology that tries to get the walker out of the boredom of the city by luring him deeper into it. He might end up in a state of utter *anomie*, or he might enjoy the kind of doused insight that saves W.G. Sebald's several books about walking across Europe from the trudge of despair: 'in the middle of this vision of imprisonment and liberation I could not stop wondering whether it was a ruin or a building in the process of construction that I had entered' (*Austerlitz*, 2001).

A more exuberant kind of magical thinking seems to have prompted the walk recounted in Werner Herzog's *On Walking in Ice*, a short account of a three-week walk undertaken in November 1974 in the spirit of Rousseau and told in the manner of Bruce Chatwin. On hearing that his friend the German film historian Lotte Eisner had been hospitalised with a serious illness in a Paris hospital Herzog, director of films about mildly loony loners and psychopomps in the baroque and megalomaniac tradition that is second nature for Bavarians, set off on foot from Munich in order to 'save' her. While most morbid walkers, like Kierkegaard, walk away from their own illness, Herzog, by an act of transferative virtue, hopes to heal someone else's. By the end of the book (when Eisner does leave the hospital) Herzog is no longer walking: he knows how to fly.

The elating 'anti-gravity' induced by the muscular effort of a long walk as related by Herzog finds visual expression in a splendid oil painting by Marc Chagall now hanging in the National Museum in St Petersburg: of the couple walking out together it is the man (in a reversal of the male's usual *Luftmensch* role) whose handclasp serves to hold down his buoyant red-dressed female companion. One limb of a partnership, at least, needs to feel native ground beneath its feet.

It would seem, Roth and Adorno notwithstanding, that the true enemy of the walker is not so much the sedentary habits of the city-dweller as the WALK DON'T WALK of the orchestrated social life: it is no accident that the rise of the gym is contemporaneous with the decline of walking. Machines have become faster, and people identify with their speed: the body is often experienced, sometimes with resentment, as being slow and lumbering.

New technologies change expectations, rather than emancipate human beings into that spontaneous reprieve from routine that is the essence of the festive. What Rebecca Solnit in *Wanderlust*, her indispensable vade mecum to all aspects of life at four miles an hour, has called the 'aerobic Sisyphus' is unlikely to register the irony of his treading a machine that allows him to replicate as empty gestures movements that were productive work for a farmer or stoker a century ago.

Many gyms are actually refurbished factories. People don't work there, they work out. As often as not they work out on the tread-mill, designed in 1818 (not long after Bentham's panopticon) as a method for rationalising the minds of inmates. The gym may even be a kind of hothouse for the preservation of a rare species. As Solnit puts it: 'the gym (and home gym) accommodates the survival of bodies after the abandonment of the original sites of bodily exertion'.

So, does the walk have a future? Well, as the poet Edouard Jabès said, we get to where we are going, and then there is still the distance to cover.

Cinema Verities

THE FILM EXPLAINER: A NOVEL BY GERT HOFMANN

After a long career as a writer of radio plays Gert Hofmann came late to the novel, just a few years short of his fiftieth birthday. Widely respected, but never a literary lion or trend-setter, he turned out almost a novel a year in the fifteen years before his death from a cerebral haemorrhage in 1993. Such a furious rate of production is belied by the brilliant surface of his fiction, which is limpid, neutral, hyperrealist, and often strikingly indifferent to psychology. He has often been compared to the more pugnacious Thomas Bernhard in his modernist insistence on ironic multiple perspectives, and dismantling fictive pieties, but Bernhard's books seem a long gripe compared to Hofmann's rapid-fire humour, which upends conventional props and hangs the narrative, as in the present book, on the speech of his characters. It is a skill presumably acquired from the years of radio work, and it gives his work a lightness of tone which is captivating, heady, and sometimes devastating.

When it first appeared in the original German in 1990, his tenth novel *The Film Explainer* was immediately hailed as a comic masterpiece. Like most of Hofmann's novels it places itself firmly within the mainstream post-1968 German convention of questioning the moral pusillanimity of the preceding generation. The voice of ten-year-old Gert Hofmann starts up with what seems a set of recollections out of the family photograph album: 'My grandfather Karl Hofmann (1873–1944) worked for many years in the

Apollo cinema on the Helenenstrasse in Limbach/Saxony.'
Grandfather, as the grandson explains, 'was the film explainer and
piano player in Limbach. They still had those, back then. A lot of
them came from the fairgrounds, from the "apish origins of art"
(Grandfather).'

Grandfather has all-round talents, 'but they're no use for
anything'. Clad in the tails and waistcoat purchased by Grandmother as a working outfit 'at Hagen's Gentlemen's Outfitters, in
the Helenenstrasse, reduced to 39 billion marks' – this is the
Germany of the Depression, we should remember – he creates the
perfect atmosphere for every film, pointing up the action with his
music, 'and his explanations, especially in the dramatic moments'.
Grandfather puts words together for a living, and tries to make a
philosophy out of it. The natural world bores him; he is looking
for his 'second world', and can't find it. Or if he does it is only for
an hour or so at a time, and always in the cinema. That is where
this virtuoso of the Word finds his niche. Not that the seventh
art really needs explaining, since film-explaining, in the words of
Herr Theilhaber, the Jewish owner of the auditorium, is as superfluous as a third nostril.

It was only around 1925 that cinema developed its galactic
dream-images and overwhelming point of view, and movie-
theatres started to resemble mystery grottos and bordellos: before
that, in the early days of cinema, films were still rowdy music-hall
'turns' and had to compete with song-and-dance routines, magic
tricks, performing animals and other extempore acts. Theilhaber's
auditorium is evidently of this early type. Every day at six, except
for Mondays, Grandfather appears before dwindling audiences at
the Apollo with its standing room for seventy and desultory rows
of seats and explains such classic cinema as '*The Indian Tomb*, 1921,
with Conrad Weidt and Mia May' or '*The Honeymoon*, 1928, with
Erich von Stroheim', not forgetting that Alpine drama '*The Blue
Light*, 1932, with Leni Riefenstahl and Matthias Wiemann'. All of
which is delivered in a memorably terse manner, grandfatherly
dicta and pedantic film-buff citation sitting cheek by jowl.

Grandfather is the last in a long history of artists without an income and not much of an art either. There is, inevitably, a dark side to his explaining; and that is where the audience sits. The dark is Plato's cave: those watching may take the moving images for substance, but the reality of which they are monstrous phantoms is beyond their ken. The French novelist Céline described it as 'the mean little factotum of our dreams, which can be hired for an hour or two like a prostitute'. The dark offers a kind of refuge, a voyeuristic disengagement from the usual social meaning of what is being acted out on the screen, but it is also a threatening, almost preconscious territory: the projected image also has the power to enthral in a manner so complete as to possess people.

Modern art, wrote Nietzsche, is the art of tyrannising, and never more so than in the twentieth century's quintessential form, the cinema — short for *cinematograph*, a kind of writing in images that requires hardly any conventional verbal literacy. Cinema emerged when the other arts had already matured into modernism and were able to bestow on the neophyte all the possibilities of the new forms of expression they had so laboriously acquired. The nineteenth-century passion for increasingly realistic dioramas of external reality was therefore able to appropriate, in the years when the modernist novel was touching its apogee, a mode of representing lived experience that had actually been first sketched out three centuries earlier, in the designs Leonardo da Vinci made in his notebooks for a camera obscura. Osip Mandelstam dubbed cimema 'a metamorph of the tapeworm': the social body had been infected by a tapeworm which helped the host digest its history.

Momentously, and not just for Grandfather, the sound-film era is about to arrive — '*The Jazz Singer* (1927, with Al Jolson)' — an event which threatens to discount his employment entirely. It was precisely the coming of sound which put paid to experimentalism in film-making and established the cinema as a popular artform. Grandfather starts attending political meetings and fraternises with Herr Götze and Herr Friedrich, who wear brown shirts and talk about the time they met HIM. Grandfather's interest in politics doesn't extend beyond the first person, but he sees National Socialism as the possible saviour of silent film. External events are oppressive for being scarcely mentioned: when Herr Theilhaber 'disappears' the event is summed up in the theatrical phrase 'He's over the hills and far away!' The rhetorical blankness of the screen accommodates any sort of explanation, not least the denunciations Grandfather's Nazi cronies obtain by trickery and menace. Sent to Berlin as a deputy 'flag-waver' in the Deutschlandtreffen of 1 May 1939, and in the capital for the first time in ages, he decides to go and see a talkie at the Gloria Palais instead of assembling with the other flag-bearers. 'The film Grandfather saw and was to rave about until his death was of course *Gone With the Wind*' – which happens to be the glorious Technicolor film the Führer himself watched with admiration in the first year of the war. Hitler ran his own epic project for 'a civilisation gone with the wind' like an eccentric mogul: he never visited the front but he watched the rushes, in the days following the events, in his private screening room. Germany might go under, but it could all be reinstated as a glorious lost cause in a motion picture classic. On the afternoon of 24 May 1944, Grandfather dies when a stray bomb falls on the Apollo cinema. Grandmother attends the burial, and as the grandson records, '"out of anger at such a stupid death," hadn't even changed or put on a hat'.

There is no gainsaying the fact that the Führer now seems like an escapee from the closed Gothic shadow-world of expressionist cinema, less a contemporary of the dashing Clark Gable and Gary Cooper (Hitler was a great admirer of both cinematic swash-bucklers) than a sinister version of the down-at-luck and irrepressibly droll figure of class resentment portrayed by Charlie Chaplin, whose early caper films were entirely devoted to kicking or pushing all other male characters in the rear so that he, the undisputed hero, could walk off with the girl. Power relations are never so naked as in a Keystone film. One of the sources of Hitler's control may be that he successfully projected not what W.H. Auden, to his later embarrassment, once termed 'the truly strong man' but the ordinary weak man so far down the social ladder he was able to take it out on his perceived victimisers without anyone raising objections.

Without ever making their conscription seem forced or merely literary, Hofmann's memorable little novel alludes to Kafka's ironic late story *Josephine the Singer* and the frequent references to films in his letters (Kafka was a film buff who enjoyed reciting the plots of French, American and German melodramas to his sisters while they were in the bathroom), spans the glory years of Babelsberg and German celluloid and comments wryly on the spectral effects of the cinema as a form of cognitive tyranny, all the while lovingly sending up Grandfather's art of forcing meaning from the self-evident. It is, as in Kafka, the self-chosen and there-fore ironic fate of the artist to have to dedicate his life to accomplishing painstakingly and deliberately what everybody else does as spontaneously as breathing.

While Eisenstein remarked that cinema techniques were prefig-ured in Dickens' novels, fiction itself has hardly remained uninfluenced by cinema techniques. Robert Musil, one of the greatest novelists of the period as well as one of the first serious film critics, was moved to observe that the explosion of activity in early films undercut the idea that passions and events could speak for themselves: 'even in one's personal life the *outer* attitude is no more than a makeshift and expressively poor translation of the *inner* mindset, and the essence of the person resides not so much in his experiences and feelings but in his protracted, silent arguing and coming to terms with them'. The cinema is a kind of ventila-tion shaft for personal-public ambiguities and double-dealings too complex and intricate to be aired by more conventional means. In Hofmann's novel, Grandfather's last-gasp theatrics surrender to a new aesthetic of the widescreen that perpetually threatens to over-flow its frame of reference. The post-war cinema will invite all kinds of ironic voice-overs, notably a popular culture uninhibited about learning its ethics from the bad guys. But that is another metamorph of the tapeworm.

Nothing captures better the tragicomic allure and brutal deflation of this novel, which is Englished, in a further biographical twist, by Gert Hofmann's son Michael, than a throwaway line near the end: 'Grandfather at seventy said: In the beginning was the light. The light was switched off.'

DOWNFALL: A FILM BY BERND EICHINGER

Controversy attended the release of Bernd Eichinger and Oliver Hirschbiegel's film Downfall (Der Untergang, 2004), in France as well as in Germany: the distinguished historian Claude Lanzmann, director of the painstaking nine-and-a-half hour-long documentary film Shoah (1985) which created a new idiom for talking about the Nazi extermination policy in eastern Europe, felt that the crimes committed by Hitler overwhelmed any reason which could be advanced for making a big-budget (13 million euros) film about him. Lanzmann may have been baulking at the thought that the last days of such a detestable régime should be experienced as an *entertainment*, although given Hitler's penchant for theatrically restaging events on celluloid, indeed for banishing the footlights and making everyone an actor in his universal Saturnalia, film may actually be the obvious medium in which to portray the downfall of a man for whom reality – the reality of the 1930s – was a theatre of universal credulity. Some critics took the view that the film 'humanised' Hitler, as if it were scandalous that he should turn out to be a man rather than an alien; or even that it made him seem 'affable', as if Hitler's unctuous Viennese courtesy towards his secretarial staff and maudlin affection for his German shepherd dog Blondi were traits somehow not in keeping with the man who sent millions of people to their deaths. Kitsch and cruelty get along famously, as W.H. Auden reminded us in his poem 'Epitaph on a Tyrant' (1939): 'And when he cried the little children died in the street.'

Downfall is a study in domestic claustrophobia, a Götterdämmerung in a hole in the ground. It draws heavily – perhaps too heavily – on the eyewitness account of the last twelve days of Hitler's life written in 1947 and published just before her death in 2002 by Hitler's young Bavarian secretary, Traudl Junge, whom we see being recruited at the beginning of the film, as well as on Joachim Fest's solidly scholarly work, in particular his volume *Inside Hitler's Bunker*, which was published in English translation last year. If our notion of Hitler's strength and power is inseparable from the sight and sound of crowds, from what might be called the community of expectation, here he is seen exclusively in his meagre inner circle; and it is a circle in crisis.

It lives out this crisis in the notorious Führerbunker which, with its fifty small and sparsely furnished rooms (twenty in the inner circle), was hardly the most enticing of hide-outs. It was cold and stank of kerosene, sweat and urine from the poorly ventilated toilet blocks. This was Hitler's bolthole: Albert Speer had noted in 1933 that when they met to discuss the architecture of the future Reich the Führer was fascinated above all else by the plans for underground defences and the closed spaces of caverns and warrens. If the terrace at Berchtesgaden with its view of the Obersalzberg mountains was one of his Happy Places, then the underground has to be the other. Here he could be himself alone, while the city died above him. In his short story *Der Bau* Kafka remorselessly explored how the paranoid mind constructs a burrow for itself, making out of the underworld, stricken as it might be by alarms and panics, a dwelling-place, even quite a cosy one. The bunker can even be seen as a kind of inverted ivory-tower. In the documentary film made before her death, Traudl Junge admitted that when she arrived there to assume her duties as scribe and stenographer, she immediately felt safe. Lucidity only came later: 'When I took up my position in his service, I thought: "Now I'm at the very font of information." In reality, it was a blind spot.'

Hitler is played by the Swiss actor, Bruno Ganz, perhaps best known for his role as the disconsolate chief angel in Wim Wender's film *Wings of Desire* (1987). Ganz provides one of the few convincing Hitler impersonations other than Charlie Chaplin's, in what was a rather different film-genre — *The Great Dictator* (1940) was Chaplin's first full talkie, and his most profitable film at the box-office: documents now show that Hitler himself tried to obtain a copy of the reels through diplomatic channels in Portugal. Ganz runs the gamut of Hitler's autodidactic oddities, one moment digressing on some aspect of natural history to ram home a point of strategy, the next withdrawing into sociopathic coldness with a remark about the deaths of his soldiers being 'what they were there for'.

All the big noises who attended the Führer in the prison of his own myth are there: the gentlemanly Minister for War Production Albert Speer, who drops in from organising what will eventually become the new Europe, along with Hitler's 'press chief' Josef Goebbels and his thuggish adjutant Martin Bormann. Battle-weary generals enter the bunker in field uniform to announce the bad news only to emerge, half-convinced even at that late hour, by the Führer's victory rhetoric. Final triumph could only be a matter of time once the Nibelungen were on their way. Right up to the end Hitler believed in the 'miracle weapon' that would reverse the course of the war (the V2 rocket); he even saw the war as a conflict between him and his personal enemies: his view of history was comprehensively that of Carlyle's 'great men'. Eighteen days before his death, Speer found him in a state of exaltation: news of the death of Roosevelt (whom he scorned as a 'paralytic') was a sign that his fortunes were about to turn at the last moment, much as the unexpected death of the Russian empress Elizabeth had saved in extremis his hero Frederick the Great. Carlyle's biography of the Prussian king was the last book he read.

One lesser figure absent from the film's gallery of rogues is Hitler's Leibartz or personal physician, Dr Theodor Morell, a sinister and generally detested dermatologist-venereologist who was at least partly responsible, thanks to his benzedrine and morphine cocktails, cocaine eyedrops and barbiturate sleepers, for the lamentable physical state of his patient. Hitler had also, on

Morell's advice, been taking pills containing low-dose strychnine to ease his flatulence. He was therefore in an advanced state of toxaemia, though little of his drug consumption is shown in the film. Everybody remarked on how pasty and bloated he looked; at times he was drooling and incoherent, his usually tidy uniform spattered with stains. He lurched rather than walked, grasping at furniture for support. Documents that required his personal attention had to be typed on a special typewriter to enlarge the script. Hitler celebrated his 56th birthday in the bunker, but it was an older-looking, unmistakeably ill man who walked out into the chancellery gardens, left hand flapping behind his back, to decorate the boys who were defending Berlin. That was to be his last public appearance. In the streets behind the chancellery ordinary Berliners were dying in their apartments or being hanged for insubordination from the lampposts. The war was being fought to the last, without a thought for the necessities of everyday life. The Red Army was less than twenty kilometres away. (It is a historical irony that the film exteriors were all shot in the shabby courtyards of St Petersburg, that 'unreal city' that served as permanent residence to Dostoevsky's superfluous and abject heroes and, as Leningrad, barely survived the terrible siege by the Wehrmacht in the winter of 1942.)

The women around Hitler are exceptionally well played, especially Magda Goebbels (Corinna Harfouch), who veers from idolatrous Führer-worship to cold detestation of her husband: after Hitler's suicide on 30 April, she alone undertakes the terrible task of killing her six blond children, the parade family of Nazi eugenics; this she accomplished by drugging them to sleep and then crushing phials of prussic acid between their teeth. Theirs had been the only innocent life in the bunker, playing games and singing in its concrete corridors. Amidst the coming and going of military personnel, and the pounding of heavy shelling, Eva Braun strikes a flippant note: her role in Hitler's life is still, to put it mildly, enigmatic. She was what P.G. Wodehouse would have called a 'flibbertigibbet', though her devotion to Hitler, like that of Goebbels' wife, was absolute and unquestioning. Ganz dares to portray a Hitler who might conceivably have inspired such devotion. Eva Braun's presence in the bunker adds a touch of flapper absurdity to a situation teetering on the grotesque (though she was never seen by anyone dancing on a table). A civil registrar is summonsed to marry her and Hitler a few days before their joint suicide. 'Are you Aryan?' the registrar nervously asks the bridegroom, following the standard Nazi protocol for the civil marriage ceremony. Hitler's hesitation momentarily deflates the tension of the film, though it hardly offers comic relief. As the chronicler Emil Cioran wrote, if Hitler had replied in the negative to that question, 'it would have been the most extraordinary reply in History'.

Ganz's uncanny mimicry steals the show: so theatrical are his tantrums that the dull Nazi leather-coats administering to his needs come across as almost reasonable men. Hitler's every move in his final months showed him to have been a tyrant who believed his right to govern resided in his person: he was the 'one man' who had stepped forward 'to form granite principles from the vacillating world of the imaginings of the broad masses'. In fact, it's not his supposed 'humane qualities' which repel, but his 'Saubermann' inhumanity: he made it clear to his staff that he was embarked upon a great, difficult and necessary work – in the testament we see him dictating to Traudl Junge he calls it 'my unique contribution to history'.

Like an artist, he expected posterity to absolve him. Hitler never displayed any interest in seeing the practical effects of his policies, and refused to witness the aftermath of the bombing raids on Germany's cities. Yet the fairly elaborate preparations for his own death (should he shoot himself in the mouth or the temple? should he take poison too?) and precise instructions for the disposal of his post-mortem remains suggest that, at least in part, he knew the truth about himself: destruction was the empty core of his vision. By April 1945, it hardly mattered to him if those being annihilated were Germans or Russians: all deserved to die. 'If we go down the others will go down with us.' Throughout his public career Hitler never changed: he meant what he said, and said what he would do, way back in that turgid act of self-vindication *Mein Kampf*, published in 1925. It sold in the millions; nobody, it seems, ever read it. But Speer noted in his diary that Hitler himself mistrusted the written word; it was the spoken word that put people under.

Deep insight into Hitler's tactics and behaviour is not prominent in Eischinger's film, which, in its opening sequence, invites us to adopt the perspective of the wide-eyed Traudl Junge as she nervously waits for the job interview with the man who was to prove such a considerate boss. Is this how contemporary Germans – those who make films at least – see themselves? It is curious, too, that the one exitus not shown in the film (in which many brains are blown out) is the Führer's. Hitler, alas, lives on. For all its liberal-mindedness, *Downfall* colludes with the fact that the brown gang's black party has entered the realm of myth, where legends never have a final shape, a development fully anticipated by some of the more Wagnerian members of the Third Reich, including the top Nazi himself. Film is glamour, whatever its characters get up to. That must have been in the Führer's mind, when he asked to see Chaplin doing him as Adenoid Hynkel in that once innocuous lampoon with the 'thrown' globe.

Candour and Hygiene

LOUIS-FERDINAND CÉLINE

> M. Céline scandalise. A ceci, rien à dire, puisque
> Dieu l'a visiblement fait pour ça.
> Georges Bernanos, 1932

Louis-Ferdinand Auguste Destouches was born in 1894, the year of the Dreyfus affair, in Courbevoie, an old working class area on the fringes of the Seine which has been wrenched out of recognition by Mitterrand's city-planners' grandiose schemes for the mini-Manhattan that now blocks the western skyline of Paris *intramuros*. His parents were hard-working *petits commerçants* who aspired to middle-class respectability but lived in fear of poverty. Theirs was the tormented sense of place in the economic pecking order that has always afflicted the petty bourgeoisie, deprived of the consolations of working-class solidarity and driven to aspire to a style of leisured living that, in truth, is alien to them. The family stares into the camera in a rare photo: father plump, bombastic moustache, a hail-fellow-well-met air about him; mother severe and thin-lipped, her right hand keeping her son in place. The older the son became the more he acquired of his mother's animosities and dislikes: he must have caught something from her, the pinch-faced woman whom he remembered sitting in her little lacemaker's shop in the Passage Choiseul facing 'a mountain of work that would bring in only a few francs. It never ended. She had to do it so we could eat. It gave me nightmares, and her too. I've never forgotten it. Like her, I come to my desk and see a huge pile waiting for me – a pile of Horror that I have to mend before being done with everything.' His writing is, above all, a laden monument to the class resentment that ate her away, and perhaps even to the injustice she felt at being born a woman. It was the maternal name, Louise-Céline, which he took as a pseudonym when he decided to become a producer of luxury items himself.

Unusually for the times, he was sent for periods to Germany and England to learn the languages, which suggests his parents at least lived a good slice above the breadline. Engaged as a cuirassier in the 12th Regiment in the First World War on that already anti-quated engine of war, the horse, he was invalided out of the army for life after sustaining a fractured arm. He claimed to have suffered a head injury (subsequently trepanned), but the story turned out to be a complete fabrication: it was perhaps (in view of the trepanning) a kind of darkly Gnostic joke. Decorated with the *médaille militaire*, he spent a period at the French Embassy in London in 1916; and then set off for Cameroon where he worked for a year as a supervisor in the employment of the Compagnie Forestière Shanga-Oubangui. He qualified as a mature student in medicine at the University of Rennes in 1924 with a thesis on Ignaz Semmelweis, the maligned Hungarian physician who, in 1847, introduced regular antiseptic hygiene to the Vienna General Hospital and almost overnight brought down the abysmally high puerperal fever mortality rates. Céline quickly separated from his wife (daughter of his professor of medicine) with a letter which read: 'I'd rather kill myself than continue living with you... I detest marriage, it gives me the baulk, I spit it out...', and left her to bring up the daughter he never saw again. He had a number of liaisons with dancers in the 1930s, including the red-haired American Elizabeth Craig, to whom he dedicated his first novel, and her Danish friend Karen Marie Jensen. Desultory practice in Nantes was followed – improbably enough – by three years' work for the health division of the new League of Nations in Geneva which brought him on a study visit to various sites in the US including the Ford factory in Detroit (Henry Ford's anti-Jewish campaign impressed him as much as his health care provisions for the workers). In a relatively restrained period from 1928 he did some private practice, combining clinical work with providing promotional material for a pharmaceutical company, later working at the municipal health clinic in the Parisian suburb of

Clichy-la-Garenne. Medical articles written in the 1930s advocate a kind of nationalised health system not dissimilar to what would emerge in various European countries after the war. Hygiene is a favourite topic. He claimed to live in poverty; in fact, Céline was never short of a bob or two.

For someone of his generation, these might have remained the early external facts of an unusual, but not exceptional life. That life, and the history of French literature in general, changed irrevocably in 1932 when Destouches, as Louis-Ferdinand Céline, published his first novel with Editions Denoël in Paris: it was a book whose deliberate philistinism aroused nearly as much offence as admiration, and almost won him the Goncourt prize. *Voyage au Bout de la Nuit* (1932) was callous, vociferous and mordant; its grimly disenchanted view of the human condition and the world's hebetude was put into relief only by the sheer imaginative verve of the writing; 'it wrung the neck of positivism', in the words of Henri Godard, editor of Céline's work. Its theme is the horror of war, and man's inability to possess it imaginatively while experiencing it; it was based, with only thin dissimulation, on Céline's own wartime experience, although its main protagonist Bardamu is even more cynical than Céline himself. Most of the critics thought *Voyage* a refurbished kind of realism, Zola without the fatted calf. In fact, although there are moments of quite sumptuous, almost Dickensian descriptive realism in the book, Céline's writing pushes beyond verisimilitude to a something more convulsive. Its language is both mannered and colloquial, or brilliantly parodic of the colloquial, in a manner anticipated most distinctively by Eugène Sue in his famous novel *Les Mystères de Paris* (which the young Marx vehemently disowned) and, closer in time, Eugène Dabit in *Hôtel du Nord*.

The very first sentence of the novel – 'Ça a débuté comme ça' – with its nonchalance about the conventionally well-shaped sentence, whistles in the action with what is functionally a pronoun, and then reinstates it as an adverb. It was surely a gibe at Proust's famously languid phrase at the beginning of *A la*

Recherche du Temps Perdu. Céline was advertising his allegiance to the popular idiom, in open defiance of the cool reasoned language enshrined in the Academy, which he later sent up as 'le langage flagorneur et vantard et redondant et de haute fatuité pontifiant auquel les Français seront toujours infiniment sensibles'. As far as he was concerned the French had, for more than two centuries, been speaking translationese: he wanted to uncover the vulgate again.

Despite his huge success, Céline kept practising medicine, 'cette merde'. He began to travel widely, an experience which seems to have hardened his prejudices rather than opened his mind; one of the trips he made was to transfer his royalties in the form of gold bullion to accounts in the Netherlands (seized to his rage, by the Nazis, in 1940) and Denmark. By 1936, he had completed his second novel *Mort à crédit* (Death on the Instalment Plan) and started supporting his mother, 'cette emerdeuse'. Like 1916, 1936 seems to have marked a decisive moment in his life. Initially claimed for the Left after the bleak indictment of capitalism in the *Voyage* (although Trotsky's review of the book makes it clear he never saw Céline as a fellow socialist), his almost obligatory trip to the USSR, as much as anything to spend the royalties he had earned there, brought into the open his complete disillusion with any system of social betterment. *Mea Culpa*, the tract he published on his return, provided in effect an abstract of his first two novels, and vaunted his disbelief in any idea of intrinsic human goodness. 'Man is human is the same way a chicken is able to fly: both need a good boot in the arse to get them there.' He had witnessed the rise of an ideology, and if he was not going to be taken in by the Soviet Union's promises to the future, *Mea Culpa* hardly prepares us for what Céline did next.

In 1937, with the government of Léon Blum in the Elysée Palace, Céline published the first of his anti-Semitic 'pamphlets', *Bagatelles pour un Massacre* (1937), which would be followed in similar vein by *l'Ecole des cadavres* (1938), and *Les Beaux Draps* (1942). ('Polemic' is a better word in English, since none of the three books is less than 200 pages.) *Bagatelles* is a rattle-bag of a book; it is also a work of quite extraordinary spite and recklessness. Avowedly pacificist in intent, it goes to vituperative lengths to settle scores with communists, Freemasons, Jews – the usual suspects. Aside from the French literary world, Hollywood and 'Ben' John Bull, individual targets singled out in his linguistic pogrom include Louis XIV, the Pope, Montaigne, Stendhal, Racine ('Quel emberlificoté tremblotant exhibitionniste! Quel obscène, farfouilleux pâmoisant chiot! Au demi-quart juif d'ailleurs!') and Proust ('prout prout'). 'Juif' is used egregiously, as an intensifier and invective-raiser: it is assigned to all establishment figures. The bibulous French, for their part, deserve to be well and truly shafted: 'C'est la vie des anges par le pot!...' And these are the people Céline expects to read his diatribe!

Despite the whiff of parody, the editors of the right-wing journals initially tripped over each other in their haste to recruit Céline to the cause. Soon, however, Robert Brasillach, editor of *Action française*, while trumpeting the book as the first salvo of a 'native rebellion', expressed misgivings about Céline's rationality and queried the utility of such a vitriolic approach to his 'moderate' platform: he was not mistaken, since Charles Maurras was added to the 'Jews' in the next book. Céline was not out to score political points. He wasn't really a political thinker at all. Nobody expected him to be, and the reception of *Bagatelles* was mild, even amused. But what were his readers really laughing at? Gide commented that his book clearly advertised itself as tilting at windmills, and made his famous comment about Céline painting not reality, 'but the hallucination it produces'.

Typical of Céline's mixed genre are passages like the following, at the outset of *l'Ecole des cadavres*, where the narrator meets an old siren crawling out of the Seine between La Jatte and Courbevoie – 'Tâteurs de situations! Chiasses! Je m'enfulmine je l'avoue! Je brouille! Je bouille! Je taratabule plein mon réchaud! Je fugue! Je m'époumone! J'essouffle! J'éructe cent mille vapeurs! J'outrepasse le convenant branle!': a volley of translation-resisting invective is followed by screeds of execrable name-calling – 'youp' and 'youtre'

– and passages filched from the spurious pseudo-scientific broad-sheets issued by the anti-Semitic press of the time. Alice Kaplan in her various scholarly works has shown that nearly every claim made by Céline in *Bagatelles* was lifted straight from the publications available at the time; some of them are advertised on the book's dustcover. What he did was to *syncopate* them.

'Qu'avons-nous à perdre dans une alliance franco-allemande? Les Juifs'; 'Le Juif doit disparaître'; 'Milles fois Racisme! Racisme suprêmement! Désinfection! Nettoyage!'; 'Intégralement! Absolument! Comme la stérilisation Pasteur parfaite!': even in a tradition which offers a mandate for intellectual terrorism Céline's harangue is appallingly irresponsible. His anti-Semitism is a kind of social therapy, and it includes Christians too: 'toutes les religions à petit Jesus, catholiques, protestantes ou juives, dans le même sac!' The pamphlets, it finally emerges, are projects for reforming society: utopian blueprints for future communal happiness. Céline offers his pennyworth on new kinds of urban planning, property rights, medicine, health and diet, and the cinema; and it doesn't really matter if anyone takes them seriously, for this is the anarchic and excessive laughter of a licensed clown who has exchanged apocalypse for a utopia. Utopia, of course, is the reverse side of all Ends-of-the-World; and neither is terribly mindful of reality. The truly peculiar feature of Céline's urbanism is that once the perceived evil is overcome nobody, it seems, will be able to inhabit his utopia. He doesn't believe in anything like a master-race. Rest assured, the future will be so hygienic nobody will be able to experience it.

Visiting Paris when the bookshop windows were full of *Bagatelles pour un massacre*, Gershom Scholem noticed what he called 'a wild anti-Semitic polemic… of extravagantly vulgar vocabulary', and mentioned it in a letter to Walter Benjamin. 'That Céline's nihilism had found a natural object in the Jews was bound to give one food for thought.' Benjamin had yet to read the book, but he told Scholem, under no illusions about the extent of the phenomenon in France, 'admirers who were influential on the literary scene got around taking a clear stand on the book with this explanation: "*Ce n'est qu'une blaque*'". The 'just-a-joke' line of defence continues to the present day, though expressed a little less nonchalantly than it used to be. There is even a Lacan-inspired version of Céline that has him as a precursor of the 1968 rebellion: if clarity, that traditional virtue of French thought and expression, is actually a vehicle of repression and authoritarianism, then Céline must be one of the liberators. Indeed, his mannerisms are a model for some contemporary French writers resentful at a society that ever less often obliges itself to notice them.

Reading the pamphlets more than fifty years later, it's not just the gratuitously offensive and lurid insults which are striking but Céline's levity of tone: he writes capriciously, as if he had found a kind of freedom on his way down to the Cloaca Maxima. His verbal high jinks suggest a form of mood dissociation, the outpourings of an author who has elected to play Satan to Proust's attempt to write the autobiography of God. Céline was calling up the old eschatological demons for a European civil war that promised to be even more terrible than the one he had fought in himself, but calling them up with a kind of satanic glee or carnival levity. But carnival is not *just* a spectacle. It is a lived event; and it acknowledges no distinction between actors and spectators — and as such betrays its alliance with Hitler's attempt to bring the front into every living-room. Nobody can read the pamphlets now (they have never been reprinted although thousands of copies of the original edition must be mouldering in attics all over France) and claim that he was an honest pacifist trying to prevent war by decrying its effects, or a man of truly furious compassion in a degenerate world. Céline's pamphlets are *guignolesque* versions of a form of writing that had been appearing in the bookshops of France for almost a century (Alphonse Toussenel's *Les Juifs rois de l'époque* is generally credited, if that's the word, with inaugurating the genre in 1845). But the Nazis didn't want to have anything to do with his ejaculatory language: there was no propaganda value in Céline's diatribes. They wanted to put the social order on a different basis;

Céline calls for a plague on all houses. Bernard Payr, head of Alfred Rosenberg's propaganda service, right-thinker that he was, put it like this: 'he has dragged almost everything of positive value in human life through the mud'. Even the Nazis felt they had to have 'moral' reasons; Céline slays even that sacred cow. His haranguing yields to the incantatory power of words themselves: rhythm runs slipshod ahead of meaning. And his 'arguments' are simply propositions tacked on to bogus facts and figures. (For someone who had been through the rigour of medical school, Céline's attitude to the empirical is cavalier: even his doctorate on Semmelweis is full of blatant factual inaccuracies.)

Céline did have some ideals though, notably the therapeutic attitude itself. Money was reliable, too, provided he could get his hands on it. His biographer Philippe Alméras notes that, in 1936, his revenue from his books was four times greater than it was from medicine. It was his alibi. Under the *profession libérale* tradition in France he could set up shop wherever he could find premises, without governmental say-so in the provision of services and, it would appear, little sense of accountability. Patients came or patients stayed away. His biographer records that on the outbreak of war he attempted to open a practice in St Germain-en-Laye. Not a single patient visited Dr Destouches in three weeks; and he was forced to take on a number of locum positions, before spending most of the war working at municipal clinics in Sartrouville and Bezon, on the far side of Asnières.

The truth is that for most of his working life (even in the 1950s in Meudon when he worked under the new Sécurité Sociale system founded by the Vichy government), Céline actually subsidised his doctoring by writing. His reluctance to abandon the profession altogether surely stems from the fact that medicine gave him an access to the sensationalism of the sordid, to the authentic underground: working at the frontline between the social and the biological he could look down on other writers as mere bourgeois poetasters. Philippe Muray notes that Céline is the first writer to have dared suggest that he had no peers ('Il faudrait que je vive mille ans pour dégueuler tout ce que je pense de mes confrères'). He'd been there, done that; they'd only written about it.

The dispensaries he worked in were, by all accounts, principally those of Lucette Almansor, another dancer who was to become his wife in 1943, grim places. He seems to have been a compassionate enough doctor, solicitous of his poorer patients, but his writing displays little interest in the drama of individual suffering: his experience in the clinics is always used metaphorically, to expose the diseased body of the world. General medicine was never more expansive than *chez Dr Destouches*. His attitude resembles that of Chandler's policemen: 'Civilisation had no meaning for them. All they saw of it was the failure, the dirt, the dregs, the aberrations and the disgust.' When he does notice the suffering – 'the old codgers who inevitably get cold quicker than anyone else... being nearly frozen to start with... who were so happy with their hot drinks... how were we going to get them warm again?... their rheumatics?... their laxative?... these are problems too big for humans to solve...' (*Les Beaux Draps*) – it is nearly always from the perspective of the community health officer. Again and again in the pamphlets he returns to ideas torn willy-nilly from their context in public health or hygiene. Céline's rhetoric, with its harping on extirpation as a *therapeutic* necessity, is part of a biomedical vision that in Germany legitimised Nazi doctrine: the medical profession as a whole played a significant role in obliterating the barrier between healing and killing. To advance an imagery of killing in the name of healing, as he does in the appalling ABC of surgery/germ theory chapter of *L'École des cadavres* (quoted from above), was crucial to a furthering of that ideology. Goebbels used exactly the same imagery: 'our task here is surgical... drastic incisions, or one day Europe will perish of the Jewish disease'. But perhaps the incompatibility between Céline's nominal humanism as a physician and his contribution to political biology is only an apparent one. Pity and misanthropy have always cohabited quite snugly.

The other great trajectory of Céline's life was his role as actor and witness in the final sputtering-out of the thousand-year Reich. Rightly suspecting that he would be the target of recriminations in the *après-guerre* (his publisher Denoël was assassinated at the close of the war), Céline fled with his wife in 1944 to Baden-Baden, and then to the Kafkaesque castle of Sigmaringen, where the last of the Vichy régime was holding out in pathetic hope of a German counteroffensive. There he tended the thousand-or-so-strong French community, acquiring morphine on the black market, rather happy to be treating lice and scabies in the way he had years before in Clichy. He had nothing but contempt for the remnants of Pétain's government around him. Examining the prostates of politicians seems to have been a particular relish. In the topsy-turvy of these last days, he asked for the Vichy Governorship of Saint Pierre-et-Miquelon, the tiny French island dependency off the coast of Nova Scotia he had visited before the war, should Laval be returned to power. It was a characteristic whim from the man whom the BBC now proclaimed an 'enemy of Man' – straight out of *Don Quixote* in fact. In March 1945, with a visa for Denmark, he and his wife and their enterprising cat Bébert set out for Copenhagen: it took them five days (eighteen, writes Céline to his friend Dr Camus) by cart and train strafed by Allied planes, through Nuremberg and Hanover in flames and past the empty German cities glowing on the night-sky. 'Je serai pervenu... à passer à travers la plus grande chasse à courre qu'on ait organisée en Histoire.' It was a hectic, hallucinated bass line, a *Götterdämmerung* that inspired some of his most bebop lyrics in the three novels of the flight; ellipses and ecphoneses are shot at the reader like machine-gun fire while the comic-book onomatopoiea of aerial bombardment thuds in the background: '*Uuuh!... brang!... broum!...* des bombes... des bombes, oui.'

Perhaps the best way to read Céline's elliptic style is as a kind of trickster's announcement that the narrative has moved on in scene or tempo or emphasis – the famous 'three dots' are a brief stuttery cough. The aposiopesis is more than just a form of pointillism. Godard has suggested that Céline's blend of violence, laughter and emotion represents an irruption of the Shakespearean into French culture – a suggestive line of enquiry given that Céline's real venom seems to have been goaded by a language whose modern form lacks the *plaisante plasticité* of Shakespeare's premodern French contemporaries. Rabelais is the one writer unreservedly praised by Céline; and some of the venom he reserved for James Joyce was surely spurred by his realisation that what Joyce had taken from Rabelais was untouched by his rage and bile, indeed was immune to misanthropy.

It is not often observed that, Céline, who has some memorable passages about London in his novels, comes close to several great English writers in the sly way he manipulates the expectations of his readership. How much did he learn from the hypocrisy-hating Jonathan Swift – to whom he refers in one of his medical pieces of the 1930s – and his *Modest Proposal* (1729), a recommendation to settle the Irish crisis with infanticide and cannibalism, or even Daniel Defoe, with his *Shortest Way with the Dissenters* (1702), a satirical pamphlet which seemed to propose large-scale extermination of religious troublemakers? If the latter was irony it was taken straight at the time; and Defoe ended up three times in the pillory for disturbing the peace. Their pamphlets, no less than Céline's, raise the question: do authors working in a satirical or moralist vein put their finger on something furtive but merely potential in the subjects of their parody or do they actually provide an alibi to allow men of truly murderous intent to go about their business? (It is difficult to forget Luis Buñuel's provocation, when asked about the intent behind his surrealist film *Un Chien Andalou*: 'that crowd of imbeciles who find the film beautiful or poetic when it is fundamentally a desperate and passionate call to murder'.)

The real scandal about Céline, according to Godard, is that we take pleasure reading an author whose ideas we condemn. In the double-game of replicating tutored responses and cultivating impertinent ironies we are always reading – queasily perhaps, but reading nonetheless – to see how just far the monster of an author is going to push his luck. It is a trap that Céline, the writer 'without ideas', has primed for his readers – 'I despise them' – who are left to tread their way around a vicious circle. Céline has learned by heart the lesson of Diderot's dialogue *Rameau's Nephew*: in a democratic age, upward contempt is more secure in its legitimacy. If the socially elevated feel contempt for those lower, it is likely to be accompanied by excruciating moral handwringing. None of this pertains to the man from the underground. For morality, in the modern world, is a game with rules, and he refuses to play by them. They are rigged for the benefit of others, and asking to be outwitted. As Edwin Muir wrote, reviewing the first English translation of the novel in 1934, 'there is such a seductive absence of complexity about such an explanation of existence that when it is expressed in the language of the street and with complete candour it sounds almost convincing'.

That Céline could write a scabrous, insulting letter to a close friend and concluded it with a breezy 'Rigolade et amitié' fits with the story of the public writer who feigned surprise in post-war interviews that his public writings should ever have had anything to do with the Final Solution. Céline's strategy to stay one move ahead of the game is to act on the knowledge that humiliations befall us all, sooner or later: so aim low, and the lower the better because the more secure. But if such a strategy succeeds (and if the word 'success' is to retain its conventional meaning), it is only at the subjective level of the novelist himself; its costs are borne by those who experience its effects in the social world. 'Tous les autres sont coupables, sauf moi': this is the voice of the son of Rousseau railing against a 'société des méchants', a pioneer of victim-chic brandishing his stigmata before the unbelievers. No wonder he makes such a show of his sincerity. Céline is actually one of the earliest and most adroit practitioners of victimist *inversion* – I annihilate you to show you that I am your victim, and you ought to feel guilty as I do so.

Imprisoned and then put under detention in Denmark, Céline

was fortunate not to be extradited (and worse). He lived there with his wife and cat in meagre circumstances until he was amnestied in 1951, partly on account of his status as a disabled First War veteran. When he came back to Meudon, where he set up again in practice in order to be able to claim his pension, he was a forgotten man. He and his wife, who gave dancing lessons, lived in seclusion with a menagerie of birds, cats and dogs. The work he had begun in prison in Denmark, *Féerie pour une autre fois*, was published in 1954, and is his most experimental novel; content is exploded, leaving a breakneck discourse to develop by free association. It has the kind of balletic poise and movement he had always hankered after. If Céline's writing had always been about the body, functioning and failing, now its tics and automatisms almost seemed scripted by it. *Féerie* and its sequel were ignored but in his last years, with his wife as amanuensis, Céline completed the trilogy – *D'un château l'autre* (1957), *Nord* (1960) and *Rigodon* (1969), which restored him a measure of fame and public attention. He knew how to exploit it. He himself was a part of its history that France didn't want to know about; his novels were the 'repressed' returning anywhere but in the psychoanalyst's office. Since everyone else denied they ever had anything to do with Vichy, he drew attention to himself: here was the sole authentic 'collabo' voice of the national disgrace. The trilogy is one of the few sustained works in European literature which deals with the war's end; Céline's sense of danger, heightened by the knowledge that he was writing his own testament, is tellingly transmitted even though the clear line of descent between his technique and the pow-zap-kerbang of a *bande dessinée* tyro point to successors in a different form of writing altogether. The word 'blabla' is his invention. He knew exactly what he was up to: 'the precise point of all my work had been to try and make French prose more patently "raidie, voltairisée, pétante, cravacheuse et *méchante*…"', he wrote in a 1949 letter to Jean Paulhan. He was never delirious. His touchstones were the part-truth of his poor beginnings, his persona as the 'médecin des pauvres', his frankly pagan appreciation of the physical beauty of

Third Person to Herself

MARGUERITE DURAS

Her life was her best novel, and M.D. – or 'La Duras' as even she referred to herself in old age – knew it. She kept ransacking it, covering her tracks, refining her ability to confuse the issue, 'for having us believe lies she then ended up believing herself'. So says Laure Adler – historian, French television pundit and acquaintance of the older Duras – in her scrupulous biographical reconstruction not just of M.D.'s life but of the many other visible and not so visible lives subsumed in 73 books and nearly 20 films. One of the last sacred monsters of French cultural life, award of the 1984 Goncourt Prize for her most conventional novel *The Lover* – it sold more than a million copies and ended up as a film she detested – brought M.D. fame. So much, in fact, that a writer who believed writing was the opposite of telling a story had to resign herself to the maddening way a personal truth tends to reveal itself – in the breach: *The Lover* was read as her life story.

Born in 1914 in Gia Dinh in French Indo-China Marguerite Donnadieu was brought up, after her father's early death, by her mother, one of those rod-of-iron schoolteachers who was roundly disliked by her colleagues and nicknamed Madame Dieu by her pupils. Mother was a very partial parent, and a fierce presence in her daughter's writing. She indulged her disturbed, opium-addicted elder son, beat her daughter, looked on as the elder son beat her up too, and then put the family in financial straits by purchasing a plot of uncultivable land in the Cambodian region of Prey Nop. The concession flooded regularly; and one of Duras's early successes, *The Sea Wall* (1950), tells the story of how a party of Vietnamese workers was engaged by her mother to erect a mangrove barrage against the incoming Pacific, to no great avail. The book was later made into quite a successful film with Anthony Perkins. Duras loathed it.

Cochin-China was a lush, overpowering place, in which a stiff colonial society did its best to ignore the extraordinary riot of poverty and natural beauty outside the mosquito screens — newly arrived colonists, the novelist noted, were revolted by the overpoweringly heady odour of jasmine, tamarind and organic decay, but spent the rest of their days back in France trying recapture the sensual assault of the 'terrifying tropical jungle'.

M.D.'s other big theme was sex: it entered her life unsought at the age of four, when she was abused by a Vietnamese boy, though she claimed that she had later initiated her other brother Paul. She was fifteen when, on the Sadec-Saigon ferry, she met a French-speaking Chinese businessman called Leo: despite the fact that fraternisation was frowned on in the colony, they embarked on a two-year affair. He wasn't prepossessing, in fact was quite ugly, but he had a big diamond ring, limousine and the trappings of conspicuous wealth. Money was the motive, and the schoolgirl at the lycée Chasseloup-Laubat in Saigon had her mother's connivance: 'Marguerite was for sale.' The physical tenderness in *The Lover* may well be reserved for the brother who was close to her: he died under mysterious circumstances in Saigon in 1942.

As with many French intellectuals of that era, Duras's war years have their murky moments. A clever law student in the 1930s, she could easily pass for a *congaï* (a Vietnamese girl) and had 'extraordinary powers of seduction'. After a string of lovers, she married Robert Antelme, a literary 'saint' with a masochistic streak (her witness at the wedding was another lover). Their circle included the young François Mitterrand, then an ambitious right-winger: the dynamism of the new Germany was a siren-song for him, too. Daladier's abandonment of the little fish, Czechoslovakia, to the big one had sealed France's own fate. For the first time in its history, the Occupation exposed the shabby pretensions of *la grande nation*: France felt, at least for a few years, the shame of being a small nation, a state on the marches – like Poland – that might very well disappear from the map of Hitler's Europe.

Occupying a desk job in the Paper Allocation Agency attached to the Bureau of Propaganda (i.e. the censor's office), Duras was a small-scale collaborator, though no more of a collaborator than Sartre or the publishers who had to toe the German line. Like others, she joined the Resistance in 1943. The year before she had fallen in love with Dionys Mascolo, a Gallimard editor. Mascolo also happened to be a friend of Antelme, though it didn't stop them embarking on an intense secret affair; much later they had a son. It seems that following Antelme's arrest, Duras had an 'ambiguous' relationship with a Gestapo informer called Delval, allegedly in order to find out from him where Antelme had been deported. Less than two years later, with the Allies in the saddle, Antelme was rescued from Dachau, weighing 35 kilos, and driven back by his friends in a pitiable state to Paris; gradually he was restored to 'solidified living being', and wrote a book about the camps comparable in its hurt and lucidity to Primo Levi's. Delval was arrested as a *gestapiste* and tortured – apparently with gusto – by Duras and others: much of this can be found in *La Douleur* (1985) in which Delval crops up under the name Rabier. When he was finally shot for treason in early 1945, his wife was three months' pregnant with Mascolo's child. Around about this time Duras also claimed to have saved Mitterrand from a Gestapo raid; they stayed lifelong friends.

After the war, in a Paris down-at-heel, suspicious, demoralised and unrecognisable as the degrimed city Malraux left to posterity, Sartre and Camus suddenly discovered the human condition. Where had it been hiding all this time? Some very abstract premises about that condition as first set out by Marx et Cie had been brought to the Latin Quarter for reholstering: in 1953 Mascolo published a book on values and needs which Gombrowicz shrewdly noted offered 'a communism for the Elite', and Duras, who had joined the Community Party in 1944, had the obligatory flirt with Uncle Joe before going on to develop her own more idio-syncratic brand of armchair authenticity. Despite their common position against the war in Algeria, she detested Sartre and Beauvoir and their steadily growing influence on the intellectual scene; and despite a certain similarity of outlook tried to stay aloof from the practitioners of the *nouveau roman*. Only Nathalie Sarraute among woman writers met with her full approval. Duras never forgave Sartre for telling her bluntly: 'I can't publish you. You're a bad writer. But I'm not the one who said it. If you don't improve, you won't get published in *Les Temps modernes*.' So that's how it's done! 'The-one-who-said-it', she always suspected, was Beauvoir.

In the 1950s Duras set to writing with a vengeance, developing her trademark convoluted style with its hiatuses — not silence exactly, but a muteness from which emotional truths rush out of their lair and ambush the reader. Profound for some, vulgarly Freudian for others, her reflections on men and women trapped in geometri-cally variable relationships could easily slacken to corny pulp romance. Her big discovery was that the defeated rival or excluded other person always occupies the most powerful, because stable, vertex in any geometry of desire. Her own strategy as novelist was to defend the jilted appendage of a love triangle, as in *Le ravisse-ment de Lol V. Stein* (1961), a novel which is dominated by the paradox of desire: desire seeks to take on structure, but the very emergence of stability is fatal to the seductive force of its appeal. Duras' talent for dialogue gave her books compositional rigour and pushed her towards the stage and films, one of the best of them, *Moderato Cantabile*, appearing in the same year as her famous cinematic co-production with Alain Resnais *Hiroshima Mon Amour* (1959), a film in which members of the two aggressor nations in the war are transformed into victims by a narrator from a defeated nation that, by luck and guile, has been able to end up on the winning side. Historical amnesia enables the guilty narrator to identify with the adversary as a means of evacuating what she regards as the 'Nazi' violence of her own society. *Hiroshima Mon Amour* might be seen as the lyric overture to the decade in which we were all encouraged to become 'humanitarians'. Duras' period of acutest insights into the nature of the coming commercial society coincided with the death of her mother, propelling her into six months of 'violence, alcohol and eroticism' and to a change of publisher from Gallimard to the new Editions de Minuit, whose editor Alain Robbe-Grillet persuaded her to be more experimental and do away with 'certain naïveties in the style of romantic magazines'.

By 1970, M.D. was third person to herself, a verbal tic shared in France only by the General. The Duras cult is its practical expression (her work has apparently cornered the world PhD market in French studies). A voracious taker, the success of *The Lover* brought the imperious streak in her character to the verge of megalomania. Not a word of criticism was brooked from editors, and a barb like Robbe-Grillet's would have been regarded as lèse-majesté. The sisterhood acclaimed her, despite what seems like a female version of intellectual machismo: it doesn't matter what you say as long as you say it with conviction. She fell out with almost all of her old friends. Old affairs were vampirised for the page as her life became more solitary. Nothing was to remain hidden from her reader-voyeurs, though in a Zen-like moment she told friends her films might be easier to follow if they shut their eyes. She proclaimed her film *India Song* a swansong – 'unequivocally the end of the capitalist world'.

Shuttling back and forth between Paris and her house in Neauphle-le-Château she was cared for – *tant bien que mal* – by a much put-upon and far younger homosexual man, Yann Andréa. (In the time-honoured manner, he has recently published his own account of the relationship.) It was an abject decline. The only lover she was really faithful to, Adler says, was the booze: encouraged by her mother to drink beer in order to gain weight, she had survived cirrhosis at 50 and a period of abstinence to consume as much as eight litres of wine a day in her seventies. By then she was speaking as she wrote. Near the end she said: 'It would appear I have genius. I'm used to it now.'

Adler's biography (which won the Prix Femina) remains sympathetic to the writing while registering the all-consuming nature of the writer's 'narcissisme de midinette'. Her taped interviews and access to the original papers housed in the Institut de la Mémoire de l'Edition Contemporaine bring her as close to M.D. as anyone will get or want to get, though some lovers and friends are still alive and may wish to amend the record. The subject of Adler's remarkably level-headed book is that supremely French object of idolatry, the writer, and the occupation Duras called tragic; Adler forgoes psychoanalysis, even though M.D. positively invites long slouching detours to the Kingdom of Ends. Though she was friendly with Lacan, Duras steered clear of the couch. She had her reasons: Narcissus in the myth didn't just fall in love with his reflection in the still pool of selfhood; the very borderline between reality and image became a blur.

Duras brings to mind Hemingway, a writer she greatly admired – her friend Madeleine Alleins said she knew whole chunks of *Green Hills of Africa* off by heart – and the way in which he became a victim to his manipulations of the plot of his own life. That Duras managed to work hard through a permanent low-octane drizzle of depression and paranoia resulting from a staggering alcohol intake is out of the Hemingway book too. Mind you, he wouldn't have had a clue where to find 'the best and cheapest pigs' tails in Paris' or what to do with them once he'd got them squirming home.

Believing in Architecture

Rubble Berlin. People keep mislaying things in Berlin, even the city itself. While every European city offers the historian a biography (the history of Europe is, in large part, the history of its cities), Berlin, since 1870, has acquired an archaeology, too. Some of its layers are made of compressed nightmare, deposits of sordid misery and not just the eerie atmospheres of the 'weird tales' that made E.T.A. Hoffmann famous in the days when Berlin was a most respectably enlightened regional capital. A couple of weeks ago I stood with my son flying a kite on the top of a large sandy hill in the Grünewald area, between Berlin and Potsdam. The hill is called Teufelsberg. The only incline for miles, it offers a superb vantage point across the city from Spandau and Reinickendorf in the north to Tempelhof and Kopenick in the south. In winter it becomes a ski resort. But Devil's Mountain is no ordinary hill: pipes, bricks, tiles and other detritus can be seen poking out from beneath its sand and scrub. This 120-metre-high heap is the derelict body of prewar Berlin; this is the city carted away brick by brick at war's end by the famous 'rubble women'.

Prairie Berlin. In Wim Wenders' film *Wings of Desire* (1987), a fantasy about angels watching over the lives of modern-day Berliners and hearing their thoughts not as a vast cacophony but as random strands of monologue (some of which were written by Peter Handke), an old man potters across a warren in the middle of Berlin. He can be heard to mutter to himself, 'It must be here some-where. I can't find the Potsdamer Platz.' The old man was wandering across what had once been Berlin's commercial hub. Hitler, who had big plans for Berlin once he had conquered Europe and established an empire on the backs of those who failed to meet criteria for belonging to the master-race, ended his life in this spot: as a troglodyte. In 1953, the East German workers confronted Soviet tanks on the same stretch of ground, and Brecht wrote (but didn't publish) his famous poem about the government that ought to dissolve the people and consider electing another. By the time Wenders came along with his 35 mm camera and two philosophical angels with overcoats and pony tails (the actors Bruno Ganz and Otto Sander, who, in the course of the film, relinquish the tedium of immortality among the angelic orders for an existence in the realm of necessity) the presence of the nearby Wall had turned the Potsdamer Platz back to what it had been before Bismarck made the city capital of his united empire in 1871: sandy prairie.

The New Berlin. Only a few years after Wenders' film this stretch of waste ground has become Europe's biggest construction site. Amid some controversy, the leaders of the newly united city sold off plots to multinational companies including Sony and Daimler-Benz. The government complex slowly being erected around Sir Norman Foster's glass-domed Reichstag is flanked by new embassies built on the same imposing scale. Inside, the graffiti from the Russian soldiers who occupied the building in 1945 has been preserved; it thrusts the violence of the past into the present more effectively than any purpose-built monument could have. Monstrous grey Potemkin blocks stand gloomily waiting in the other half of the city: they will have to be stripped of asbestos before anything else can be done with them. The more luxurious Berlin is now an 'edge city', one of those dazzlingly aseptic confections in steel and glass that can be found the world over: modernist certainly, but not fired in the crucible of conviction. After the euphoria over the fall of the Wall, overspeculation, mismanagement and an economic slump in the mid-1990s have made it difficult to lay comprehensive plans for the new capital.

Hitler's Berlin. Plans? Even the word induces nervousness. Yet Berlin's scale imposes its own logic: following Bismarck's adroit military campaigns against Denmark, Austria and France, the city was laid out, its roads diverging like Ixion's axles, on a scale to rival Vienna, Paris and London. 'Hyperthyroid neoclassicism' is its default style. Hitler didn't like Berlin, but he needed its bigness. With the help of Albert Speer, his general inspector of buildings, he intended to transform it into a cultic city which, by 1950, would contain the crowds whose arousal was the secret of his power. The whole thing was to look like a vast, militarised Ufa premiere. Germania would have a new north-south axis, a triumphal arch four times bigger than the one at the top of the Champs-Elysées and a central dome, the Kuppelberg, sixteen times bigger than St Peter's. Other European cities would be lilliputian by comparison. In fact, he was planning for a mausoleum on the largest possible scale, a Piranesi doom-machine made with an eye for its own sublime destitution. Hitler wanted to see what his Rome would look like once its thousand years of glory had passed. Visiting the ruins of the Chancellery in late 1945, Stephen Spender noted the reams of building manuals above the Führer's bed. Hitler didn't believe in much, but he believed in architecture.

Hauptstadt Berlin. It is therefore not entirely surprising that one of the figures which haunts the history of the city on the Spree from its 1871 promotion as Reichshauptstadt through to the year 2000 is a ghost: self-doubt. (Much of Berlin is built on aquifers, which adds literal unsteadiness to the figurative: visitors to the city cannot fail to notice the purple-coloured drainage pipes coiling down Unter den Linden: these have been installed to remove bog-water from the foundations of new building projects.) Bismarck, like his sovereign, distrusted the new capital's bombast and swagger: it was a hotbed of liberalism, sucking in new people from the eastern marches. Thousands of enterprising Jews from the marches were drawn there, and many poorer Jews too: the Scheunenviertel ('barn district') north of the Alexanderplatz became a haven for refugees from Russia and Poland. Joseph Roth opens one of the chapters of his book *Wandering Jews* with the bold assertion: 'No Eastern Jew goes to Berlin voluntarily. Who in all the world goes to Berlin voluntarily?' Roth did, and made a name for himself. The rest of Germany found Berlin alien, both parvenu and preposterous – an attitude that has never entirely disappeared. It resembles the shudder some Americans used to get at the sight of Chicago, though they have never had to live with it as their capital. Seafaring Hamburgers mocked Berlin as an outpost on the pampas; ecclesiastically conservative Bavarians loathed it for being northern and Protestant. Berliners replied with their famous blunt cheek, the Berliner Schnautze (hence place-names like Devil's Mountain).

Wilhelmine Berlin. Within a few decades of its inauguration in 1871, Berlin had become an urban laboratory: it was the world's newspaper capital and home to its first fast-food chain (Aschinger's). It stood at the cutting edge of scientific progress: Koch, Ehrlich, Planck and Einstein made some of the most important advances in modern science in the city, despite their misgivings about the grip of the Prussian military on the academy. Indeed Elektropolis, as it was known in the early years of the twentieth century, heralded the ascension of the empirical sciences over the older humanistic disciplines and the new international image of Germany as the 'machine nation'; even the Kaiser, who presided over Berlin's odd blend of uniform worship and urban modernity, exhorted his subjects to participate in the game of power. Knowledge was power for those who wanted to achieve more than truth. Tradition always had a caricatural quality in Berlin, such was the city's thralldom to hard facts, to the lure of efficiency and Technik. This very modern amalgam of feudal attitudes – no other European industrial power was so dominated by the landed aristocracy and traditional military figures – and an almost unquenchable belief in the power of machines was to prove the undoing of the Kaiser, and Germany itself, in the longer run.

Weimar Berlin. Long before the wild Twenties, Berlin was renowned for its strenuous hedonism and armies of prostitutes: it was the great Babylon of the East. The collapse of civil order that followed the end of the Great War, with violent street battles between the Spartacists and government troops culminating in the murder of Rosa Luxemburg and Karl Liebknecht, convinced the rest of Germany that its capital was not just corrupt, but dangerous. The novelist Alfred Döblin, working as a doctor in the working class Lichtenberg district, wrote in disgust at the indifference in the better heeled parts of the city to the bloodshed around him. The First International Dada Fair, in 1920, took art more seriously than anyone had hitherto thought possible, and instructed dilettantes to rise up against it. Overthrow art, and society would be easy game. Social conditions in Berlin were not helped by the draconian terms imposed on Germany by the treaty of Versailles, which led to the hyperinflation of 1922–3; in November 1922, the mint was printing 100 trillion mark notes. Their value depreciated before the printer's ink was dry: in what became known as the Great Disorder a loaf of bread cost 80 billion. Doctors began to talk about 'zero stroke' or 'cypher stroke', a kind of nervous break-down induced by contemplation of the spiralling currency figures. Berlin's streets began to dominate the screen in Fritz Lang's films, the stage in Brecht's dramas of the 'jungle of the cities', and the newspapers in the articles of Egon Erwin Kisch, the first journalist to turn the reporter into a recognisable figure: the entertaining crusader. The cynic was no longer someone outside the city: his mindset was inextricably part of the social substance. Tucholsky, Roth, Kafka and – perhaps most surprisingly of all – Nabokov (whose father was shot at a political meeting when he tried to protect the speaker, one of Kerensky's ill-fated Russian cabinet of 1917) all lived and wrote there during the 1920s. In fact, Berlin was the first cultural capital of the Russian émigré community: it had Russian theatres, bookshops, hairdressers, grocers and even a foot-ball team (with Nabokov in goal). At the end of the decade Berlin could claim to be the most progressive city in the world:

Stresemann, Germany's conciliatory foreign minister, son of a Berlin innkeeper, was perhaps the first prominent politician to be genuinely fond of the capital: his death in 1929 deprived the Weimar Republic of the one person who might have held it through the terrible year of the Wall Street crash, which allowed the Nazis to make their bid for power. What are often thought of as Nazi projects, such as Berlin's new airport at Tempelhof, and its elevated trains, roads and egalitarian housing were all launched during the Weimar years. Weimar Berlin was modernity's advance post.

West Berlin. After a collapse so total it ended up as a hill, half of its population dead or dispersed, Berlin became extraterritorial. The city had come into its own. The doctor and poet Gottfried Benn wrote to a literary journal, in July 1948: 'It is the city whose brilliance I loved, whose misery I now endure as that of the place where I belong, the city in which I lived to see the Second, the Third, and now the Fourth Reich, and from which nothing will ever make me emigrate. Indeed one might prophesy a future for it now: tensions are developing in its matter-of-factness, changes of pace and interferences are developing in its lucidity, something ambiguous is starting up, an ambivalence such as centaurs or amphibia are born from.' The amphibian city was oxygenated by the famous airlift a few years later when – after the Soviets blockaded all road, rail and canal routes – food, medicines, fuel, building materials and other necessities had to be supplied by air: the operation was so successful Berliners started putting on weight. While the rest of the world moved into the era of mutually assured destruction (MAD), Berlin became a kind of conservatory for espionage and counter-espionage. The visit of the young Augustus of the new American age ('I am a doughnut,' Kennedy told the packed crowds, though nobody seemed to mind), and the overnight construction in 1961 of the thirteen-foot high 'anti-fascist protection barrier', as they called it in the DDR. Berlin never regained the array of industries that had made it the nerve-centre of the Nazi military-industrial complex, but it became the vitrine of the free world. It was a city on the take. The communist half of it was drab, virtuous and uninspiring, the other heavily subsidised by Bonn and rather self-conscious about its decadence. Draft-dodgers flocked there, and it seethed with anti-establishment sentiment and student provocation. Bohemians dressed in black. Stoned out of their minds, Iggy Pop and his friend David Bowie sang about having plans for everyone. Here was all the dark glamour of the twentieth century, pretty much risk-free. For others, Berlin was a hope of heightened sentience. In Wender's film about the sky above the city, a startled angel becomes human, and acquires colour vision in front of a portion of the Wall transformed into graffiti art by members of a Kreuzberg movement that called itself Fast Form Manifest. Only Johnny Rotten thought of going over the Wall, and pleaded, in a hair-raising punk refrain, 'please don't be waiting for me'. But the world didn't end again. Subsidised Berlin won out in 1989, and vice triumphed over virtue for the benefit of mankind.

Berlin Redux. Now the Wall is gone and Berlin has, for the first time in its recent history, the chance to grow bit by bit as a national capital, rather than an international showcase – as a 'capital-redux'. The fact that unity ultimately came about not through anything like Bismarck's 'blood and iron' but through the implosion of an ideology and that singular event in modern history – the peaceful withdrawal of an undefeated army – offers grounds for some confidence in the future. Germany's place in the world is quite different from what it was in 1870; or is it? The common European home seems to be extending eastwards, and Berlin is bound to dominate it. So what about Germany's commitment to the west? A restrained or uncertain modernism is quite in order. Nobody wants to have to look for the Potsdamer Platz again.

The Last Culture Broth

Bernard Pivot's Bookshow

How does the Brassens' charity song go? – 'Quand le croqu'-mort t'emportera...'

The undertaker's mute came on 29 June for the 407th transmission of Bernard Pivot's famous Friday night programme, *Bouillon de culture*. For the past eleven years, for an hour and a half around 11 p.m. on France's second public channel, France Deux, *Bouillon de culture* offered little more than the prospect of an affable middle-aged man with sartorially suspect ties talking to guests about books they had written. For his last outing on air before retiring, 'Stock-taking before final closure,' a panel of twelve guests commented on highlights from a decade of Pivot's being passionate about books. He had even invited the American talk-show host James Lipton, who does a good funeral, to talk in English. Lipton was apparently doing public penance for having purloined for his own show Pivot's questionnaire, a series of trite questions tossed to guests at the end of proceedings. 'If heaven exists what would you like to hear God say when you arrive at the pearly gates?' (Answer: 'Get off my show.')

Pivot's television career started in 1973 with a programme called *Ouvrez les Guillemets* ('Open quotes'), which lasted two years. This was followed by the famous *Apostrophes* which ran for fifteen years before being replaced in 1990 by a programme that was similar in format but more eclectic in scope – hence, culture broth. An initial concession to showbiz proved to be a mistake and Pivot quickly returned to his original style: four or five guests would sit with him round an oval table talking about books. One point of

Pivotian etiquette: guests were expected to have read the other invitees' books. It made for a kind of radio with visual mimicry; no bad thing since radio is a medium for which, as Mavis Gallant once observed, 'the French have a rather daft talent'. Pivot disarmed his guests with charm and never pretended to be a know-all, though I do recall him pointing out to the Belgian writer Amélie Nothomb that she had bodged the imperfect subjunctive in one of her novels. She took the reprimand most graciously. Sitting in on Pivot was a civil affair; and only Charles Bukowski ever got shown the door – live – for being drunk and disorderly. Courtesy, good manners, wit and a degree of frankness (Michel Driot: 'Miró? An idiot!') made his programme unfailingly interesting.

Le Roi Lire is a celebrity in France, where he seems a projection of the idealised figure of the teacher, though the French have been meeting just for the pleasure of talking together at least since Baron d'Holbach's salon in the eighteenth century, when Europe's philosophes would 'Shandy away' in a hôtel in the rue Royale. Pivot must have been a teacher out of Chateaubriand's century then, the century after, for teachers in France are now members of an increasingly harassed profession, like workers in the public sector almost everywhere. Indeed, Pivot radiated an old-fashioned confidence in the book as a means for reflecting on the morals and society of one's time, even though the pleasure of reading is not what our society calls pleasure at all. He himself is a general reader from the provincial middle-classes, a grocer's son from Lyons who used to write copy under Jean d'Ormesson (present at the final night jamboree as Pivot's most-invited guest) at the conservative daily *Le Figaro*. Were he still alive, Barthes would surely have written a barbed mythology about Pivot's 'poujadist' good sense, though Friday nights with Pivot were little mythologies entirely by themselves. His appeal was classless, and he could entice a Renaud-le-Parigot to talk as volubly as the President of the Republic (an ashen-faced Mitterrand went on camera with Pivot just days before his death). After three decades of serving as 'the interpreter of public curiosity', his influence on the book trade (*pivotisation*) has been immense: every bookshop in France used to have its shelf of 'Pivot's books' (and this month things have come full circle with a paperback entitled *Le métier de lire*: it offers Pivot in interview with Pierre Nora). Some complained that his was little more than a kind of punditry: after Pivot visited the chaotic apart-ment of the historian of religion Georges Dumézil in 1986, the ailing but intellectually sprightly thinker had the ironic pleasure of seeing his *Mythe et Epopée* in stacks beside the latest novels. (Pivot forgot to warn his audience that a Sanskrit primer and half a life-time were required before so much as broaching the book.) Pivot could have founded his own production firm fifteen years ago and become, I imagine, spectacularly wealthy. But money wasn't what moved him; in any case, partiality of that kind would have fatally wounded his authority. Nor did he ever call himself a critic. He believed in reading as an exaltation, and in speaking well about books as a part of living well: his greatest pleasure, he once said, was having Nabokov as guest, although there was no shortage of famous names on his podium: Aleksandr Solzhenitsyn, Marguerite Yourcenar, Julien Green, Albert Cohen, Marguerite Duras. Vladimir Nabokov's drolly magisterial appearance in 1975, shortly after the publication of *Ada* in French translation, has recently been made available on video: Nabokov responded to all Pivot's ques-tions by reciting his answers from index-cards, even when reminiscing about Mademoiselle O, the French governess from the Doubs who figures in *Speak Memory*. That is the cost of 'style'. Only a very few writers – the reclusive philosopher Emil Cioran and the novelist Julien Gracq – refused to appear in the studio. They no doubt had their reasons: you wouldn't go on Pivot if you thought of writing as a conspiratorial activity or of books as rele-vations of the demiurge. Television destroys that kind of mystique. Philippe Sollers, a professional *écrivain maudit*, used to sit on the platform smoking a cigarette in an old-fashioned cigarette-holder – which gave him the air of someone picking words up with a set of tweezers. Younger Parisian intellectuals talked proprietorially about 'passer chez Pivot' as if he were a special uncle who liked to slip down to the cellar to bring up an especially good bottle of claret. Often he did, and they sat there chewing. They were fascinated by the spectacle of an 'honnête homme' surviving in their dog-eat-dog milieu: after all it takes great skill to defuse the ritualised contempt of the bohemian for bourgeois culture in France, because intellectuals are at once the fiercest enemies of the bourgeois and the ultimate bourgeois themselves.

Pivot's show, even for those who don't like their culture done in ninety minutes, was a kind of anthropology in action. In a programme on the French-speaking nations of Africa the Malian writer Aïcha Fofana put things in a Montesquieian perspective by observing that, in her community, writing was regarded as 'an anti-social act'. By removing herself from the group she would become, by virtue of her apartness, a potential threat to it. So she wrote at night. Pivot indulged British writers, and helped to obtain wide audiences for William Boyd, Theodore Zeldin and Julian Barnes. The latter once remarked that it would be impossible to find a programme with five writers, and foreign ones at that, on British television. A theme evening in December 1998 followed the history of the chanson from the Middle Ages to the aforementioned Georges Brassens, with guests providing extempore versions of classic chansons. It gave me a keen sense of how the deliberate archaicism of 'la douce France' serves as a balm for the wounds of a hypermodernity France believes it has to embody, as the nation of the revolution. One of the best recent programmes was themed 'Against Hate'; it brought together George Steiner, as silver-tongued in French as he is in English, Roberto Benigni, director of the film *Life is Wonderful*, Gottfried Wagner, a disaffected member of the Wagner clan, and a brave man called Emile Shoufani, a teacher and curé from Nazareth. Shoufani pointed out, at a time when France was embroiled in heated discussions about multiculturalism, specifically about whether Muslim girls should be able to wear a headscarf to school, that all religious accoutrements were banned from his non-denominational school in

Nazareth: teaching would be impossible in such a charged political setting were signs of religious affiliation to figure in the classroom. The irony was loud.

The generalist tradition, which Pivot represented, used to live in horror of specialists, though even Pivot couldn't avoid inviting some of them on his platform. Even in France intellocracy is not what it was, according Régis Debray, who wrote the obituaries for the generation that died out with Sartre in 1980, and criticised Pivot for presuming to talk about books he didn't understand. The generalist tradition may have died out not, as everyone says, with that great concert speaker Sartre, but earlier still: a figure like Gaston Bachelard – a postman who became a highly influential philosopher of science at the Sorbonne – or Simone Weil's teacher Emile Chartier (Alain) would be high on my list. Figures like Bachelard have been obscured by a psychoanalytically-fuelled culture of suspicion: everything he wrote had a naïve trust in the works of the imagination, as if the mere act of perception could, of itself, provide a guide for good living. The phenomenologist of literary daydreams once called himself 'an addict of felicitous reading'; Bachelard's term would fit the Pivot who used to spend up to ten hours a day reading. But if the generalist has gone from French culture, the philosopher-writer has not, nor the vanity of pretending to be a 'maître' – intellectual empire-building was a conspicuous activity in the heady years of structuralism. Now, in a culture adrift between the all-purpose vocabulary of the professorial mandarins and media 'peepoll' (the English word 'people' is used in French to signify media *celebrities*), Pivot's retirement is like the end of an institution.

And the literary scene itself? Well, in 1968, French students were reading Mao, Althusser and Marcuse; now some of their children are accusing them of arrant hedonism and egocentricity, for failing to grasp that aligning themselves with a society of mass consumption was the broad road not to liberation but to subjection – as when Pivot invited the whisky-drinking, chain-smoking Michel Houellebecq (born 1958), author of one of the most read books of recent years *Atomised* (*Les particules élémentaires*). A million copies of his book have sold, and Houellebecq, an angry if not-quite-so-young man, has discovered that you can bank on the allure of being a last man. Look how ugly I am! Physically and morally! And you too! Houellebecq describes what the 'anything goes' of the 1960s has done to the republic built on Rousseau's founding paradox of a humanity forced to be free. Total liberation from religious, cultural, social and political determinations has made everyone a specialist bit player on the market, not least the sexual; the prized subjectivity of the generation (*the* Generation) now occupying all the plum jobs looks empty and comformist – helplessly manipulated by the system it thought it was protesting against in 1968. The disquieting thing about Houellebecq's critique is its quietism: he can see nothing to do other than 'be abject, in order to be genuine'. Experimentum mundi is over. A hundred years ago Jules Renard could dismiss Nietzsche by suggesting his name was a typing error; Houellebecq takes the historicism of the secret master of twentieth-century French thought, Hegel – transmitted to a generation of French students through the teaching of the Russian-born philosopher (and, it would seem, Soviet spy) Alexandre Kojève – as destiny itself. His depressed narrator, having first relieved humans of the pain of knowing themselves to be the wrong job lot by creating a line of untroubled immortal clones, drowns himself in the Atlantic under a 'shifting, gentle light' off the coast of Ireland: history has gone west. Twenty-five hundred years of metaphysics hauls itself from the Ionian Sea, lurches to Jena, only to drown off Mizen Head: Houellebecq's cynicism is as reductionist as that of any logical positivist who mistakes reason for a form of scientific calculus.

Perhaps it was symptomatic – don't we wilfully confuse cause and effect by talking about generations anyway? – that the conversation on the last Pivot show circled around two aspects of the French exception: the supposed decline of the language, and the reputation of Louis-Ferdinand Céline, Proust's only challenger to the title of the greatest twentieth-century novelist. These days, it seems to be the Québécois who get upset about French laxity with their language: Denise Bombardier was no exception. On a previous programme with the polyglot linguist Claude Hagège, it had emerged that some French companies, even when anglophones are not present, insist on their managerial staff convening in English. The global market is exposing young French people to terminologies that bear only the most tenuous link to their historic culture or the self-readings that give literature top ranking in the same culture. French pop singers record in English; the self-indulgent but sometimes wonderfully idiosyncratic French film industry seems to be dwindling away; French commercial radio is unyieldingly American in its inflections; a French scientist who can't write his papers in English has no career. A recent lexical study showed that two per cent of *Le Monde*'s current vocabulary is loaned from English. What is staring at the French is the prospect that their language – once thought to be a superbly honed instrument for mediating thought and perception – might one day become a kind of folklore for patronising the grandparents.

That, of course, was precisely the attitude taken by the Jacobins towards France's regional languages in the nineteenth century. Now a nation that conceived itself as the producer of modernity has woken up to find itself consuming it, too. When, by reciting by heart a passage from the book he turned into a successful one-man-show in 1994, the actor Fabrice Luchini proved himself to be, like many Parisian intellectuals, a venerator of the said Louis-Ferdinand Céline, it took a comment from one of the other guests, the scientist Georges Charpak, to remind him that Céline, aside from his anti-Semitism, despised intellectuals and writers. 'Why do I write? I'll tell you: to make the others unreadable.' Céline's invective is a racist version of Captain Haddock's spluttering rages in the Tintin comics: 'représentant de l'Union des Cinglés, diplomatiques, politiques, coloniaux, et ectoplasmiques…' Hatred made him lyrical; hatred was reliable. But first Céline had to overcome the formidable problem of having French as his literary hate-language – its empty abstractions, its pouting mellifluousness, its *dulce*. So he duffed it up good and proper, force-fed it the upward contempt of the Paris poor, and taught it lots of swear-words out of Villon and Rabelais. He was its anti-Descartes. But Céline's assumptions aren't really that different from those of the Academy that stifled Rabelais' 'français gras': a culture demands certain rituals of belonging and self-surrender, in return for which it magically effaces doubt. 'The French language is royal! The rest is glibawful gibberish!' Here be fleecy sheep, there be very smelly goats. What lends for a certain paranoia in France's defence of its linguistic purity is surely a suppressed realisation that, at a certain period in its history, it produced great stylists precisely because, convinced its language existed outside history, it could ignore the cacophonous others, not least the speakers of that ghastly patois across the Channel.

Even as Bernard Pivot unquoted himself – 'les guillemets sont fermés' – I couldn't help but recall an arresting passage in *Democracy in Europe*, published last year by the Oxford historian Larry Siedentop (not invited to this or any other literary supper). Siedentop, who is American in origin, suggested that if the French wish to continue to dominate Europe in the civic and bureaucratic sphere, as they have done since the days of the Fourth Republic, they may be obliged to accept English as Europe's lingua franca. With a Machiavellian flourish – or perhaps a misplaced confidence about how many cultural ingredients are to be found in a language thinned to a gruel of cognitive essentials – he went on to suggest that by adopting English as a shared language the French would be better placed to emancipate themselves from American cultural and political influence.

Back to the soup kitchen, Auvergnat?

Windfowl and Their Advantages

GUNTER GRASS IN 1999

Günter Grass stands so prominently in the line of fire of Germany's still polarised and politicised cultural life, and has been sniped at so often since *The Rat* (1986) – his novel *A Wide Field* (1995) was literally ripped up for the benefit of the press by that other Grand Old Man of German letters, the critic and TV personality Marcel Reich-Ranicki – that it comes almost as a surprise to find a barely noticed survivor: Grass the poet.

As the cover of his modest *Selected Poems* attests, Grass was a poet before he had his colossal success in 1959 with the first of his three Danzig novels, *The Tin Drum*: indeed, his first publication was a book of lyrics, improbably named *The Advantages of Windfowl*. It announced some of those obsessional objects which dominate Grass's writing: ready-assembled furniture, Polish flags, prophets and flapping nuns. Wit is an angel of connection for Grass: his exuberance of mood, association and image suggests a poet drawn to a Surrealist code of practice, a member of that Aesopian line that extends all the way to Arp and Holub and Popa. Even early on, Grass works as a moralist, not by means of direct statement or logic, but by manipulating imagery. Oskar Matzerath's refusal to grow up into a world of fallenness in *The Tin Drum* is prefigured in 'Family Matters', a short poem in which a collection of briny foetuses observe the secular attitudes of Sunday culture-goers:

> In our museum – we always go there on Sundays –
> they have opened a new department.

Our aborted children, pale, serious embryos,
sit there in plain glass jars
and worry about their parents' future.

The Advantages of Windfowl appeared in 1956, a watershed for German
poetry. Both Brecht and Gottfried Benn died that year; the first
famous for his moral exhortations, cigars and artful-dodger
support for the fledgling GDR; the other a more acquired German
taste: a former Expressionist, a dermatologist-venereologist in
private practice in Berlin, and an *esprit fort*, who flatly declared as
far back as 1926 that 'works of art are phenomena, historically inef-
fective, devoid of practical consequences. That is their greatness.'
Benn's star seems to be in the ascendant again, judging by the urban
topographies of the young, hard-nosed and very productive East
Berlin poet Durs Grünbein, though it is surely the case that
however much his reputation as a dramatist is eclipsed, Brecht's
example as a poet will always serve as a beacon to chase away poetic
self-absorption, especially of the German variety.

Grass's distinction was to tread a wary path between the positions of Brecht and Benn throughout the turmoil of the Sixties. It
was a balancing act with a superficial resemblance to the one practised by Seamus Heaney a decade later in Northern Ireland, in
which the poet had to pay lip-service to the claims of the 'cause',
while the poetry insisted on occupying a free state of the imagination. If anything, Germany – and certainly German literature –
has been politicised in more far-reaching and radical ways than
Ireland: Grass's response to those who insisted on 'commitment'
was to involve himself in party politics, campaigning in 1961 for
Willy Brandt's distinctly unrevolutionary Social Democratic
Party; what he wanted from his growing readership, he claimed in
his essay 'On the Lack of Self-Confidence among Scribish Court
Fools in the Light of Non-Existent Courts', was the freedom to
be a jester. 'Poems allow no compromises,' he said in that lecture,
'though we live by them. Whoever can endure this tension every
day of his life is a fool and changes the world.' It is, as Michael

Hamburger remarked in his survey of postwar German writing, *After the Second Flood*, an earnest of Grass's sophistication as a dialectician: by putting his shoulder to the wheel of gradual social change while insisting on art's autonomy he was demonstrating to his critics that he was that unusual thing in Germany, a cook who tasted as he cooked, not one who followed the book – even if he did tend to overdo the salt.

In fact, one of the poems in this bilingual edition, more than half of which replicates the Penguin selection of thirty years ago, is a recipe for jellied pig's head – *Schweinekopfsülze*, one of those echt German dishes like the *Saumagen* (haggis) Chancellor Kohl once had served up to a bemused Margaret Thatcher. As with so many of his early poems (it comes from his second book *Gleisdreieck*, 1960, named after a junction on the Berlin S-Bahn line), its pseudological structure recalls the poet's debt to Dada; a key term in the standard recipe is replaced by Grass in a manner than is both comic and purposeful. The ingredient that makes this gargantuan pig's head suitable for consumption is the addition of a level tablespoonful not of Maggi sauce, but 'mittlere Wut' – medium rage. After boiling and the dissection of edible portions, the head is left to set 'all by itself and communicated rage,/ that is, without power and gelatine paper'. Whatever else it is, this disintegrating and not entirely apolitical head is as powerful an image as those complexes and fetishes that Grass fed into the short lyrics of his first collection. Not all his catalogue poems have the gusto and verve of 'The Jellied Pig's Head', however; some of them wander aimlessly through registers of meaning that were either pretty empty to start with or which have been evacuated by subsequent events.

Other poems from *Gleisdreieck* and *Ausgefragt* (1964) suggest that, after the success of his trilogy of novels, Grass felt less at liberty to let metaphor carry him towards that child's-eye suspension of moral judgement that had been so successful in *The Tin Drum*. The pervasive influence of Kafka's parables on his writing of these years is quite apparent, much as it is in American poets writing at the same time, such as Elizabeth Bishop; this is Oskar's legacy, the intrusion of self-consciousness. Given Grass's involvement with the Social Democrats, and the hundreds of podium speeches he delivered for them in the 1965 electoral campaign, the publication of his third book was as much a political as a literary event. For all his attempts to steer his 'third way', in 'Powerless, with a Guitar', Grass seems pressured by the decision to air his private dilemma about public protest.

> We read napalm and imagine napalm.
> Since we cannot imagine napalm
> we read about napalm until
>
> by napalm we can imagine more.
> Now we protest against napalm.

In contrast to the agonising of 'Powerless, with a Guitar', some of Grass's poems of this period are too overtly polemical and haranguing – 'Do Something', for instance – and it is almost a relief that the cook who wanted to recite 'The Jellied Pig's Head' as an attack on the morally complacent should have been seduced by his salivary glands. The radical Left, meanwhile, saw 'Powerless, with a Guitar' as a slight.

'Catholic deep down I smoked', Grass writes in a later poem: some of his best poems, like 'Family Matters', verge on the blasphemous. Repeatedly, it is the briefest lyrics which draw the reader up short, and which exhibit the fool free in a realm of moral compunction. The title of 'Müll Unser' (Our Litter Which) parodies the Lord's Prayer and closes on another kind of blasphemy:

> Looked for pebbles and found
> the surviving glove
> made of synthetic pulp.
> Every finger spoke.
> No, not those daft yachtsman's yarns

but of what will remain:
our litter
beaches long.
While we, mislaid,
will be nobody's loss.

One of the most intricate poems in *Gleisdreieck* (and Grass's own favourite, according to Hamburger's introduction) is a sinister 'children's song' with quadruple rhymes and an intricate play on bureaucratic language: 'Wer spricht hier, spricht und schweigt?/ Wer schweigt, wird angezeigt', which is Englished adroitly by Hamburger as 'Who speaks here or keeps mum?/ Here we denounce the dumb.' No criticism can be levelled at a translator who has to work at such a density of compaction, in which it is impossible to convey the full finger-pointing menace of that ordinary German verb *angezeigt*, especially when here, as elsewhere, he shows such resourcefulness in responding to the challenge that makes translation worth doing in the first place. Hamburger's skill with German idiom is sometimes inspired: he equips the abstraction at the end of the poem in praise of cigarettes, 'Coffin Nails', with a set of dentures it doesn't have in the original – 'That's why I smoke/ in the teeth of all reason.'

Formal restraint is the predominant quality of the last section of the book, a suite of thirteen sonnets about Germany after Reunification. Essentially, it represents all the new work in the collection. 'Novemberland' is Grass's portmonteau term for the country that has contrived to have a number of events in its recent history fall on 9 November: Hitler's putsch in 1923, the Kristallnacht riots in 1938, and the fall of the Berlin Wall in 1989. Novemberland, a late mutant form of Thomas More's Neverland, is a dismal place of *Konjunktur*, overcrowding, inflation, fat old Germans and younger ones with pension plans, a fortress to fend off 'Black, Fellah, Jew, Turk, Romany'. And if the pressures of intrusion aren't bad enough, Novemberland is plagued by enemies within – among them, the threat of 'imminent Christmas'. Citizen

Grass has turned grumpy OAP, and left his fool's garb in the drawer. Not to mention his cook's apron. A bit of bluster about talk-show society – 'quite glibly on their stools now they debate/ why on occasion humans lapse from the human state' – is a insider reference to the fact that Grass himself famously writes at a lectern, standing up: it sounds from the poem as if sitting on stools is a sin as heinous as debating human lapses. Several poems evince a curmudgeonly resentment about having to pay what others write off against taxes. Altogether, the tone is indignant and peevish, and the poems topical in a way that binds them to their recent occasions: the asylum in Mölln set on fire by Neo-Nazis in 1992, for instance, or the utterings of the carnival figure of the former Government, employment minister Norbert Blüm. Hamburger has chosen to pour the original poems straight into English, although the results are anything but fluid. His initially baffling line, 'That changeably remains the same', does duty for 'Das bleibt veränderlich sich gleich': surely a case of *plus ça change, plus c'est la même chose*. Another poem has the tortuous sentence 'Yet on returning to the home control/ to market I must carry still my dyed-in wool', which, apart from hobbling the hearer, is slavish in its concessions to the German rhyme (*Kontrolle/Wolle*) and word-order. Not only that, but the unhappy 'home control' suggests some kind of domestic surveillance rather than a simple customs shed this side of the frontier.

Hamburger is not entirely to blame. The original poems are a long way from Grass at his best: they are turgid, bilious, and their intentions on the reader all too obvious. Rhythmically tongue-tied, they have little in common with the wit and linguistic poise of poems such as 'Nursery Rhyme'. Oh for windfowl and all their advantages! Nor is it just the poetry. Grass's lack of literary acumen since reunification seems to be confirmed by his prose work *My Century*, published in English in 1999. The very neatness of its conception – a book containing a hundred three- or four-page vignettes – betrays a publisher's brain-child. Frustratingly, they include an imaginary meeting between Benn and Brecht at Kleist's

and dread. While *The Man Who Disappeared* is recognisably 'Kafkaesque', the humiliations and letdowns reserved for the seventeen-year-old young Karl Rossmann (in other places he is 'sixteen next month'), banished from Europe 'because a maid had seduced him and had a child by him', have less of the irrevocable finality that marks his other two novels.

It is easy to see why America as an aspiration – and Americans as the other chosen people (Hebrew and German were both considered as a language for the fledgling Republic) – would have fascinated Kafka, who never travelled the Atlantic, though many of his relatives did: some entered the family lore like his uncle Joseph Löwy who worked on the construction of the waterway between the Atlantic and Pacific first proposed in 1830 by Saint-Simon in his journal *Globe* and endorsed by the elderly Goethe, the Panama Canal – incidentally, the last construction project paid off in full by the American Congress. Berlin, which Kafka often visited, was then the European capital closest in spirit to the most dynamic cities of the United States. He recorded having read accounts of a journey through America by the journalist Arthur Holitscher, which included a visit to the Elgin clock factory in Chicago, as well as Oskar Weber's 'colonial' novel *The Sugar Baron*: a graphic description of a copperplate-piercing machine in the former points towards the harrow that inscribes punishments into the flesh of the condemned man in his story 'In the Penal Settlement'. Kafka also apparently drew heavily from the writings of the Czech socialist František Soukup, who, in June of the same year, gave a lecture and slide presentation in Prague on 'America and its Civil Servants'. Some of the more mythic features of Kafka's New World came from the pen of that bilious visitor Charles Dickens (whose melodramas of family life he parodied to grotesque good effect in 'Metamorphosis', written around the same time as *The Man Who Disappeared*) and the fantasist Karl May, whose invented stories of frontier life – Cowboys and Saxons – thrilled generations of children in the German-speaking world. In Kafka's America, for instance, San Francisco is in the east and a

bridge links New York to Boston. There are other strange transformations, or perhaps portents. The name of the old Egyptian
pharaoh Rameses becomes that of a town (somewhere like
Memphis perhaps). The Statue of Liberty seen by his hero on
entering New York harbour holds in her hand not a lamp but a
sword – a sword that 'seemed only just to have been raised aloft'.
America may be an 'exploded Bohemia', as its latest translator
Michael Hofmann calls it, but it is also a peculiarly expressive
dislocation of Kafka's imagination.

What are we seeing then? A nation that tries to escape history,
to make a radical break with its colonial father, to orphan itself,
to empty the mind of acquired disposition, offers an obvious
parallel with Kafka's neurotic obsession with the shape that ruled
his life. As the Russian film director Sergei Eisenstein admitted,
the reason he came to support that other Revolution, the Bolshevik
one of 1917, 'had little to do with the real miseries of social injustice... but directly and completely with what is surely the
prototype of every social tyranny – the father's despotism in a
family'. Necessity might have been the mother of invention for an
earlier civilisation; for a society of brothers, father is the very necessity of invention: the need to come up, fraternally, with reasons to
stop the Paternal Presence coming back, like the Commendatore
in *Don Giovanni*. Yet it is among Americans themselves that we find
the sternest critics of Oedipus Indulged. The philosopher George
Santayana thought it utter misfortune that revolutionaries should
set themselves adrift from tradition in this way – 'and their folly
is that they wish to be disinherited even more than they are'. In
1947, the recently naturalised poet W.H. Auden observed disap-
provingly of his pushy students at Swarthmore College, and what
he saw as the indomitable American matriarchy, 'it isn't that they
shouldn't eventually find out the limitations of the father substitute and eventually discard him; that's quite as it should be. But
they begin with the idea that they are the important ones to be
pleased not taught and that their untutored reactions ought to be
their final judgement on their instructor.'

Kafka understood, without any help from Freud, that the urge to transcend the past might itself be determined by that past: the reader is pulled up short by the apprehension that the values of liberal America, its size and wealth and confidence, are more obviously those of his shopkeeper father Hermann, a man who had worked his way up from modest circumstances in his native southern Bohemian village to solid respectability in the Prague Old Town. His son, by comparison, was a member of a generation that shrank from the 'will to life, business and conquest'; indeed, shrinking itself was ever an escape route. Perhaps Kafka was paralysed by the vertigo of realising, as he wrote further into the novel, that wide-open America paradoxically represented not the prodigal son's freedom but the primordial father's triumph, a symbolic force very nearly unassailable because so completely bound up with the abstract power of money. 'Freedom, freedom above all else,' Kafka once wrote to Max Brod; yet even as his protagonist Karl confirms his liberty to the cook who befriends him in the Hotel Occidental, 'it seemed the most worthless condition'.

Had Kafka read that other Herman, Herman Melville, especially his subtle meditation on the prophets of faith and faith in profits – as espoused most famously by that quintessentially modern American trickster Phineas T. Barnum – in his last novel *The Confidence-Man: His Masquerade*? Surely he had: in August 1912, he finished a story about the unmasking of a confidence trickster that ended up in his collection *Meditation* ('to them I owed my first inkling of a ruthless hardness which I was now so conscious of, everywhere on earth, that I was even beginning to feel it in myself'). Both of them wrote stories about bachelors. There are nightmarish passages in Melville that point hysterically at Kafka: 'At rows of blank-looking counters sat rows of blank-looking girls, with blank, white folders in their blank hands, all blankly folding blank paper' ('The Tartarus of Maids'). Both writers were deeply concerned by the ethical responsibilities of being a creator. They were product liability testers of the art form that was itself originally construed as a guide to good living. Private life in America, Kafka would have been aware, is both under greater threat *and* less constrained than in Europe. 'Trust men, and they will be true to you,' Emerson had written in his essay 'Prudence' (1847), 'treat them greatly, and they will show themselves great, though they make an exception in your favour to all their rules of trade.'

To which Melville had appended, in his personal copy of the essay: 'God help the poor fellow who squares his life according to this.'

A Rational Advent

Kafka left six completed chapters and a number of additional scenes, two of which can now be read in English for the first time. One effect of restoring Kafka's original title – aside from getting back to the pristine *draft* actually written by Kafka before Brod 'corrected' it – is to point up how much this is a novel about a person, not a place. Kafka gives his main man, Karl Rossmann, a full name rather than just a sign. Even then, Brod's title *Amerika* (the 'k' spelling was put on placards to taunt the administration during the Vietnam War) is still appended to Michael Hofmann's translation (1996). It seems a peculiarly modern phenomenon in that what are properly *concepts* should be remembered as geo-historical tags or outlandish place-names.

Kafka's working title is significant in another way: *Der Verschollene* recruits as a substantive the past participle of the verb *verschallen*, used to describe a sound fading away into the distance. This is a novel about a man who is never heard of again, a cast-away. About to disembark in New York harbour in the opening chapter, Karl realises he has left his umbrella 'down below' and retreats to the lower levels of the ship to find it: already the story is enacting its title. (Taking figurative language literally, in the way he does with his title, was a deconstructive technique Kafka was to develop more pointedly in his later fiction: fatally enough, the word was to become an euphemism for Jews who 'disappeared' during the Second World War – the new synagogue in Berlin keeps a Gedenkbuch of the names of the 55,969 persons who are listed as deported, fate unknown, lost or 'verschollen'.)

There is, at any rate, no going back. Events shunt Karl forwards, generating a specious kind of momentum and expectation; for every new door that opens takes him downwards, cyclically, through the strata of American society where status, unlike in Europe, is an easily convertible thing. An immigrant with high hopes, guest in a country-house, elevator-boy, factotum: every incident in the novel forces Karl to replay his original expulsion from the parental home. 'Guilt is never to be doubted' as Kafka famously wrote: innocence is no defence against the original sin of having been born, and banishment to a lower region follows inexorably from offences that appear to have no judicial standing at all. The world is its own tribunal. Nothing could be less American than the doctrine of original sin, that stock-in-trade of the cultural conservative, for America is a code-word for a way of being in the world that has exchanged theological despair for actuarial hope and, in the process, managed to sell insecurity as opportunity (though it has its creed of anger too, as Tocqueville noted: 'it must never be forgotten that religion gave birth to Anglo-American society'). Karl Rossmann is 'an atom that must journey alone through the world': the phrase was once used to describe the genial Charlie Chaplin, and it is fascinating to register the cinematographically precise quality of Kafka's descriptions of showers, gramophones, electric lighting, five-lane roads and striking workers.

This is Kafka's description of Karl on a day out with Therese Berchtold, a girl from Pomerania who works as secretary to the manageress of the Hotel Occidental. She discovers that he is a considerable asset now that she has a list of errands, and gets him to shout orders 'in his utterly distinctive, over-precise English across walls of humanity'. Youth and energy, Karl knows, are what America is all about; and the orchestration of life under time-and-motion studies seems to exert an effect on Kafka's legalistic phrases, too: 'They would almost run, Karl carrying her bag, to the nearest underground station, the ride was over in a flash, as though the train was being pulled by an irresistible force, and already they were out, clattering up the stairs instead of waiting for the lift which was too slow for them, the great squares appeared, out of which the roads flew apart in stellar patterns, and with them a bewildering confusion of traffic all of it flowing in straight lines, but Karl and Therese hurried, close together, into various offices, laundries, storerooms and shops, to place orders or make complaints where it wasn't possible by telephone, things that were usually less than momentous.'

Kafka might have had an Old Biblical mind but in other respects he was thoroughly conversant with his historical moment (he became the first person in German literature to describe aeroplanes in a report, incidentally his first published article, sent to the Prague newspaper 'Bohemia' from a flight-show in Brescia in 1909): much of his desk work as an actuary for the Arbeiter-Unfall-Versicherungs-Anstalt in Prague was devoted to assessment of damage claims and devising ways to prevent new technological devices from causing accidents to the workers who used them. He was a clerk inside the great empire of chance which, even before the First World War, had come close to realising Daniel Defoe's meliorist dream of insuring against 'all the Disasters of the World'. It did so by making the very *credibility* of the future tense a rational advent: what had once been an explicit religious tribute to the act of hope was now forced to be on nodding terms with the claims of social justice. Shortly after Kafka wrote his novel, the development of the automobile, in the train of the mass production of the Singer sewing machine in the late nineteenth century, ensured the triumph of the instalment plan (or hire purchase, as the British called it) in American life. Some time before he was born, perhaps around the time of the California Gold Rush in the 1840s, and certainly with increasing rapidity after 1865, the sober religious utopia forced into being by the Puritan work-ethic had been transformed into a dream economy kept going by consuming more and more. America's first colonists had spoken about thrift, restraint and prudent household management; their revolution had been one against the dependency produced by trade and commerce with the Mother Country, their rectitude the moral fervour of an old-fashioned moralising crusade against extravagance and luxury. They would barely recognise their successors. For the price, and not just monetary, of bringing heaven to earth is a kind of vertigo, traditional causality and the materiality of money being over-turned by those great institutions of credit called banks that invite us to reap before we sow. Though able to secure the world's resources at knock-down prices, the country that was once its cred-itor can't pay its way. External debt was 500 million dollars in 1910; it had swollen to no less than 1.3 trillion in 1998.

Let's be frank. It's not just that American policy-makers regard their country as the best model for the resolution of social and economic conflicts: America needs our entrancement to maintain its own lifestyle. As that great monument *The Education of Henry Adams* suggests, America will get it, for we are edging into a phan-tasmagoria in which the tiresome separation between mind and body has been replaced by that between image and reality. If money is going to work for you have to *believe* in it: a moment of doubt, and it vanishes like the dew on the new-mown grass. It is Calvin's conviction – of being saved.

SELF-MADE

Karl is far from being the solitary atom he might think he is (or even like to be). Initially welcomed to New York by his uncle Jacob, he is taken to the iron skyscraper his uncle owns where 'his uncle was kind to him in every little manner, so Karl never had to learn from bitter experience, which is the lot of so many when they begin life in a new country'. Where exactly this skyscraper rises from the ground we never learn. Karl seems to spend all his time in a small room with a limited view on anything resembling 'New York'. After two months his situation seems about to change for the better, when he accepts an invitation from one of his uncle's business associates, Mr Pollunder, to visit him in his country house outside the city and meet his eighteen-year-old daughter Klara – not only sexually experienced, it turns out, but a practitioner of ju-jitsu. On the very threshold of being admitted to their world, he is expelled from it. A note from his uncle is read out to him at midnight in one of the rooms of Mr Pollunder's labyrinthine mansion: it instructs him that for reasons of principle (he has failed to return home by midnight) his uncle wishes never to lay eyes upon him again. As in the opening scene with the stoker, the 'offence' seems quite gratuitous. Even as he strikes out on his own, the solitary atom is about to learn that the basic social unit is never the supposedly autonomous individual beloved of social contract thinkers but at least *two* persons. Experience (will it be bitter? will it be sweet?) is about to teach him individualism's first lesson: should Karl pursue happiness he will soon find that he is being assessed by other solitary atoms in terms of his role in their pursuit of quite disparate private ends. That assessment of rights will be conducted in the egalitarian manner familiar to us all; its great contradiction being that its perceived fairness of opportunity and merits is actually its unfairness: it cannot recognise the individual, because to do so would imply a hierarchy, a scale of values, and all the other rankings and distinctions which gave force to it in the first place. It will make Karl an inconveniently sensate object, while for him other people will come to resemble impersonal forces.

These are the billiard-ball gyrations of eighteenth-century cosmology, as much at the mercy of chance as of determinism. Karl's *dégringolade* bears comparison with a fiercer universe: the terrifying diminishment of Lear, in Shakespeare's tragedy, by his vulpine daughters. With words Lear himself has invoked, words of the new language of accountancy and commerce, in which all natural relationships are translated into monetary terms and love is a thing *produced*, he is urged by his daughter Goneril to 'disquantity' his feudal entourage of knights and squires. His elder daughters want to cut overheads, to reduce his gothic kingship; and suggest a progressive halving of his train from one hundred to fifty to twenty-five, then to ten, and one, and with Regan's 'What need one?' he arrives at zero. It is the point in the play at which Lear knows he will lose his mind.

On the road to Rameses, Karl acquires two comic-sinister travelling companions whose names seem to reinforce his own status as itinerant and castaway in the big sea of society: Delamarche, a domineering Frenchman, and Robinson, a feckless Irishman. (Robinson is a popular name in the European novel: in *Voyage to the End of the Night*, a first novel which offers many parallels with Kafka's, including a stretch in an America experienced as a giant cloaca, Louis-Ferdinand Céline chose the same name for his cynical wanderer, a kind of nocturnal *double maudit*, who so often seems a jump ahead of the hero Bardamu.) Soon Delamarche and Robinson touch the young immigrant for money and pilfer his suitcase, divesting him in the process of a photograph of his parents, one of the few tangible remnants of his old life. As ever in America, opportunity beckons; but hardly has Karl become proficient in his job as a lift-boy in the Hotel Occidental (ever the loving pedant, Kafka makes being a bell-hop sound, before Karl becomes fully acquainted with 'his servile role', the most fantastically elaborate occupation) than the attentions of the drunken Robinson ensure he has lost it, in a tribunal scene that portends the more ominous one in *The Trial*, for 'dereliction of duty'. What seemed to be an offer of fraternity edges close to brothers turning on each other. After heartbreak hotel, the only place left to go is their apartment, where he meets Delamarche's mistress, the large and simpering Brunelda; she agrees, after a little persuasion, that Karl would make an excellent char-boy.

With her red dress and quivering double-chin, Brunelda is one of Kafka's most imperiously baroque creations: she is the Fat Lady, one of those props Mack Sennett claimed were indispensable for good slapstick. Her 'hot and apprehensive form' does a lot of complaining and ordering about. Brunelda used to be a diva of sorts, but now she only shouts for hours – 'like a man'. She is a creature of caprice, her choices uncomplicated by any reason why they should go *this* way and not *that*. The four of them form a kind of negative community, in which no obligation is incumbent upon its members other than staying in the same room, and corporate life is entirely given over to complaining about it. Not all the time, however: when Brundelda and Delamarche canoodle in the apartment, Robinson and Rossmann are evicted, as it were, to the balcony, where they discuss what to do next. Perhaps that's putting it too actively: they discuss what *might* happen. The bath scene, in one of the fragments at the end of the novel, in which Brunelda has her back scrubbed by Delamarche while Robinson lusts over her in the adjoining room, is one of the most deliciously funny in Kafka's entire oeuvre.

Just how Kafka planned to end his novel after the appearance of his bulkily captivating Queen Quintessence has often been discussed. Since Karl never introspects about the nature of his serial 'accidents', the reader is in the dark too. Max Brod claimed that the novel's final scene, the Nature Theater of Oklahoma, set, after some time has passed, on a racecourse in a town called Clayton, with winged women on pedestals blowing trumpets and posters proclaiming 'All welcome' would bring all the loose ends of the novel into triumphant resolution. 'The great Theater of Oklahoma is calling you! It's calling you today only! If you miss this opportunity, there will never be another! Anyone thinking of his future, your place is with us! All welcome! Anyone who wants to be an artist, step forward! We are the theatre that has a place for everyone, everyone in his place! If you decide to join us, we congratulate you here and now! But hurry, be sure not to miss the midnight deadline! We shut down at midnight, never to reopen!' *The Divine Comedy* has been choreographed by Busby Berkeley, and everyone gets to blow his own trumpet. 'It was a confused noise, the trumpets weren't playing in tune, there was just wild playing. But that didn't bother Karl, rather it confirmed to him what a great enterprise the Theater of Oklahoma was.' The angel-girls play for two hours, doodling hypothetico-deductive arabesques on the ether, whereupon they are relieved by the men 'dressed as devils'. In the old days, making a tintinnabulation was a way of driving off the devils; not any more. The greatest theatre in the world seems boundless, and Karl can't tell whether he's among the footlights or backstage.

A Truly Minimal Event

Theatricality, as Montesquieu had understood in the most influential political tract of the eighteenth century, *The Spirit of the Laws*, is the world-picture awaiting individuals whose social actions fail to tally with what they profess to believe. It was one of the world-pictures of the ancient world recovered by the sixteenth century, the great age of theatricality; yet barely half a century after Shakespeare, anti-theatrical prejudice reached its zenith with the abolition of the very institution in Puritan England. Lawyers weren't held in high esteem either. A detestation of staginess (the original meaning of hypocrisy) made the religious thinkers of the Reformation adopt strange positions as drama critics. Calvin's prescription of a single public role, that of the repentant sinner, put a severe brake on the spontaneity of his flock: the great mechanist of the will was endorsing a rather studied form of theatricality even as he strove, dogmatically, to escape it. (He would have known that the ancient Hebrews, who so often served him as model, had no theatre.) His remedy was the notion of an 'inner calling', the vocation that led the individual to the station assigned him by God in the structure of society. The origin of the will lay outside the world — *in coelestibus*. Yet from autonomy guaranteed on theological grounds we have passed, almost without registering the immensity of the change, to a kind of self-moving magic whose origins are veiled from us.

Two hundred years later, d'Alembert noted in his article on

Geneva for the *Encyclopédie* that there were still no theatres in the city. Calvin's townsman Rousseau, for all that he called into being a form of moral life in which cosmic angst was displaced by the outpourings of feeling, was no less suspicious of the sophistries of self-presentation. Rousseau was not against entertainment, he insisted, especially those uplifting events of happy communality that would bind people in the sense of themselves as citizens, nor did he subscribe to Plato's belief that the soul of the actor was contaminated by the parts he played. His complaint was more subtle: the actor, by impersonating himself, was negating his true person, engaging in the art of 'counterfeiting himself, of putting on another character than his own'. Civilisation, once thought to be Europe's crowning glory, was the real source of corruption. Kant, a keen reader of Rousseau, echoed him almost to the word: 'the more civilised men become, the more they become actors. They want to put on a show and fabricate an illusion of their own persons'. Authenticity was the thing. Since the influence of Rousseau, and even Kant, on American life is still prominent, especially in the belief in 'honest souls' following the promptings of their passions and being all the more virtuous for it, it is not surprising that self-presentation has become the great American theme: in a culture where the salesman cannot help but parody the preacher (and how bitterly Melville knew that too), modern personality organises itself around the gospel of self-fulfilment. Two hundred years after Rousseau, Andy Warhol, the celebrant of personal vacuity, couldn't tell the difference between reality and show-time, and certainly didn't lose any sleep over it; he now seems like a sage prophet of reality television, which claims to put on show 'real people' for the delectation of other people while effacing the idea of theatre altogether: welcome to the inanity of living forever inside a billboard! Welcome to your afterlife in Main Street!

A strangely aseptic atmosphere hangs around the Nature Theater, as if Kafka anticipated that one day the typical American would think of himself less as an actor-citizen than as a pious

patient. It is no great surprise, therefore, to learn that the paraphernalia of the Nature Theater come from a 'health farm' in the
Harz Mountains at which Kafka spent a bemused three weeks in
July 1912: the naturopathic sanatorium Jungborn, or Fountain of
Youth, seems to have been years ahead of its time with its daily
routine of group gymnastics (eurhythmics), raw vegetables and
ablutions (detox), and vaguely solar religiosity (holism). Nudism
being the rule, Kafka distinguished himself by his prudishness –
'they call me the man in the swimming trunks'. Most critics have
had a surprisingly soft spot for the high absurdity of Kafka's vision
of the world as a stage, in which the entire Far West opens up as
an arena for making the illusory look natural. Walter Benjamin
called it 'the World Theatre which opens towards heaven'. The
loveliest dreams, wrote his colleague Theodor Adorno, have a
blemish in them, precisely by dint of the fact that they are dreams.
'Such an impression is captured superlatively in the description of
the Nature Theater in Kafka's *Amerika*.' It is the campiest moment
in all of Kafka's fiction, as if an austere twelve-tone composer were
suddenly to begin writing a sumptuous entr'acte in the style of
Puccini's *La Fanciulla del West*.

In spite of the fact that everyone is eligible for the Theater
(genuine talent is beside the point *pace* Warhol), Karl has difficulties being an 'actor'. Asked his name by the recruitment officers
who seem to double as casting directors, 'as nothing else came to
mind just then', he divulges the nickname acquired in previous
jobs: 'Negro'. And that is how he enters the books: 'Negro, a
secondary schoolboy from Europe.' In French, perhaps adventi-
tiously, the word *nègre* is used to describe a scrivener or
ghost-writer. It is precisely the occupation, and the most discreet
madness, of Melville's Bartleby, the clerk who keeps repeating to
the discomfited attorney who wants to give him things to do: 'I
would prefer not to.' And not long before Melville wrote his story,
Dickens had portrayed an abject copyist of legal documents in
Bleak House who calls himself 'Nemo, Latin for no one'.

It is equally plausible, however, that the source for Karl's new name was the Czech socialist speaker, who, in his lecture on New World Man in June 1912, would surely have mentioned the black American thinker and activist W.E.B. DuBois – he launched his famous journal *The Crisis* in the 1910s – on the master-slave dialectic in the age of sympathy: even on the verge of acquiring freedom through 'playing himself' in the Theatre, Karl insists he is not ready for apotheosis. He refuses to pursue happiness, to become part of the success story written by Jefferson, which is tantamount to saying that he refuses to be an American. If traditional ethics is a matter of telling us whose wants should be *sacrificed* for the sake of social cohesion, then Karl votes against himself, quite matter-of-factly. (For the self-esteem school of American philosophy, or 'Objectivism' as it is sometimes called, this kind of selflessness would be seen as a kind of depravity: the truly moral person is the person committed to acting in his own self-interest.) How could Karl play himself anyway, when progress in self-consciousness demands more than mere self-assertion?

Karl's revelation – a form of political statement as much as personal confession – also reveals the striking resemblance between Kafka and his older contemporary, the Swiss writer Robert Walser. It was an affinity underlined by Robert Musil in a 1914 review of one of Kafka's collections, although the comparison had already been made by Franz Blei, who published Kafka's first stories in the review *Hyperion* in 1907. Even Herr Eisner, Kafka's perceptive superior in the first insurance company he worked for, Assicurazioni Generali, thought he resembled Simon, one of the Tanner brothers in the novel of the same name by Walser. Walser is perhaps best known in English for his novel *Jakob von Gunten*, which Kafka once gave to Max Brod as a birthday present. This slim, disturbing, nearly unclassifiable novel in the suicidal discursive mode turns all the fat pedagogical novels of the Enlightenment, of which Rousseau's *Emile* and Goethe's *Wilhelm Meister* are the blithely chubby precursors, on their head.

Walser, who had once worked as a butler in Silesia, makes servitude his great theme: his short stories and novellas often start with a kind of giddy panorama that swiftly descends to the 'lower regions', with little to remind the reader of the great avenues his characters had started out on. His novels are comedies of under-involvement. Pupils in the mysterious Institute Benjamenta in Walser's novel are repetitively trained to know their thoughts do not belong to them: donning the mask of the servant is life's supreme possibility. The school curriculum in the Institute aims to erode meaning, inculcate automatism and exclude the symbolic. The pupils aspire to be zeroes. In Hegel's famous dialectic of self-determination the underling strives to free himself of the double consciousness imposed upon him by his superior: he first inter-nalises the painfully acute sense of his diminished reality as a responsible agent (to know oneself is to alter oneself in the very act of knowing) and then seeks to overcome his handicap by doing what it takes to assert his freedom. The typical Walser hero, though unmistakably subordinate, suffers from a kind of extreme 'personal tidiness', as if only those who can do without freedom really merit it. But just imagine – the absolute thought, the supreme moment of consciousness, the very crux of ethical rela-tions in modern democracies; and a literary hero slips through the hole in the middle! He thereby transgresses what John Stuart Mill said was the only non-negotiable limit to self-determination: a liberal society cannot permit a person to abolish his own liberty.

In short, Walser's prankish training scheme for errant school-boys doesn't sound too far removed from Karl Rossmann's stake on his claim to freedom: if the Nature Theater is salvation and last refuge, as Walter Benjamin claimed in his 1934 essay, a stage-set where every one of Kafka's short stories would be acted out, then it is also a place where the self is disquantitied.

So the question asks itself: is this a cheerfully assertive antici-pation of the Kingdom of God on earth (renamed the Nature Theater of Nevada it could be developed as a religious theme park on a spare lot outside the shimmer of Las Vegas) or instead a back-drop of the Last Judgement as heralded by the sword-brandishing Statue of Liberty glimpsed by Karl as he enters New York harbour? Get real, man! Even Las Vegas sprawls on one of those uranium-drenched scrublands where America rehearses its wars. 'History moves towards the realisation of the Kingdom, but yet the judgement of God is upon every new realisation,' wrote Luther's man in twentieth-century America, the theologian Reinhold Niebuhr. Kafka's novel rushes to a similar vanishing point, but runs out of track in the middle of Karl's passage through the mountains on the two-day journey west to Oklahoma, which happens to have been the arid destination for the 50,000 Cherokee rounded up in the rich Florida basin at the behest of President Andrew Jackson (in defiance of the Supreme Court) in 1838, and sent on a harsh winter trek westwards.

'Only now did Karl begin to grasp the size of America.'

Paris, France

An Afternoon with Mavis Gallant

At her suggestion we met up on the terrace of Le Dôme. In several years of living in Paris, I'd never been there. Too much the mythic sanctuary perhaps, too obviously smart-set these days to attract a novice. And climbing up the stairs at *métro* Vavin just outside the café, it occurred to me that there couldn't be too many writers left in Paris bold enough to be so *obviously* literary. It was clearly a refuge for Mavis Gallant; one of her press photographs shows her sitting with a demi-tasse in front of her. The lettering on the cup says it for Le Dôme. And once inside, I could see it was a strategic choice – a neutral zone just round the corner from her apartment in the *sixième* with a view down the boulevard Montparnasse, an area of Paris which serves as setting for several of her stories. Choose a coffee-house and you announce to the world what you think of it: Le Dôme's fame started back in the 1910s, when the patron of the nearby La Rotonde refused to serve a young American woman who had the *culot* to sit hatless and smoke on his terrace. Before the First World War it had been one of Apollinaire's haunts; the early *dômiers* were principally German painters, *Französlinge*, and as he noted in his *Paris-Journal*, the café's name to 'tedescan' ears has the sonorous boom – *der Dom* – of an actual cathedral. And wasn't this the café that had made poor young V.S. Pritchett feel 'cast down', having sat there while the Twenties span dizzily about him?

Mavis Gallant was gazing out through the vitrine at the crowds pushing across the boulevard Montparnasse. A taut, alert, solar face. Coats on against the winter cold, even in Le Dôme, we sipped our coffees. She warmed immediately to the names of a couple of writers I knew she admired, Céline, one of the bad boys of French literature, and Joseph Roth, reporter before he became a successful novelist. I discovered we had both been reading a French translation of one of the few biographies of Roth, a book of recollections dictated after the war by his friend Soma Morgenstern in his New York exile. It is a wounded, repetitious book that has never been properly edited. 'But why is it a Roth revival never gets off the ground?' she asked me, referring to the recent publication of one of the Austrian writer's novels in translation. I didn't have an explanation. In fact, it suddenly struck me as odd we should refer to both writers in the same breath, even though they'd lived in Paris at the same time: one infamous for his *petite musique*, the other a fastidious artisan of the line, a Jewish exile. She interrupted with a mantra, the nonchalant opening of Céline's great hallucinatory novel of the first war: 'Ça a débuté...' – then lingered on the last two words with relish – '...comme *ÇA!*' It reminded me how hard Céline worked to make his biliousness appear a Fact of Nature just as Roth, after years of journalism, had a cuffmaker's facility for the perfect phrase. My subject's admiration for them was collegial, a stylist's feel for their punctiliousness and dedication to the *métier*. But it was the good government of Mavis Gallant's fiction I wanted to talk to her about.

In fact, our conversation the evening before hadn't been promising. 'I really don't know what I can tell you,' she had confided to me on the phone, 'that isn't already in the preface to the book.' She was referring to her *Selected Stories*, which appeared in 1996. Having already agreed to meet me (during the afternoon she rued the daily stack of mail she has to deal with on her own – some of her contemporaries in a generation of gifted female Canadian writers have assistants 'and even personal secretaries') it was a gentle warning that however wide-ranging our chat might be I shouldn't expect disclosures. 'The language of the imagination has its own roots. It feeds on something quite different from what one knows and what one is,' she'd written once in *Le Monde*. A conviction similar to a line I'd underlined in her review of Simenon's

Intimate Memoirs: 'A writer's visible life and the root of imagination do not connect above ground.' In fact, the eleven-page tour of her life and times in the preface to her *Selected Stories* is one of the few direct statements about herself anywhere in her work. Most of it deals with childhood. There are hints and suggestions about the importance of her early life in the body of the work itself: the emotional weight in her reference, in an essay on style, to the 'grief and terror that after childhood we cease to express', or her judicious barbs against inflated reputations: in a recent review she shot down St Exupéry's morbid fable *Le Petit Prince*, whose Orphan Annie waif of a character – now immortalised on the 50 franc banknote – ensures that it continues to sell every Christmas to the harm of vast numbers of hitherto visually uncorrupted children.

Manifestly I wasn't Miss Pugh in *A Painful Affair* who didn't believe in the arts, only in artists; yet for all that Mavis Gallant's work is reticent and well-mannered, it arouses curiosity about its sources in autobiography. Not only do some of the stories, such as the *Linnet Muir* sequence, seem to tread in the footprints of lived events, but the 52 (from an oeuvre of about 150) printed in the *Selected Stories* are arranged not under their original titles or dates of composition but under decades – decades of their author's life.

A linnet, *Linaria cannabina* of the family *Fringillidæ*, the ornithologically astute reader will have realised quicker than I did, is a song-bird, a bird all of feathers, just like a mavis, while Muir is hardly a stone's throw from Young, the perfectly ordinary Scottish surname she grew up with as a girl in Montreal. Not to mention the name she acquired when she married, and the way it shifts its freight so decorously between English and French. It embraces a concept: *gallantry* was that generous attention to others praised by the philosopher David Hume as a way of civilised living, of strengthening the bonds of sympathy – it is a quality in short supply now that 'authentic' emotions carry the day everywhere.

It's not every writer – even in a century that has compelled writers to adopt escapism as a mode of selfhood, and then censured them when they did – who sloughs off an existence, friends and profession in order to cultivate a new sense of self. Mavis Gallant may guard her deep secrets, but we talked for a long time about the oddness of a child's life, hers in particular. The facts are broadly on record. The flighty mother, the tubercular father dead at a young age, the mysterious boarding out to the Pensionnat Saint-Louis de Gonzague, a French-speaking Catholic school only just down Montreal's Sherbrooke Avenue from her Protestant and English-speaking home, the various schools, the cub reporter's job for the now defunct, left-leaning *Montreal Standard* she started in the penultimate year of the war and which gave her the opportunity to interview Jean-Paul Sartre on a visit to Canada in 1948, the early marriage, divorce and the big break as a writer, a story accepted by *The New Yorker* in 1950 that finally pushed her to make the break. Canada – 'where a *Mac-* was always better than a *-ski*' as someone said to her once in Toronto – must have been a stifling, caste-ridden place for a woman with literary ambitions. Nonetheless, to up everything and go to Europe to write: friends told her it was a folly. But how can a writer's life assume a shape other than the one it has? Her decision is the very substance of her writing: self as a flame of determination above a dark Piranesi architecture of the partially knowable. But perhaps destiny is a species of tautology – you are the way you are because you get that way.

After a few years drifting around the continent, selling her spare clothes once in 1950s Spain 'because money was so tight', put off by the drabness of London under rationing, seeking out the company of the many impoverished 'displaced persons' still foot-loose on the continent years after the war because she 'didn't want to get caught up in the Anglo-American expat thing', she finally settled in Paris in 1960 after living for several years in a small cottage in Menton, near Nice. It was an obvious choice, but perhaps not for the obvious reasons. Despite astonishingly outmoded legal provisions – dating from Napoleonic times and still in force – which denied suffrage to women until as late as 1945 (and this in the country of universal suffrage!) and still make widows effective wards of their parents-in-law or children, it is oddly easier for a woman in France in one regard: if she is an intellectual. On more than one occasion Mavis Gallant has referred with astonishment, and certainly gratitude, to the fact that in France she might be asked what she did for a living and, on replying, not hear a guffaw or snort or the incredulous 'But what do you *really* do?'

By the time she became a Parisian, she was already a regular *New Yorker* contributor: one of the remarkable aspects of her literary career has been her long-standing association with that magazine. All but three of the stories in her *Selected Stories* were first published there, sign of a symbiosis between life and ambition few of her characters ever achieve. It is hardly a secret that the brashly revamped magazine of the mid-1990s was no soul-sister for the moral dramas at the heart of Gallant's stories; they must have seemed dated, chaste and flat to a magazine intent on advertising its hipness. 'The whole *New Yorker* business left me at a loss: I haven't published anything there for four years.' Happily the situation has been remedied by its recent change of editorship.

Of course, there are those, and not just professional critics, who feel the *New Yorker* is stiflingly predictable, its role in literary history monumental in the wrong sense, on the assumption that any cultural icon is bound to be cloyingly self-conscious about its status; yet it is also a survivor, last of a whole gallery of widely-read magazines that went into steep decline in the early 1960s and were finally undone by the 'new' journalism. Whatever the *New Yorker*'s role in cultural history, the short story has proved to be a resilient genre – the only literary form modernism has not over-hauled or repackaged. I quoted Mavis Gallant a passage from the introduction to a copy of I.B. Singer's *Collected Stories* I had with me; it offers the traditional objection to the niche conditions of experimental writing. 'Imagination is one thing, and the distortion of what Spinoza called "the order of things" is something else entirely. Literature can very well describe the absurd, but it should never become absurd itself.' She nodded her assent; she had rubbed shoulders with a number of experimental writers in Paris including Beckett who, from Spinoza's crystalline view of things, might even appear to be a much more traditional, unproblematic writer than the slate-wiper he is usually thought to be: a pietist haunted by his past – and his Dublin mother.

'I'm not a popular writer, you know,' she insisted. Too writerly, she meant, to be popular, if popular meant resembling St Exupéry. Her stories are nothing if not crafted: the phrases worked over, the mordancy growing amber-coloured with the years, the urge more pronounced towards that Jamesian need to define the 'state of being of the American who has bitten deep into the apple of "Europe" and then been obliged to take [her] lips from the fruit'. Her own forcefulness and strength derive from a creative life that has first outfaced and then refashioned its own sense of disjunction and displacement; it has left her – like Colette – with a merciless, acerbic eye for all forms of self-deception. Hers is unflappable writing, quite sharply critical of its characters but not unsympathetic to the pathos and comedy of their lives – lives distracted by romanticising delusions, finely tended gardens of anachronism and silvery pools of narcissism, with homelessness as a thick acid cud that threatens to corrode every escape route. Her technique has been compared to that of the French writer Patrick Modiano – a comparison she didn't much care for; justifiably, I think, since Modiano plays and plays his one mellow B-flat note (*bémolisation* is the pseudo-curatorial putdown in French). Her characters commonly live in hothouses, but exotic décor is rarely allowed extended description and never claims a commanding place in her stories. It is the human element that interests Mavis Gallant. Most of her stories are nests for that curate's egg, the expatriate condition – the condition she didn't like when she saw it first in Menton in the 1950s. Children often look in on it as if it were all under a glass dome, and sometimes they do more than that. Her first novel, *Green Water, Green Sky* (1959), originally four separate stories, is about American tourists in Venice and Paris who also happen to be tourists in their own lives. The fourteen-year-old

Flor McCarthy, dragged around a Europe of cloudless skies, cocktails and not so clandestine affairs by her vain mother, wonders whether instead of an emotional *Festland* 'it might be possible to consider another person one's home'. That she slips from her sanity in the course of the novel gives the lie to that illusion.

Sober realism is perhaps the right generic term. It is a realism not without its magical moments – in 'Lena', my own favourite among her stories, a husband serenely recounts the turmoil of his flamboyant wife's struggle to overcome her terminal illness in Paris: she has already 'died' twice and come round 'just when the doctor said, "I think that's it"' – but in general it aims for astringency and a clear head. Only one story, 'Kingdom Come', leaves the moral domain of what it means to be a consumer of persons, or a person consumed, and invents a tiny Baltic sociopolitical entity of its own, the Republic of Saltnatek. More freighted than her character studies, it nonetheless has the telling line: 'Europe had grown small, become depleted, as bald in spirit as Saltnatek's sandy and stony islands.' Whatever nationality they affect to claim, all of her characters secretly bear Nansen passports, that League of Nations' invention grudgingly accepted by the European nation-states between the wars to allow the stateless to cross their borders. Like so many writers who came to maturity after 1945, Mavis Gallant's stories are haunted by the depredations of recent European history; there is a laying bare in the lives they describe, lives of the young jostled in barely understood ways by the sins of their elders. It is the unspoken event that binds them. A kind of fecklessness is the fate of many: 'Baum, Gabriel 1935– ( )', a young man from Potsdam typical of many of these exiles and drifters, ends up acting the war in television serials, his own life unreal to him. One parenthetical foot in nothingness, as the title suggests. 'The Pegnitz Junction', one of her best stories, relates the chronicle of a 'bony slow-moving German girl from a small baroque bombed-out German city' whose overriding concern is to forget the past. The more she tries to, the more it points the finger. Only the thoughtless seem at ease in their lives, those who have lost their souls and committed their lives solely to survival. In the vitrine of Le Dôme, I caught a glimpse of a shocked 22-year-old reporter briefed to write an article on the very first pictures of the concentration camps to arrive in Canada.

Astonishingly, it took forty years for any of her books to be translated into French. Bernard Pivot, the literary chronicler whose television show is a barometer of book reading in France, has only ever invited her once in front of the cameras, in the days when his programme was called *Apostrophes*. Canada's nationalist revival in the 1970s didn't pay her much attention either. Such inattention when she was in her prime partly reflects the recent prestige and domination of theory in French life, though it can't be the only reason, as I reminded her, since Jane Austen – declared enemy of that virtue-faking, modern quality of charm – has still to set a firm foot on French soil. She was withering about interest from academics, but relative obscurity didn't seem to have been too much of a worry. Quite the reverse. It has allowed her to work in anonymity, at least in France. What more can a writer ask for? Besides, nine of her titles are now in print in translation. Her *sur le vif* account of the street riots of May 1968, for example, which takes up most of her *Paris Notebooks*, is one of the best things on a summer that fixed the shape of institutional life in Europe for more than a generation. It reveals a writer with a journalist's instinct for the telling moment, and amply demonstrates Mavis Gallant's flair as a chronicler: it touches on the postwar brightening of Paris, the Algerian war, *l'évènement du mai 68*, the architectural gutting of Les Halles, the pharaonic Mitterrand years, and not least the resurgence of right-wing politics in France.

Paris is a battlefield between what human geography aspires to do with a city and the rationalising blueprints of townplanners: she has been just as eloquent as Richard Cobb in defence of the city cleared over the years of much of its traditional populations, an exodus that began at the start of the century when Paris *intramuros* was all the city, and only a few tens of thousands lived outside it, beyond what is today the six-lane *périphérique*: now four in every five Parisians is a *banlieusard*. Walter Benjamin called Paris the capital of the nineteenth century, as indeed it was, but the solid bourgeois city that Haussmann planned has continued to exert an almost archetypal hold on the twentieth-century literary imagination, to take only four stylistically innovative North American writers who have been drawn there: Stein, Hemingway, Wright and Baldwin. The list for South American writers would be even longer. Then there is the debilitating, vapid Paris – the genteel museum of world nostalgia. Mavis Gallant's evocative piece on Beaubourg and the gentrification of the old Jewish quarter of the Marais, 'The Taste of a New Age', is bravura social commentary that exposes just that trend, in its officially-sanctioned 'urban renewal' form. 'The past,' she observes, 'belongs to those who can afford to turn it into an urban fairy tale.'

Last year, in the silly month of August – the month when almost all of Paris descends like a tide-race on the Midi – she was asked by *Le Monde*, along with another five expatriate writers, to tell the French how she saw them. It was an unusual move, keeping others at arm's length being what the French think of as a condition for civic life; not exactly a coldness, as she has written elsewhere herself, but a form of minding one's own business quite alien to the easy familiarity of North Americans. In a piece titled 'Ecrire à Paris, France' she observed that she has now been living so long in the country – thinking more in French than in English, however bound she might be to the latter as her creative language – that 'she can no longer conceptualise it, a country being made up of nothing other than the individuals who knit its history'. Which is a way of saying that she is no longer merely living in Paris – Paris lives in her.

Loss of access to the *New Yorker* has brought a change of focus in what is a disciplined working routine. Despite the hint of a empty writing cabinet in the preface to her *Selected Stories* – 'I keep the sketchiest sort of files, few letters and almost no records' – she told me she has been busy the last few years revising her diaries, 'scoring through the predictions I got wrong with a black pen'. In Canada there is now a Mavis Gallant Award for non-fiction – 'nothing to do with me really, but I read a chapter from my diary at the inaugural ceremony in 1992 and it pleased me enormously to be able to keep the audience glued to its seats for almost two hours'. When it is published I suspect her journal of half a century in literary Paris will be a work to rival that of the forthright Paul Léautaud she once wrote of, and the 'carnal delight' he took in writing.

She pursed her lips with a gesture as mischievous as it was disdainful: 'after all, at the age of 76, it's really high time to put things in order'.

We got up to go out into the chill of a February on the boulevard Montparnasse. I was momentarily struck, not having seen her standing, by her physical frailty; her conversation had been so purely expressive of a life looked back on as the will to write it. At the door she pointed out to me the apartment across the road that had been home for the wet-nosed Henri Grippes, one of her serial comic creations – a writer who, in the time-honoured French manner, devotes more energy to avoiding the Fates, in the singular form of the *contrôleur des contributions*, Monsieur Poche (a wonderful name for a tax man), than actually writing. 'You didn't think it was me, did you?' I hadn't thought so, but now I would have to consider why she thought I might. Whereupon she was gone, an indomitable curve of the air, walking towards Montparnasse-Bienvenuë, another of the *métro* stations on the map she had pinned to the wall of her apartment in a distant city more than fifty years before. One of the earwitnesses, who, in Elias Canetti's words, 'knows all the places where there is something to be heard, stows it tidily away, and forgets nothing'.

Russia and the End of Time

Natasha's Dance, the title of Orlando Figes' brilliant diorama of Russian culture, in eight thematic chapters from Pushkin to Stravinsky, derives from a tense scene in Tolstoy's *War and Peace* (1869). Natasha Rostov, filigree product of the largely French education favoured by the Russian aristocracy, finds herself with her brother in the home of a distant relative who has embraced the 'narod' and taken a peasant wife, as many Russian intellectuals were to do after the emancipation of the serfs in 1861. Once the homely meal is finished, 'Uncle' strikes up a melody on his guitar, and although Natasha has never learned to dance in the Russian way, this slim, graceful, French-speaking countess finds herself, to her relief and general applause, doing 'the right thing'. She dances, self-surrendered, with perfect atavistic poise.

Written in the very long shadow cast by the French invasion of 1812, Tolstoy's recounting of Natasha's dance is a fine illustration of his aim to construct a patriotic epic illustrating the fundamental unity of the Russian people. Napoleon's advance on Moscow, which had been razed on the orders of General Kutuzov to deprive the Grande Armée of provisions (a devastating typhus epidemic was to follow), introduced a new sense of 'the nation' based upon the virtues of the common man. The standard European upbringing had corrupted the nobility, many of whom could hardly speak more than a few words of Russian; salvation, if it were to come, could only come, like all things organic, from below. Tolstoy was interested in the experience of history as something new in human affairs.

This awareness produced a kind of historical hiccup: rather than becoming a nation-state in the European mould, the Tsarist state emerged as God's chosen agent in a new historical dispensation. The problem with the tsars, most of them, was that they tended to move back into the past in order to shield themselves from the future. The problem with the peasants was that they, not having acquired the narcissistic will to power of the burghers, weren't in the least political. That was precisely what made them attractive to the intellectuals; and a kind of piety about truly authentic (self-sacrificing and other-redeeming) proletarians was to be found among Marxist intellectuals for generations. If those same intellectuals hadn't forgotten the songs nanny had taught them on her lap they might have suspected that the proletariat would 'negate' itself more times than those gaily-painted Matrioshka dolls now sold to tourists everywhere.

No other nation has ever been quite so obsessed by defining what it is, or troubled by the idea that reality might not measure up to the ideal. (In the United States, by contrast, most intellectuals except Walt Whitman had mighty difficulties adoring the folk culture, although it might be said in their defence that the folk had pre-empted them: American populism is – uniquely – lived in person.) What was at stake, after all, was salvation, and not just Russia's: Dostoevsky expected the 'Russian soul' – with its basic need 'for suffering, incessant and unslakeable suffering' – to redeem the rationalist west. Joseph de Maistre, the great French antimodernist, came to Russia in 1810 hoping to find people uncorrupted by the *philosophes*, and found St Petersburg chattering away in French. He defended cultural tradition on transcendental (rather than pragmatic) grounds; in the next few decades, it was the notion of the ensouled nation that was to be imported from Germany, especially as found in the writings of Schelling: he enjoyed cult status among the young blades of the 1830s, who so closely resembled Lermontov's 'hero of our times'.

The conviction that something has been lost in becoming

civilised has shadowed civilisation at least since the ancient Greeks, who had it with respect to the Egyptians; only the Russians dared make something messianic out of their own divided nature. In a world-historical order in which the British stoked the economy and the French commandeered the politics, admiring themselves ever more loudly in the process, the best the Russians could hope for (like the Germans) was inner consolation: speculative idealism provided a kind of intellectual ferment to the dead weight of public life. Hegel, *primus inter pares*, set off the decade known in Russia as the 'philosophical epoch' in 1838: it ended with the notorious 1848 Pan-Slav congress in Prague at which the Polish version of Pan-Slavism turned out to be a call for protection from the Russians: according to the Poles, they weren't Slavs at all but Tartars! In no time at all we run smack into the vertiginous ironies of Dostoevsky's Grand Inquisitor, the very model of the modern politician. 'Go, and don't come again – never, never!' he tells Jesus, who, like the original cynic he was, had come to cause trouble again in the benighted sublunary world. Denying the faith he outwardly represents, the Grand Inquisitor chides Jesus for not knowing how to think politically. Freedom! People go in horror of freedom! His vision of the future is a nursery: hundreds of thousands of happy children in a technological Eden where only the administrators are burdened by the curse of knowing good and evil.

Some called history's bluff in a different way. Petr Chaadaev was declared insane in 1836 and placed under house arrest on the orders of the Tsar: he had had the temerity to suggest that Russia was essentially a void. He had discovered the West, and as the poet Osip Mandelstam wrote, 'only a Russian could discover this West, which is far denser and more concrete than the historical West itself'. Chaadaev lays bare the conflict built into imitative desire, or what is called 'culture cringe': imitation, the least sincere form of flattery, cannot keep its illusions warm without generating ways of thwarting its desire, because it needs failure as proof that it was right to choose the model in the first place. Gogol even became a martyr to what he claimed was the 'beautiful Russia of his heart':

the trouble with his great novel *Dead Souls* was that the characters kept butting in to remind him, with rude gusto, that Russia was anything but what he thought it was. 'God, how sad our Russia is!' said Pushkin, when he read the manuscript; but Gogol's Russia is quite as phantasmal as the dead souls 'bought up' by his hero Chichikov in a country where live men were still sold and purchased. In his later life Tolstoy practically renounced his enormous creative gifts, preferring instead to espouse the Christian idealisation of ignorance that started with the Apostle Paul's attack on philosophy in his first letter to the Corinthians. Tolstoy was a Christian anarchist who was at times uncomfortably aware that politics could not lay claim to a critique of social conditions and, at the same time, venerate the people whose standing it hoped to change as the source of all sanctity.

Ideas themselves seem to have the power of icons for Russian writers: Orlando Figes tells us that the principle of 'inverse perspective' was used by icon-painters to focus the worshipper's gaze on a point just in front of the picture space, thereby reinforcing the impression that 'the action taking place before one's eyes is outside the laws of earthly existence'. In Orthodoxy worshippers pray with their eyes open, gazing at an icon: God is being worshipped *through* the image. Iconic art had flourished in Andrei Rublev's icons of the fifteenth century, the era that coincided with the repulsion of the Tatars: what defined the Russians at this crucial point in their history was their Christianity. Only in Russian is the word peasant (*krest'ianin*) a near homophone for Christian (*khrest'ianin*): in all the other European languages peasants are bound, with etymology as witness, to the earth. This idea of the peasant as a natural believer (and later natural socialist) underpinned the ideas of Tolstoy and the Populists, no doubt abetted by the fact that Orthodoxy had always preached the virtue of humility and passive suffering.

Being suspended within its liturgy, so to speak, it must be said the Russian church is very distinctive. Last year I entered on a morning service in the same beautiful golden-domed Russian Orthodox church in Geneva which figures in Conrad's *Under Western Eyes*. Apart from the incense and guttering candles, and the deacon's booming bass, I was struck by the continual coming and going as people entered, came back, wandered on, and crossed themselves before various icons; most worshippers seemed, like myself, to be hanging around. There are no pews or social rankings, for the Russian church is a kind of holy marketplace.

Of all the great writers of the nineteenth century only the agnostic Chekhov, whose grandfather had actually been a serf and father was a pious bully, and who had a bit of medical experience to fall back on (Gogol, for instance, had few dealings with ordinary Russians, insisting in his *Selected Passages from a Correspondence with a Friend*, the follow-up to *Dead Souls*, that the peasantry should be kept in the holy state of illiteracy), was not undone in some way by the power of myth and illusion: he knew, as several of his stories suggest, that the idealisation of the Russian peasant was itself substantially a townee's projection. Chekhov built three schools, donated his skills to the peasants on his estate at Melikhovo, and worked without remuneration to provide famine and cholera relief. Icons might be good aids to prayer, as the great critic Vissarion Belinsky pointed out in his famous letter of 1847 to Gogol, but for the average peasant they also made pretty handy lids for pots on the stove.

The tension between different kinds of Russia goes back much further in time than Tolstoy. Peter the Great's decision to build a new capital on swampy coastal land was a negation of medieval Moscow – the 'big village' as it is still called – and the geography of old Muscovy. (Peter's decision was an act of heresy for the Old Believers who continued to observe the orthodox rituals that had been superseded in the ecclesiastical reforms of the 1650s: Peter was their Antichrist.) St Petersburg, the city that bears his name, symbolises Russia's eighteenth-century aspiration 'to reconstruct the Russian as a European'. It was an act of brazen cultural engineering. Built at great human cost, its grid plan, zoned districts and splendid Nevsky Prospect created a strange kind of hyperborean vertigo in those who contemplated it: crowds, for the city on the Neva, were to become its floods.

If Peter built it, Pushkin created its image – one that has haunted generations of writers (see Gogol's story 'The Overcoat', out of whose sleeves all subsequent Russian writers dropped, according to Dostoevsky). But the tension was more than just a tale of two cities. Which way was Russia actually facing: east or west? The eighteenth-century westernising movement was called into question by the Slavophiles, who believed in what the soil taught; they, in turn, were outraged by the pioneering work of the historian Stasov in the 1860s, which suggested that Asian influence was widespread in all aspects of Russian culture. This was an affront to Russia's 'civilising mission' to the East, which was partly fuelled by fear and partly by the bitterness many Russians felt at the betrayal of the Christian cause in the Crimean war, when Britain and France had sided, for strategic reasons, with the Ottoman Empire. Stasov's brave colleague, the painter Vereshchagin, had to flee the country after an exhibition of his paintings depicted the violence of the 1874 Imperial campaign in Turkestan so realistically that he was accused of slander by the very general who had awarded him the commission. His paintings bulge with horses. Horses had become symbols of the apocalyptic in Russian art in the wake of the devastating Tatar invasions that had overran Rus' in the thirteenth century: Blok's 'Scythian' poems of the 1910s still drum with their hoofbeats.

Even the level-headed Chekhov was attracted by what Mandelstam later called 'the watermelon emptiness of Russia': his first serious story 'The Steppe' (1887) was an epic tribute to the bleak monotonous beauty of the expanse he later explored in his hazardous journey to the island of Sakhalin. Semi-pagan legends (Stravinsky had no need to turn to Africa to find source material for the 'biological ballet' that exploded on the Paris stage in 1913 with *The Rite of Spring*) had long mingled with chiliastic Christian beliefs and given rise to tenacious legends: the city of Kitezh was thought to be hidden beneath the lake of Svetloyar and could be glimpsed only by true believers. This story ended up in the opera house, which is surely the proper place for all myths; Rimsky-Korsakov, the most famous of the five 'national school' composers known as the Mighty Handful, made it the subject of his last opera.

There is a line of descent, too, from the Orthodox belief in Moscow as the Third Rome (after the fall of Constantinople to the Turks in 1453) to the Moscow of the Third International, and the great Slavic dream of the end of history. Nineteen-thirteen, the year of the *Rite of Spring*, seems to have marked a frenzied impasse: the avant-garde poet Khlebnikov insisted 'the only freedom we demand is freedom from the dead', while the modernist painter and amateur anthropologist Kandinsky, almost in the same year, claimed everything dead was trembling, 'not only the stars, moon, wood and flowers... but also a cigarette butt lying in an ashtray, a patient white trouser button looking up from a puddle in the street'.

The national idea flared briefly in February 1917, while Europe was at slaughter, and almost immediately was forced underground again, like the city of Kitezh. What people had dreamed about in the nineteenth century became possible; history was deified; and the Bolsheviks seized the Winter Palace. The light rising in the East flooded the stricken souls of a generation with a sense of meaning and redemption: something this terrible could only be the harbinger of the Second Coming after all. War ended, and society began to mobilise for a new internationalist culture based on the model of the Soviet – *Proletkult*.

Although never cultists, major artists such as Meyerhold and Eisenstein endorsed industrialisation in the 1920s, and endeavoured to make men glad cogs in the gigantic industrial machine. Soviet Russia reproduced almost every technocratic feature of Bacon's New Atlantis. What was seen as the nightmare of the production line in the west was hailed in Russia as liberation:

Lenin was a great admirer of F.W. Taylor, father of scientific management. Pavlov's dogs weren't far from his mind either. Trotsky dismissively summed up the old Russia as a world of 'cockroaches and icons', and his contempt for the usual pieties about the proletariat finds a savagely joyful echo in the Red Cavalry stories of the enigmatic Isaac Babel who enlisted with a Cossack regiment fighting for the revolutionary cause on the Polish front (doubly odd since the Cossacks were not just infamous for persecuting Jews like Babel, they were arch-symbols of Tsarist oppression). In the decade before his execution in 1940 Babel was forced to become, in his own words, a 'master of the genre of silence'. By then Trotsky had long since been seen off by the Kremlin mountaineer (the epithet given to Stalin in a poem by Mandelstam) who began to emulate Ivan the Terrible and smothered any lingering belief in the New Man.

Sentimental 'people's art' now went hand in hand with state-organised terror, though genuine culture continued to flourish underground, in conditions that sometimes beggar the mind: Shostakovich's Seventh Symphony was performed in a bombed-out and starving Leningrad (the Soviet name for St Petersburg) in 1942. Persecuted for years, the poet Anna Akhmatova managed to scrape a living in desperate conditions and still find the creative repose to write the great poem of the war years, 'Requiem' (published only in 1987): poetry was freedom when prose was so clearly identified with the state. If the Maximum Leader read the work in question (Stalin once phoned Pasternak to ask for his opinion about a fellow poet's work) the penalty for expressing this freedom was prison, exile and death.

Three million Russians left their country between 1917 and 1929, gravitating towards Berlin, Paris and New York; but many of them, like the poet Marina Tsvetaeva, *pasionaria* of the Word and no great admirer of Chekhov's grey style, were so consumed by nostalgia (she spent her exile in Paris and Prague recapturing scenes from her childhood on paper) they eventually returned. Deprived even of the minuscule readership she had once been able to count on, unable to obtain news of her husband and daughter after their summary arrests, Tsvetaeva hanged herself in Yelabuga two years later, in 1941. Her last poem was addressed to the father of the future film director, Andrei Tarkovsky, whose haunting films are themselves a kind of Tsvetaevan refusal of the 'mad world'. His last film in his native land *Stalker* (1979) penetrates so far into the dilapidation of the Soviet architectural unconscious that it leaps forward to the meltdown of communist society seven years later in Chernobyl. And during all these years, intellectual after intellectual in the West, from the Webbs to Louis Althusser, persisted in asserting that life in Soviet Russia was at least more 'spiritual' than under capitalism. Sartre, after a visit in 1954, was categorical: 'the freedom to criticise is total in the USSR'.

Now, sixty years after the battle of Stalingrad, the turning point in the Great Patriotic War in which another 25 million Soviet citizens lost their lives, Russia might seem to be a 'normal' nation: its last great prophet-writer Solzhenitsyn was recently forced to cancel his weekly television address to the nation for lack of interest. The revolutionary illusions have gone, but the disjunctive approach to reality (which engendered those illusions) lives on. Some of those Messianic beliefs in the end of history, converted into secular action after contact with Hegel's philosophy and further systematised by the philosopher Vladimir Soloviev, circa 1880, were to inspire not only the symbolist poets Blok and Bely but also Wassily Kandinsky's nephew, the charismatic philosopher Alexandre Kojève, who, as a 'Stalinist of the strictest obedience', became famous for teaching a seminar on Hegel in Paris that was attended by a roll-call of French thinkers including Georges Bataille, Jacques Lacan, Raymond Queneau, Maurice Merleau-Ponty and even Raymond Aron: their hobby-horse was the European community. The French Revolution, according to Kojève, had completed the secular development of the Christian revelation: what remained to be worked out were the practical arrangements for the Kingdom of Heaven. A hundred years before, the poet Heinrich Heine had warned the French not to be seduced by German philosophy. He didn't know of that even more potent mix: German philosophy distilled by exiled Russians.

President Putin, former KGB cadre, has coaxed old Slavophile ideas back to life, reinforced his nationalist credentials, and overhauled the old military-patriotic education of the Tsarist era. Gorbachev, the real mystery-man of Russian politics, has retreated from the public arena to write his memoirs. Many commentators have noted how, since 1990, determinism has come to haunt economic thinking in what used to be the west, giving Marxism a kind of spectrally Byzantine afterlife: the young Hegelians of the 1830s always asserted that Russia and the United States were simply different versions of the same utopia. The United States was long regarded as the pragmatic antithesis of all grand utopian movements; now it seems as if the Berlin Wall was as much a looking-glass as a blockade. But the meaning of shared misery has taken on a different freight. Last week German radio reported on the city now called Volgograd: so dismal has everyday life become in a country in which authoritarian attitudes and the military are returning to favour that the local people want to change the name of their city back to that of its glory-days: Stalingrad. Some of them do: the old soldiers, retired workers, apparatchiks and people over fifty who have stopped trying to understand how the world works and want not so much to pay tribute to the Dreadful Father as to remember their own better past...

So ends the century that began, as Mandelstam wrote in 1922 in the literary magazine *Hotel for Travellers in the Land of the Beautiful*, 'under the sign of great intolerance, exclusiveness, and deliberate non-comprehension of other worlds. The heavy blood of extremely distant, monumental cultures, perhaps of Egypt or Assyria, flows in [its] veins.' The task of those who had survived the nineteenth century, according to the poet whose own life ended in one of Stalin's labour camps in 1938, was to provide the new age with theological warmth. He was talking about opening a door on that ancient symbol, the hearth, not breaking down the walls on fiery apocalypse.

Next Year in Jerusalem

At the close of 1917 General Allenby captured Jerusalem from the weakened rump of one of the longest surviving empires in world history: thirty years later, in May 1948, the British left Palestine. On arrival, they had been welcomed as liberators by 56,000 Jews and 650,000 Arabs; when they left both peoples accused them of betrayal. The population had increased to 600,000 Jews and a million Arabs: shortly thereafter, once 'God Save the King' had stopped droning out at the Edison Cinema, as it does in the opening chapter of Amos Oz's *The Hill of Evil Counsel*, and the bagpipes, khaki and berets were gone for good, Jews and Arabs were at war. Having already been displaced from their farms and ignored by their urban élite, the Palestinians were defeated; most ended up in Jordan. It was called *nakba* – the catastrophe. Soon legislation would be passed which confiscated their land retrospectively; then the place names were changed.

Tom Segev, a debunking Israeli journalist who writes a weekly column for the paper *Ha'aretz*, has set out to correct the notion, now firmly embedded in Israeli collective memory, of the British as 'devious' – as enemies of the Jews and friends, in the mould of Lawrence of Arabia, and later Wilfred Thesiger, of the indigenous Arabs. The Mandate of 1922 was crucial to the formation of the *yishuv*, the Jewish community in Palestine; as in the 'charter' foreseen by Herzl the sheer dint of numbers made the creation of a Jewish National Home in 1948 almost a foregone conclusion. As far as Segev is concerned, John Bull in Palestine is always pro-Zionist unless explicitly acting to the contrary, starting with Lloyd

George, the lawyer engaged by the Zionist movement in London after the offer, as early as 1903, of land to Jewish settlers. Yet that tract of land offered for the 'Zionist dream map' had actually been in British East Africa, in what is now Uganda. Which raises Arthur Koestler's question: was it the business of an imperial nation to be promising another nation the land of a third?

There were indeed British lovers of the Bible who played a decisive role in establishing the new state: Richard Meinerzhagen, who fed the Ottoman troops disinformation and opium-tipped cigarettes during the First World War, and the enigmatic Orde Wingate (Ben Gurion called him simply 'the friend'), a Plymouth Brother and brilliant guerrilla commander and tactician (he distinguished himself later in Abyssinia and Burma), whose private anti-terrorist army in the Palestine of the 1920s served as an inspiration for the Haganah and the Israel Defence Force. Lloyd George himself claimed to know the geography of the Holy Land better than that of his native Wales. But Segev's desire to unseat the conventional view makes him underplay more obvious motives for British interest in the region, such as suspicion of what the French might be up to. As such, it wasn't a terribly good reason to get involved at all; and the British paid for the blunder in terms of their reputation. Segev contends that the Balfour Declaration came about because the British Empire felt threatened by Chaim Weizmann's claim that Russian Jews had brought about the Bolshevik Revolution in 1917. Zionists pulling strings across the world has always been standard anti-Semitic propaganda; most of the Jews of the time, especially those on the eastern marches, were isolated and powerless. The Zionists nevertheless tried to co-opt the myth to their own advantage, and Lloyd George played along with them. Most of the Orthodox rabbis in Britain opposed the Balfour Declaration, insisting quite rightly that they had every right to live and prosper in the United Kingdom, and the Secretary of State for India, Montagu, flatly opposed it on the grounds that it was 'anti-Semitic'.

British imperial policy sought to maintain the status quo as best it could. The administration in Palestine often felt bullied by policy from London while in practice being condescendingly protective towards the Arabs – 'our little friends' as one official referred to them. Segev devotes one of his chapters to a description of Jerusalem high society, which was out of bounds to the Jews: the visiting Richard Crossman described them as 'tense, bourgeois, central European', and lacking the romantic appeal of those upper-class Arabs who were invited to salons and cocktail parties. Zionism, with its egalitarian and socialist programme, and names like Peled ('steel'), Eyal ('ram' or 'strength') and Avni ('stone'), was seen as a wrecker of the warrior traditions of the desert (not so much 'noble savages', as Ernest Gellner quipped, as 'savage nobles'); the Bedouin, on the other hand, provided a tribal landscape on which romantic and quite often homoerotic Englishmen could project the values they saw as under threat at home. (Ironically, it was Benjamin Disraeli, the only British prime minister of Jewish descent, who, in perpetuating the Tory vision of Britain as an organic society in which people knew their place, put his considerable rhetorical skills into convincing English squires that the Jews were an ancient *aristocratic* race.) It also infuriated the Zionists that the British took an impartial and no doubt high-handed view of the first violent disturbances, such as the 1929 Hebron massacre. Eight years earlier, a sergeant major who had witnessed an attack on a Jaffa hostel for newly arrived immigrants summed up the British dilemma: 'When we found it was a question between the Jews and the Arabs we did not think it was for us to interfere... Which were we to stop?'

The real achievements of the Mandate were unexciting and unsung things which matched British efforts in other colonies: building good roads, improving sanitation and eradicating malaria from the Kedron Valley, and the introduction of an impartial judiciary and a common law tradition. An ideological war was being fought among the immigrants, not all of whom were German-speaking professors from central Europe. Hebrew, an artificial creation of largely eastern European language planners which

retained the morphology of Old Semitic Hebrew, became identified with the new man; Yiddish was vilified as 'jargon', and
identified, to its disadvantage, with the doubt, irony, mercurial wit
and dither of the Diaspora. As early as 1919, when the Chief Rabbi
of the Hurva synagogue in Jerusalem delivered a sermon in
Yiddish, a section of audience walked out; he switched to Hebrew
and another section walked out; in the end he reverted to Yiddish.
The language issue remained so fraught that Yiddish was recognised as an official language of Israel only in 1999, by which time
it posed no danger to Hebrew (although as a professor of linguis-
tics at Tel Aviv University once suggested modern Hebrew is in
fact 'a form of Yiddish with a bizarre vocabulary'). Significantly
for the future of the country, the Jews of the *yishuv* pressed ahead
with their own educational programme; since the Arab population
received nothing comparable, Segev interprets this as evidence of
pro-Zionism. Again he probably underestimates British indifference to what they saw as purely a matter for the local populations
themselves.

Though the British provided neither incentive nor assistance to
the Jews, Article 22 of the Mandate did recognise the Jewish
Agency for Palestine as an official representative of Jewish polity
(while failing notably to provide for Arab representation). That
in itself was an invitation. Unlikely as it seems, even a certain Franz
Kafka toyed with the idea of emigrating to Tel Aviv, and used to
read a magazine called *Palästina* which offered one-way tickets to
Haifa on its back pages; as the next decade wore on new arrivals
to the kibbutzim would be asked if they had come to Palestine
out of conviction or out of Germany. When war broke out in 1939
Segev suggests it proved advantageous to the Zionists. In fact, the
Arabs were now in a position, after the rebellion of 1936-9, to side
with the Third Reich against the British; and only Montgomery's
successful counterattack at El Alamein prevented Jerusalem falling
to a double threat: Germans advancing from Egypt and Vichy
French from Syria. That the rebellion's leader, Haj Amin Husseini,
found refuge in Berlin discredited the whole movement which was,

in any case, gravely weakened by its defeat and unable to resist the Zionists when the battle for territory started in 1948. The notorious White Paper of 1939 actually halted the entry of Jews to Palestine, even though they could – at least in theory – still leave the Third Reich through Romania until 1941. W.H. Auden's famous poem, written in March of that year, captures the bleak officiousness of the times: 'If you've got no passport you're officially dead,' the consul barks at the two Jewish refugees trying to leave the city of ten million souls.

Segev tells a good anecdote, but Herzl was right: the foundation of the state of Israel had reached the critical stage long before the signal year of 1948. It was radical Europe, rather than colonial Britain, which forced the pace for change: the last article of the Balfour Declaration stipulated 'that nothing shall be done which may prejudice the civil and religious rights of the existing non-Jewish communities in Palestine or the rights and political status enjoyed by Jews in any other country'. The romantic reaction in early nineteenth-century Europe had put diaspora Jews in a very uncomfortable position, and one that posed a far greater challenge than the universalism of the Enlightenment. The latter event had broken their link with the Jewish mainstream, and there was no obvious way back for them in the cities of Europe. What could they go back to? Hegel taught that world history was world judgement. The Germans demanded unconditional love, and got it; but Jewish love for Germany went unrequited. In the France of the rights of man, the Dreyfus Affair confronted the individual conscience with the essentially Roman reasons of modern statehood. It became steadily more and more difficult to be an unselfconscious citizen. Many hovered unsteadily between the two camps, others took the evidence of rejection at face value and embraced an identity founded not on exile, statelessness and the purity of the disengaged (and to which Mishnah and Talmud had been a response), but on return to the land where the Temple had been destroyed two thousand years before. Franz Rosenzweig warned against Judaism betraying its historic mission of the 'not yet' and seeking a homeland anywhere but in the Torah: for him, the Zionist ought to be a wanderer even in Zion. Yet becoming an actor in history was bound to mean a shift towards reasons of the state. Once the Zionists arrived in power they thought and argued more or less like Bismarck: Hebrew was a way to close the community, a linguistic rite of passage that emphasised the irrevocability (the Zionists hoped) of the step taken. Like the old Germany, the new Israel would be a nation based on blood kinship. It didn't matter so much what you believed in the 'Old Newland', it was what you *were* that counted. *Eretz Israel* was the last refuge. The previously unimaginable horrors of the Shoah, seen in retrospect as 'inevitable', were used to underscore the unsustainability of the *galut* or Diaspora, and the sheer folly of those who sought to assimilate in societies that were merely awaiting their chance to annihilate them.

Segev is unsparing about early Zionism's odd blend of zeal and conservatism; a Prophet of Rebuke reversed, he gives the impression of wanting to disown the careers of some of those who believed more than figuratively in the 'redemption of the land', such as the former prime minister Menachim Begin who, in his salad days as a terrorist, voiced his support for a Great Israel 'from the Nile to the Euphrates'. He knew his Book of Genesis, too. 'That day the Lord made a covenant with Abram, and said, "I give to your descendants this land from the river of Egypt to the Great River, the river Euphrates, the territory of the Kenites, Kenizzites, Kadmonites, Hittites, Perizzites, Rephaim, Amorites, Canaanites, Girgashites, and Jebusites."' Yet it was not those historical values and traditions that were invoked in defending the national territory: Yitzhak Shamir insisted that the pre-1967 borders were non-negotiable and nothing but 'the borders of Auschwitz'.

History is not fair play, and for all the partiality of Segev's account it is the British who stand as the most deceived of all – in their belief that they could govern 'one Palestine, complete'. Fair play is the world as understood by Job's comforters. But the return of the Jewish people into history as Israelis has implications

titles off. In addition to illustrating all his books, he is a notable caricaturist and graphic designer. Although he claims his style has been influenced by Americans like Thurber and Steinberg and the school of cartoonists around the *New Yorker*, his formative influences are mainly old continent. The pop-eyed, carp-mouthed satires of American dowagers he did in the 1960s have the bite of Georg Grosz, and a pandemonium out of Wilhelm Busch erupts over some of his more elaborate drawings (the notes flying off the score in Busch's 1865 image of a pianist dementedly attacking a 'finale furioso' are surely those festooning his recent *Tremolo*).

In fact, his childhood mentor was a local artist, Jean-Jacques Waltz (1872–1951), better known as Hansi. Waltz was a propagandist for the return of Alsace to France during the period of Prussian administration (1871–1918) when many Alsatians pretended to be indifferent to *Kulturpolitik*, if not to the wide-ranging social and welfare policies introduced by the Germans (which are still in force today, and distinguish local government and health care in Alsace from the rest of France: modern PR, like the welfare state, is also a development of policies introduced during the relatively liberal Bismarck period). Incongruously enough, Ungerer pays his greatest tribute to Hansi's work in his illustrations for *Das grosse Liederbuch* (1975), a million-selling collection of German folksongs and nursery rhymes: Hansi was a French patriot of a kind that died out after the First World War except in Alsace – 'la France quand même'. His famous picture-book *History of Alsace Told for Young Children* shows a succession of bespectacled and unattractive Teutons bumbling through Alsatian villages while freshly-washed local children wearing the traditional *schlupfkapp* – outsized black head-dresses with a rosette at the top of the left-hand bow – snigger at them behind their backs.

There is one other influence in his work: it is an older and more unsettling one, perhaps a kind of *memento mori*. When he was a pupil at the Lycée Bartholdi in Colmar, he used to shelter from the rain in the nearby cloister which houses the panels of Grünewald's famous Isenheim altar. Two scenes in that altarpiece would trouble even the most secular of imaginations: the savagely broken Christ on the cross, and the ruck of loathsome jabberwocks that assail St Anthony. Elias Canetti writes pages and pages in his auto-biography about the uncompromising realism of Grünewald's expressionism, and its powerful effect on the imagination.

'Expect the Unexpected', a slogan of the 1960s, is Ungerer's: it dates back to the time when he earned a living from the adver-tising agencies on Madison Avenue and shared an apartment with Philip Roth. Perhaps they'd both been reading Heraclitus: this is a motto for the Bomb as the ultimate enlightener. In 1964, Ungerer designed the poster for Stanley Kubrick's hilariously unfunny film *Dr Strangelove*. His pacifism and his posters against the war in Vietnam soon brought him to the attention of the FBI; he was on the black-list until 1993. Somewhere Ungerer quips: 'America is an SS country: Savages and Specialists. You've got to be a specialist there.' He also threw himself behind the campaign for civil rights: his strikingly simple 'Black Power-White Power' poster of 1967, which relies for its shock effect on two symmetrical figures – one white, the other black – each gnawing the other's leg, recycles work he had done twenty years earlier as an apprentice cartoonist in Alsace. This mordant comment on American racial conflict comes directly from his first-hand experience of how the Calico Cat and the Gingham Dog fought it out in Europe: he has exported Alsace's self-reflexive problems to the larger world without anyone noticing. The world has politicised itself along the old fracture line of Charlemagne's empire, and Alsace's double-negation is lifted up in the services of a higher affirmation – Europe. That may be why Ungerer, with more insight than most, takes a caustic line on the continent's presumptions to be a big global player. 'Parlement? On y parle, on y ment' (*Vracs*, 2000).

In fact, Tomi Ungerer is something of a controversialist, if not a fully paid-up *agent provocateur*. A few months ago I happened to see him being interviewed by German television on the opening night of his latest exhibition, 'Labotomica'. The venue was the

Erotic Art Museum in Hamburg. Across the walls snaked a series of collages from pornographic magazines, images cut up and reassembled to create grotesque parodies of body parts. 'It's just the same technique as butchering a pig,' he remarked knowingly to the reporters, a reference to the period when he and his wife lived on a remote farm in Nova Scotia and, as detailed in the book *Here Today, Gone Tomorrow* (1983), slaughtered their own hog. Something of the fictional Oskar Matzerath, hero of Günter Grass's *Tin Drum*, clings to the real Tomi Ungerer: scatology does the dirt on eschatology.

The exhibition is not his first venture into what we might very loosely call eroticism: Ungerer published 'adult' books regularly during the 1970s and 1980s, and a bumper edition of his saucier drawings, *Erotoscope*, has just been released by Taschen Verlag. The best of them is a humorously captioned series of ink drawings in which spoof botanical species are coaxed to develop exuberant genitalia (*Voluptiphallus delinguatus, Perivagina superba, Insoliglossa impudica*). It is a conceit which once inspired Erasmus Darwin to suggest in his poem *The Botanic Garden* (1791), a bit of poetic doggerel that tried to popularise the Linnaean system for plant classification, that the plants are polygamous and venial much in the manner of the Greek myths which, he also thought, were simply anthropomorphic versions of Nature itself. Ungerer's earlier lampoon, *Fornicon*, a series of Barbarella-like sex gadgets done in the clinical style of patent applications, overdrew his PC account a few years ago in the United States, where publishers now refuse to bring out his children's books: he was told at a convention on children's books in the early 1990s that anyone who had dreamed up a collection like *Fornicon* had no right to be anywhere near children. So what is *Fornicon* – a satire on the industrialisation of sex? Perhaps, but Ungerer seems to relish the perverse ingenuity of his dominas and their pleasure machines. He is surely more of a love-bombed Puritan than he lets on, and his occasionally cruel images and mildly shamefaced curiosity about vinyl and ritual suggest that Janus, not Eros, is the true god of sex in the modern world.

Ungerer blithely disregards the fact that the gender border has been politicised, too.

Here, again, there is illustrious local precedent: Hans Baldung's magnificent woodcut of 1513 *Beauty Swings her Whip over Wisdom* shows a medieval garden with the white-bearded Aristotle down on all fours being ridden by Phyllis, the famous Athenian courtesan. Bridle in his mouth, the humbled philosopher looks anxiously towards the viewer as if to plead for instructions; it is the naked woman with the crop in her delicate hand who looks thoughtful, knowing exactly what's coming next.

When France was Welsh

Die Gedanken sind frei (1993) is not so much a children's book as a child's book — a compilation of old cuttings and recollections about the war years, whose title recalls the conviction of a famous nineteenth-century liberty song: the body may be fettered but thoughts can stray. It was not sung during the Nazi period. The book is itself a rewrite of the original French version, *A la Guerre comme à la Guerre* (1991); the English version (1998) has the more frankly declarative title of *Tomi: A Childhood under the Nazis*. After the publication of the French and German versions Ungerer received so much material from people who, like himself, had hoarded everything from the war years that the English version, written in a lightly accented Irish-American patter, contains a substantial amount of new pictorial material. It offers, for example, an extra fifty carefully posed postcard views of the Oberbefehlshaber himself, in casual mode. (Hitler contrives to look at once daft and menacing, perhaps because his casualness is so obviously studied.) 'My mother kept everything, and so did I,' Ungerer adds. The book is crammed full of all kinds of drawings, photos, official documents and posters attesting to what it was like to be eight as the Nazis marched into Colmar.

The early part of the book is dominated by Ungerer's mother,

Alice (his father died when he was three) – a willowy, good-looking woman who had what the Alsatians call *gratl*, a sense of her own worth. Protestant and bourgeois, she nevertheless observed the Catholic saint days. A consummate actor, she used her attractiveness to get what she wanted – 'but nobody could touch her'. She had grown up in Alsace when it was Wilhelmine, and although she loved German literature she was 'practically allergic to the Germans'. Sunshine, she called her son, little tiger, darling sparrow, little goldbug, *Meschtgräzerle* (bantam on the midden) and – 'worst of all' – *Schisserle* (baby-shat-his-nappy). Hearing any of these endearments was enough to propel him under the table, just like the kitten in his children's story *No Kiss for Mother*.

At the end of 1939, in the *drôle de guerre*, Strasburg was a deserted city, Colmar lacking one-third of its population. Strasburg University decamped to Clermont-Ferrand; many Alsatians chose to evacuate to the Dordogne. The 'gallinaceous' French army believed in the impregnability of the defensive Maginot Line, built at great expense in the early Thirties in the forests of the Rhine: its concrete pillboxes were to play no role in the war whatsoever. Having defeated the France army, despite its superior tank force, in a rapid flanking manoeuvre out of Belgium, well to the north of the defensive line, the Germans eventually crossed the Rhine in rafts, in June 1940. Ceded by the Vichy government to Berlin, Alsace became part of a single province, *Oberrhein*, which included Baden, on the opposite bank of the Rhine – the river no longer served as the border. The Jews, uniquely in the Third Reich, were deported to Vichy France in convoys rather than being driven into ghettos: later the gendarmerie was to hunt many of them down and hand them back to the Gestapo. At the Ungerer house a German officer presented himself politely as a potential lodger. 'Aren't [the chestnut trees] beautiful at this time of year? One thing I promise you: the day will come when you will see a Jew hanging from every branch,' he commented to Alice Ungerer on leaving, and then pulled a piece of paper out of his pocket. 'This is a wonderful recipe for carrot cake. My wife gave it to me – it is yours.' A remark like that, we might observe, extends the violence of Nazi kitsch: politeness has become a virtue of pure form.

Teachers were sent to Germany for retraining, for now all children had to learn Hochdeutsch; the dialect was allowed only as a default. The radio became a *Volksender*. New tones entered the air. 'Don't think, the Führer will think for you.' Tomi, whose name was registered in his birth certificate as Jean-Thomas, became Johann. His first school assignment was to draw a Jew. 'Mama, what is a Jew?' he asked at home. The enemy had been stigmatised for pedagogic purposes. The Germanisation of Alsace under the Nazis went to absurd lengths. It wasn't just the changing of street names and the scrapping of the old French monuments which had survived the more tolerant years under German administration after 1870: wedding rings had to be worn on the right not the left hand, *froid* and *chaud* enamels were prised off taps, and even salt and pepper shakers had to shake it out in Gothic. Basque berets were strictly prohibited, unless you wanted to end up at the correctional camp in Schirmeck. Stiff fines could be imposed for merely saying 'Bonjour' or 'Merci'. Alsatians had to get used to saying 'Heil Hitler!' which – as old Alsatians will still tell you today – was domesticated by mumbling 'Ein Liter' (a litre of beer). Posters inscribed 'Hinaus mit dem welschen Plunder' were plastered all over Strasburg – Out with out the gallic trash! The old German pejorative, *welsch*, which comes from the same linguistic root as *wallon*, was a word the Nazis favoured for anything 'foreign' from the south or west. (In Alsace, it specifically and non-prejudicially designates the tiny language group within the Alsatian minority whose vernacular derives from Old French rather than Middle German. In 1557, the town magistrates of Strasburg, wishing to keep the city German, refused rights of property and marriage to the *welsches* – 'damit man eyn teutsch stadt behalte'. Little pockets of these 'Welsh' dialect-speakers can still be found in the valleys south-west of Strasburg.)

Ungerer's mother saw to it that he was spared most of the war's hardships. War is actually quite a lot of fun when you're a nine-year-old boy, and can't tell the difference between a Jolly Roger and the death's-head on a SS badge. The Nazis were adept at conscripting old symbols like the skull and crossbones as a way of disinhibiting an entire population: the legal theorist Carl Schmitt even drew a parallel between the Nazi régime and seventeenth-century English freebooters. Fascist virility was puerile: it exploited puberty as a source of symbolic vigour, and adolescents were central to its collective dramaturgy. Nazi gatherings might have stolen their light from religious festivities but they also trod the Scout tradition. But Alice Ungerer had the good sense and cunning to keep her son out of the Hitler Youth meetings on Sundays – to his regret at the time, since he coveted the dagger which came with the uniform. On the first page of his first school copybook he had to draw a heroic banner and laurel leaves to the glory of 'unsrer Führer': it has been marked in red by his teacher: 'too small'. That things might not be big enough was a Nazi obsession: a page from his stamp collection shows that as the Thousand Year Reich started shrinking, circa 1943, it became the *Gross-deutsches Reich*. In the four years of the Nazi occupation one hundred and thirty thousand young Alsatians were drafted into the Wehrmacht, a quarter of them to perish in the Soviet campaign; it took all of Alice Ungerer's ingenuity to stop her elder son Bernard being called up. She was a German mother now, and the Führer had a special affection for the wombs of the nation. So she argued with the local recruiting officer that, as the best student in his class, he was too brainy to go the front. He agreed, and Bernard was spared the grey-green field uniform.

In the autumn of that year Colmar was the last German bridge-head west of the Rhine. American fighters regularly strafed the area. Tombstones were manhandled from the Jewish cemetery to serve as street barricades. Ungerer was touching fourteen and next in line to be drafted into the *Wehrwolf*, one of the schoolboy brigades that rumour claimed would to be sent out in a last ditch attempt to defend the fatherland. The winter of 1944 was fierce and the family had to decamp to their coal cellar, putting snow into buckets for drinking water. Their stately, fat neighbour got his head blown off by a shell: it was the first dead person Tomi had seen. Their ordeal came to an end in the first days of February 1945, but 14,000 Germans died defending the city before it was taken. The young Ungerer watched some of the exhausted young soldiers being mishandled, the French soldiers clubbing them with their rifle butts. 'This disturbing vision cancelled out whatever hope and innocence I had left.' The Americans stayed aloof, chewing gum and not much caring if they were in France or Germany. 'To them we were part of a "zoo of savages".'

When he went back to school, it seemed to be 1940 in reverse. The Führer's portrait and the 'Out with the gallic trash' message had been replaced by a new poster: 'C'est chic de parler français.' Everything German had vanished, indeed the Nazis had achieved in four years what the French had been unable to bring about in nearly two centuries of cultural assimilation – to make the Alsatians ashamed of their dialect: the Alsatians were *sales Boches* by association. A little less than one per cent of the Alsatian population was sentenced to 'indignité nationale', often by officials whose own dealings with the war régime would hardly have stood up to scrutiny. Guilt and confusion were to deepen, as was Alsatian inferiority towards the rest of France when it came to public notice at a trial in Limousin, in 1953, that twelve soldiers from the region, recruited by force into the Wehrmacht, had been involved in one of the worst atrocities on French soil: the massacre of the village of Oradour-sur-Glane.

Nothing in their own history predisposed the French ('les français de l'intérieur' as the Alsatians say, reversing the term once used by Louis XIV to describe *them*) to show any patience with the German-speaking peoples inside their own borders. The Alsatian dialect was a 'mauvaise langue': end of discussion. In fact, the dialect of Middle High German spoken in Alsace – Alemannic is its proper linguistic tag – is one of the most compelling things about this part of Europe. Hearing it confronts the listener with a visceral life of words that has survived from an older Europe:

not a language but a tongue. Talk naturally, say the Alsatians: '*Red wie d'r de Schnawwel gewaxe isch!*' Literally: speak the way your beak has grown on you or, in more idiomatic English, the way your clapper fits. Years of assault on their linguistic identity and a feeling of always being misunderstood had made Alsatians quick to close ranks: any outsider was a potential invader. Now they were Boches by proxy. If the desire to remain true to their inheritance had come to look like original sin, there was only one option left: to learn to be impeccably French.

A whole way of life had to be reconstructed in the postwar atmosphere of suspicion and recrimination, as the stay-at-homes and the 'malgré nous' (those forced to fight on the eastern front for the Wehrmacht) mingled with returning evacuees and deportees. Many of Alsace's Jews – ardent francophiles because of the Revolution that emancipated them – never came back, one way or the other, like the poet Claude Vigée, who has talked bitterly and movingly about his father's inability to 'understand how the "noble" French government could deliver simple, loyal Alsace Jews... to the Nazis'. (Vichy's virulent anti-Jewish measures surprised the Nazis, whose initial plans for defeated France were to make it a depository for Jews expelled from the Reich.) Some of those who did come back got the cold shoulder. Although ten per cent of Strasburg's current population is Jewish, the largest community outside Paris, it is largely of recent date: many are Sephardic immigrants who came to Alsace from Algeria in 1962 – when the post-colonial crisis nearly ended up being imported into France itself – and Morocco, after the Six Days War in 1967. The empty synagogues in small towns and villages throughout the region testify to the irrevocable loss of a centuries-old tradition: very few Jews now live in the country towns and villages.

Having survived the war, young Tomi – Jean again – had to survive becoming French. Having been dragged before the local Gestapo for speaking French with his mother in the war years, he was told by his French teacher that before presuming to interest himself in French literature he'd have to lose his accent. He was learning to become a victim of history, too. School discipline was strict and some of the teachers were sadistic: 'I must obey at all times', copied out twenty times (with spelling mistakes!) is reproduced on the flypaper of the French version of his memoir. But it taught him to fuel his talent with his anger, and he remarks that the comment he received in one of his school reports – 'perverse and subversive' – indicates precisely the qualities needed to survive twisted times.

Not just those qualities, I imagine, but a heavy dose of irony too. One of his illustrations tells an anecdote about a can of bouillon. An elderly Alsatian woman on visit to Germany died during an air-raid. Her body was cremated and, with aluminium being in short supply, her ashes were sent back home in a used tin labelled 'stock powder'. The accompanying official notification of her death arrived weeks later, during which time the family had spooned grannie's mortal remains into a hearty consommé. 'This is a true story,' Ungerer asserts; and I see no reason to doubt him. Nor do I question the reliability of the older Tomi's memory when he says that in the summer of 1942 he went on vacation to a farmhouse in the Vosges run by some friends who were splendid cooks. Their pig was called Hermann Goering. On returning home, young Ungerer wrote a card thanking them for their hospitality; 'I cannot wait to visit you again once you have slaughtered Hermann Goering, and to enjoy a good hunk of the field marshall's ham.' Luckily for us, the card was not intercepted by the censors: Ungerer's career as a *zoon politikon* was under way.

Almost on the same page, he admits, a trite superfluously, to taking a certain pleasure in affronting the right-minded. It derives, he says, from the realisation that the Nazi marching songs of his boyhood are in his head, and there to stay. Not only that, but they have a driving force, and even today, when he feels 'down and discouraged' he sings one to restore his spirits. This would be abhorrent to a contemporary German, though Bismarck did say something very similar about Max Schneckenburger's nineteenth-century war paean 'The Watch on the Rhine' – that the song had been worth three extra divisions to the Prussian army. Ungerer evidently considers his anecdote emblematic of what it means to be Alsatian, even though it offers a slant tribute to the Nazi minister of propaganda who put those songs in his head in the first place. Near the end of his book, Ungerer mentions that when he entered the French army to do his national service in the early 1950s he had to train the new recruits. Then he made a discovery: 'The French marching songs will not carry you as far as the German ones. So I brought Nazi songs to my regiment, the marching improved, and I still laugh about it. It may seem tasteless, even macabre, but for us Alsatians it is our privilege to ridicule the means of persecution and oppression, thereby exorcising them as well. And our humour, even if black, is not obscured by guilt.'

A Stuttered Essay on the French

Nation légère et dure...

Voltaire

There is no such country as France. There is however a Platonic form and true beehive object of knowledge, called the Hexagon, which people refer to as 'France'.

Having nurtured two of the greatest poets of the modern age, Charles Baudelaire and Arthur Rimbaud, the French have renounced poetry. Poets are now part-time psychoanalysts, and what is left of poetry is called *poetics*. (Wholesale rationalism, as Michael Oakeshott once remarked, is like literary criticism without a literature.)

Only in France is one reminded that psychology is a branch of Christian theology, the word having been coined in the fifteenth century by theologians who sought to delimit the nature of the soul. Freud (whose name on French lips sounds like a fraud to English ears) follows in the tradition, extending this 'soul' in space while attempting to lay hold of its phantomic body and describe its surface anatomy, digestive system and visceral eructions on the basis of models drawn from electricity, hydraulics and other Helmholtzian phenomena. Descartes did the same with the pineal gland, which he considered a little bellows inflating the musculature.

The French make value judgements about sound qualities. It is, as Nietzsche noted, what gives their culture its enamel hardness.

It is a mark of pride in France to speak other languages badly, mellifluous French being the sole remedy against the cacophony of the nextdoor neighbours.

Since the French so detest each other, it would be a bit much to expect them to like foreigners. Tolerance is therefore entirely dependent on the Jesuitical strategy of complete indifference.

The French word *valeur* does duty for both valour and value, which suggests that France never experienced the advent of what Adam Ferguson identified as the decisive ethical component of civil society: the legitimation of the pursuit of interest in the marketplace over the pursuit of honour on the battlefield. So, despite its revolution France remains in some essential sense an old-fashioned aristocratic society that cannot ever contemplate the triumph of the commercial classes.

L'Invendable: the man who can't be sold. What the deuce happened to him?

France is bound to its self-image as the producer of modernity. This is a form of status narcissism – the person on top automatically thinks himself the best. This supposition subtends all its universalist ideals. Woe when the French discover they are the consumers of modernity, like everyone else.

Every century France gets a new Tartuffe.

It is a particular kind of naïve mind that conceives of order solely as the product of deliberate social arrangements.

French education: a concerted attempt to ignore the recommendations and prestige of Rousseau's *Emile* which suggested abolishing the educational programme that commenced with Plato's Academy. Fortunately for the French, the Americans assumed that burden in their stead.

Civil war or Joan of Arc.

It is hardly surprising that in a nation which believes human beings to be perfectly innocent, institutions should be bastions of privilege and iniquity.

Given the moral essentialism of the French, it becomes a kind of stupidity to seem to be in want or need. This has led to relentless social bluffing on the other hand, and to a fantastic growth of therapists, all existing to cater for the delusion of the self-sufficient citizen. As Kant suggested, nothing is more humiliating for modern people than to be dependent. No wonder the real French currency is exasperation.

Good manners are orders sublimated into hints. But if you don't take the hints, there's nothing to make of the orders.

Poverty in the midst of abundance. It is generous and an act of good faith to want to pass on to one's neighbour the good tidings. But the good tidings are not nourishing; they are stones. These stones of the most difficult intellectual truth induce a kind of anorexic bloating. Believing they have eaten something nutritious and not sensing the poverty of their diet (stones having been hitherto most useful for throwing at the police or building barricades), intellectuals feel compelled to tell others about their 'special régime', not realising that because their long and arduous training in emotional self-denial coincides with their impulse to charity they are actually spreading the most desolate kind of intellectual poverty.

Privilege was what 1789 sought to abolish: more than two centuries later, it is what ordinary people take to the streets to *uphold*.

Napoleon Bonaparte brought history to an end. Fortunately, snobbery is ever on hand to establish a new, formalised and implacable hierarchy of social rank.

Scepticism's *non sequitur*: from the assumption that pricking delusions in the realm of concepts and values is a manifestation of psychic wholeness to the inference that *every* concept or value is corrupt.

One of the attractions of analysis: the pleasure of recognising one's failings without the religious need to attend to the consequences.

A world without love in which the only possibility of genuine communication with others takes place through art: Proust.

Much in the tradition of the detective tainted by what he detects, the essential moral force of Claude Chabrol's films lies in showing what it means to be *spoiled*.

Two incompatible self-images of French society: as the glittering demi-monde of brilliant display and flattery, of words given as favours, and the Genevan interpretation of it: the real presence of the Devil.

Doesn't correctness imply corrigibility?

France is one of the three Middle Kingdoms, the other two being Mexico and China. People living in the Middle Kingdoms adopt the practice of what anthropologists call 'pseudo-speciation', and call themselves 'men'.

Aiming only to be different from each other, members of the French middle-classes end up adopting the same strategy simultaneously: the denial of reciprocity subjects every would-be hero to the rule of fashion, which is cast off at the moment everyone starts to imitate it so that uniqueness can be rediscovered emerging from a different buttonhole.

The Last Judgement secularised as the *concours*, with an examiner as God.

Can it be that the French have never grasped one of the basic principles of democratic politics: that those who hold office are the servants of those who elected them, not singular embodiments of the monarchical 'I will it so'? Jean-Marie Domenach insists that 'democracy has never been popular in France,' and that the republican tradition is in fact a counter-religion devoted to that great idol, the State.

What the French hold against the Americans: their pretending to be innocent *is* innocent.

The least likeable aspect of French culture is that the French, as predicted by Marcel Schwob in 1893, have lost their sense of humour. They want to worship themselves, and their own constitution; and for that only straight faces will do. Irony is the standard method of defending this presumption. Now and again the true humour of Rabelais bursts out of them, like a pressure cooker that can no longer contain itself, as in one of Céline's black guffaws.

Liberty – Equality – Fraternity: the revolutionary slogan is a *eulogy*, in which amour-propre slides into PR. Anyone seeking to question such a noble and fine-sounding triad is bound to seem not only obtuse but malevolent.

More Catholic than Christian: a fierce refusal to compromise or yield ground in the English way merely for the sake of social harmony.

Belief in self-sufficiency makes the individual in France peculiarly susceptible to imitating his neighbour, thereby unseating the pride that generated the assurance of self-sufficiency in the first place. And a society in which Hell is other people is essentially one in the mould not of Rousseau but Hobbes.

The whole tension of being French in the world is conveyed

through the effort of having to purse the lips to achieve open vowel-sounds.

The primordial fear of the French is that of being taken for dupes. With this fear it has been possible to initiate one intellectual reign of terror after another.

France destroyed by its philosophers: it was Joseph Joubert was first made that observation, not me.

L'*espace* France.

Five Postcards from Badenweiler for Zinovy Zinik

I

If it's true that the great spa towns, those temples of propriety from Carlsbad to Vichy, are really vantage points for observing Europe as an allegory – this was the whim of the aristocratic memoirist Charles Joseph, Prince de Ligne (1735-1814) – then Badenweiler is the continent's gazebo.

Tucked in the lap of a valley on the southern slopes of the Black Forest between Freiburg and the great bend of the Rhine at Basle, a hundred kilometres south of Baden-Baden, the most famous spa of all – where Dostoevsky tried to gamble himself out of debt in the summer of 1867 and the French collaborationists ignominiously gathered in 1944 for what Louis-Ferdinand Céline, in his novel *Nord*, called 'the "Everything Goes" Casino of History' – Badenweiler looks down onto the silt flats and water meadows, the *Ried* of Upper Alsace.

This is where the cities of the Decapolis once thrived under the Holy Roman German Empire, centres of humanist learning like Colmar, Selestat and Munster. Albert Schweitzer – organist, Bach scholar, theologian, humanitarian physician to French Equatorial Africa, perplexed author of *Civilisation and Ethics* and Goodness Personified until the 1960s – grew up in a village in their shelter when Alsace was part of Bismarck's newly unified Germany. Schweitzer knew from intimate experience that the cultural idiom of these former city-states had never aligned itself with the extended spirit of the modern nation-state, whether French or

German. So, too, did the great Basle historian Jacob Burckhardt, whose classic historiography *The Civilisation of the Renaissance in Italy* draws a parallel between the fourteenth-century Florentines and the mercantile and patrician humanism of the cities of the Rhine. 'Old Europe' was one of the highest accolades in Burckhardt's lexicon: its culture still lives on, as a kind of aboriginal memory, in the solid Rhenish cities that, as Lucien Febvre wrote, were once 'states unto themselves'.

Yet Burckhardt was forced to recognise – and the irony is a bitter one – that the flourishing of individualism in old Europe was accompanied by the advent of a desacralised view of politics and nature so corrosive in its effects as to undermine the very social order that had created lucid realists like Machiavelli and Dante. It was the new printing presses, developed by Gutenberg in Mainz, which, even as Columbus sailed west to find the Indies, made Basle one of Europe's most important centres for manufacturing and distributing the reproducible harrow-tracks of linguistic exchange: bound in animal skins and sent down the Rhine to the trade-fairs of Europe, the printed word in book form made new political communities for the continent not just possible but necessary.

In his winter lecture season of 1874–5 at Basle University, Friedrich Nietzsche, an exceedingly young professor of classical philology, rebelled against the spurious Platonism of written language, and the hardening of what was a flowing. Written language was a series of dead signs. Nothing is more alien to the nature of consciousness than moving along a single plane of narrative alertness. Not without reason had the great teachers like Socrates and Jesus avoided committing their thinking to paper.

An insight like that would drive a thinker to despair if it didn't drive him to find a fresh interplay of forces, a way of bringing the newly stressed human sense life into haptic harmony. As Nietzsche wrote, 'the time for speaking well has passed, because the period of city-state civilisations has passed'.

The remedy? 'To learn how to *write well*, and *become better and better at it.*'

2

A contested border within living memory, the land along the hundred and fifty kilometres of the Upper Rhine between France and Germany is Europe's *fons et origo*.

This was sea-bed once, millions of years ago. The broad flat-floored rille of the valley – a fault gap between symmetrical hills or *graben* as the geologists call it – bears a striking resemblance to Milton's description of Eden in *Paradise Lost*, except that the 'river large' flows northwards through the garden, fructifying, from its extensive underground tables, as in Genesis 2, the 'porous earth with kindly drawn up thirst' (a beautiful early description of capillary action).

Some medieval commentaries have even identified this part of Europe as Cockaigne, a lazy-luscious-land in which everybody went about open-mouthed, for instant gratification of appetite, and lived in the shade of their snoring bellies.

European writers rushed to translate *Gargantua and Pantagruel* in the sixteenth century, though the Reformation gave a distinctly moralising tone to Rabelais' genial transformation of 'the material bodily lower stratum'. The German version published in 1578 by the Strasburg lawyer and writer Johann Fischart seems less close to the genial spirit of Rabelais than to the stern religious conformism of his fellow syndic Sebastian Brant, who, alarmed at the imminent rupture of the Holy Roman Empire, wrote his famous poem 'The Ship of Fools' as a way of sending the errant, together with Columbus, out of the world in a boat.

It is hardly surprising that in one of his celebrated newspaper articles, Karl Marx, trying hard to bring about another Golden Age of material abundance, should charge these 'grobian' writers with using body images not to celebrate a common humanity but as a means of inspiring disgust: '. . .and suspended like an enveloping cloud over it all, the self-satisfied philistine's consciousness of his own virtue'.

While representative works of the region like Hans

Grimmelshausen's rollicking novel *Simplicissimus* (1668) suggest that the vernacular roots of the European picaresque tradition are tougher and deeper than Marx ever supposed, the rhythms of communal life in the Garden of Eden have, like everything else, yielded to the invisible hands of private enterprise: every April, teams of labourers from Poland and the Ukraine are bussed across the continent to cut the ridged fields for the deliciously delicate pale-violet asparagus shoots that poke out of the loam. Three hundred years ago, these people might have been mercenaries coming to fight in the war that lasted forty-seven but is known to history as the Thirty Years War.

Closer to Badenweiler, where the alluvium thins out, the softly billowing topsoil has been tressed and combed: these are the ancient gnarled vines of the Römerberg, all of them facing south. The Baden wine is fine, but the white wines of Alsace, cultivated on the opposite slope of the valley and not particularly well known outside France, are truly ambrosial, and much to be preferred to the sulphurous aperient gurgled by the nymphs and tritons of the spa centres. The complex geology of the region is volatilised in its wines; it can hardly be an accident that the great doctor, adventurer and medical evangelist Paracelsus, who used to tramp the roads here in the peripatetic way of the early Greek doctors, should have introduced 'spagyric', or chemical, elements to the list of largely vegetable and animal remedies that had come down from Galen.

As intimate with astral bodies as with the other kind, Paracelsus was one of the first doctors to suppose that illness might be something external, not constitutional. He believed in 'signatures', marks of a symbolic perfection written by God into the nature of things in order to spell out the underlying similitudes: this hermeneutic notion was to form the basis of his therapeutic system or *Heilkunde*, the German word drawing attention to medicine's deep connections with redemption theology.

Then again, the Rhine Valley has always attracted its vagabond population of heretics and eschatologists, its motley Kings of the Last Days.

North of the town, deeper into the Black Forest, is the log cabin at Todtnauberg where the philosopher Martin Heidegger liked to retreat at weekends from his teaching duties at the University of Freiburg: from his coign of vantage he could observe the building of a hydroelectric plant on the Rhine and ponder, as all of Western metaphysics span around him like a dizzy prayer-wheel, what he called the nihilating of Being.

Closer to the river is the medieval town of Staufen: in 1539, the necromancer Dr Faustus had his neck broken by the Devil in room 5 on the third floor of its largest guesthouse, the Hotel Löwen. The hotel is still doing a roaring trade, and proud to claim Mephistopheles among its former guests.

3

Badenweiler is stiff and wealthy, with an imposing belvedere in the centre of town which shelters a park of ancient cypresses, cedars and pyramid oaks, some of them rearing out of the eighteenth century.

What seems to be the town centre has been disfigured by a Sixties-style circular concrete restaurant in Barbarella mode. The day I visited a brass band was striking up the waltz from *Der Freischütz*. It was, I recalled with a start, the same music which accompanied the arrival of the sick party to the baths at Wildbad, another Black Forest spa, in Wilkie Collins' 1866 novel *Armadale*, a cumbersome Victorian novel expertly filleted by Franz Kafka in his eerie story 'The Hunter Gracchus'. Kafka's cross between Nimrod and the Ancient Mariner loses his bearings and ends up haunting the middle of Europe.

'My boat is rudderless,' he says, 'it is driven by the wind that blows in the nethermost regions of death.'

Next to the park is another imposing spa centre in pseudo-classical stucco, the loggia to an array of baths named after Cassiopeia, the conspicuous W-shaped constellation close to the

Pole Star. The park itself has been constructed around the remains of a large Vespasian bath complex dating from about 75 AD, built for the convenience of the nearby colony in Basle (Colonia Augusta Raurica). It features a pond with bream and turtles, and a mantle of Himalayan rock plants.

Strolling about are the superannuated descendants, great-grandchildren of the German small-holders whose prosperity Chekhov envied on behalf of his Russian peasants. He found the German women frumpish, though he surely hadn't forgotten that his wife Olga was herself of German descent. Writing to his sister on 8 June, he complains about the women in Berlin: 'There is a horrible lack of taste, nowhere do they dress as abominably, with complete absence of taste. I haven't seen a single handsome woman and not one who isn't trimmed up with some variety of absurd braid.' Three weeks later he hasn't changed his mind: 'You don't see a single decently dressed German woman, the lack of taste is depressing.'

The landscape pleased him though; the general impression 'was of a big garden, with tree-covered mountains in the distance, few people, very little movement on the streets, the garden and flowers beautifully tended'.

Then as now, places like Badenweiler are where city people come to get away from life in the stream of things, to purge their bodies, inside and out, with the reputedly therapeutic waters. Though hydrotherapy and balneotherapy died out long ago as reputable cures in the UK, the social security systems in both France and Germany make it possible for patients to be sent for a 'cure' on demand once a year, with full reimbursement of costs.

Hydrotherapy is reputed to be especially beneficial for chest, joint and skin problems, although evidence is hard to come by.

In his 1771 novel *The Expedition of Humphry Clinker*, Tobias Smollett, Scottish surgeon and vagabond man of letters, has one of his characters say: 'I have read all that has been written on the Hot Wells, and what I can collect from the whole, is, that the water contains nothing but a little salt, and calcarious earth, mixed in such inconsiderable proportion, as can have very little, if any, effect on the animal œconomy.' But people unfailingly believe what they read in books, as Smollett's character goes on to observe (and sure enough, it was Smollett's advocacy elsewhere of the beneficial effects of sea water, or thalassotherapy, which is partly responsible for the pleasure we take in holidays by the sea, a pastime quite unknown two hundred years ago).

Besides, lots of parties in our most civil economy stand to gain from the endless pursuit of what Germans now call, in a language neither fish nor fowl, 'wellness' (although the word was first used in English, according to the OED, in 1654). Taking the waters in *Wellnesszentren* is how Europeans compensate – 'sich richtig erholen' – for having to live in the historical flow, for spas offer time in an altogether more intimate, libidinous and motherly form. In the mythology of the liquid element, the word *bagnoire*, as the Prince de Ligne would have known, designates both a bath and a box in the theatre.

It could be that every underground source is really a doctrine of human knowledge.

Spas tend to bear exotic names, like Cassiopeia, mother to Andromeda, who boasted that both she and her daughter were more beautiful that the Nereids, the sea-nymphs. When their protector Poseidon sent a flood and a sea-monster as punishment for her slander, Perseus, happening by their kingdom on the coast of Philistia, was so smitten by the naked Andromeda (whose parents had pegged her out as a sacrificial victim), that he decided to unbind her and claim her as his bride. Since it kept getting in the way of the Swiss Army knife hanging from his waistband, he took the Gorgon's head out of his knapsack, and laid it on a bed of ordinary sea-weed. It was instantly turned to coral, according to Ovid, one of the resinous bronchial trees that decorate anatomy museums from Leiden to Montpellier.

Europe, always wanting to go back to first things, is littered with sublime petrifactions – with metamorphoses and monsters.

4

Badenweiler is where Chekhov died, in July 1904, emaciated, fevered, coughing and coughing, his body riddled with the tuberculosis that had been officially diagnosed in 1888.

The first hotel he had booked into with his wife Olga that June, the Römerbad, was the best in town. It is a solid, imposing building that would not disgrace a majr city. Nietzsche had stayed at the hotel several times almost thirty years before. After two days, the staff asked the Chekhovs to move on: his coughing was disturbing the other guests.

They found a small pension closer to the centre of the town, the Villa Friederike, where 'for fourteen or sixteen marks a day we have a double room flooded with sunlight, with a washstand, beds, etc'. Chekhov was eating 'butter in enormous quantities', in an attempt to regain some of the weight he had lost — but to no avail. The town was beginning to bore him, and in one of his letters to his sister Masha he asks her to find out whether he could reserve a cabin on a boat sailing from Trieste to Yalta.

A few days later they moved on to yet another hotel, the Hotel Sommer, from the balcony of which Anton Pavlovitch could sit and watch folk going to the post office on their errands. The hotel is an attractive two-storey building, its façade hidden behind wisteria; it is now a urology clinic called Park Therme.

On the railing of the first floor balcony, looking out onto a huge cedar of Lebanon, is a small plaque. It reads: 'Hier lebt Anton Tschechoff in Juli 1904.' He did; but he died there, too.

The photograph of Chekhov on his deathbed shows him incongruously tanned, his jacket buttoned up to the neck and collar pressed firmly against his chin to stop his mouth jutting open. The distended veins on his forehead confirm what we know about his symptoms: the destruction of his lungs and lung sacs was so advanced that he had developed heart failure secondary to his pulmonary TB.

Olga writes in June that had she known about his heart condition she wouldn't have insisted on his travelling. It was hot at the end of June 1904, and her husband must have been unbearably uncomfortable, hardly able to move because of breathlessness, and incapacitated by his constant fever: on 28 June he sent Olga to Freiburg to purchase him a light flannel suit, and in one of his last letters he talks about a new play set on a ship bound in the polar pack ice.

The hotel porters brought blocks of ordinary ice up to his room: Olga chopped them up, wrapped them in muslin, and laid them around his chest. All the while the stench of death was fouling the sweet air of this becalmed inner island – 'As if it had lungs, and rotten ones' (Sebastian in *The Tempest*). Doctors came to administer injections: camphor, creosote and ipecacuanha were his maintenance treatment. Chekhov made no mention of his impending death, and insisted in letters to his friends he was getting better – didn't he know Basle was the very place from which Death hops out in the famous medieval Alphabet and the Dance of Death?

'No man can admit right off that there is no way out.'

Yet the serene rationalist whose writings drove the philosopher Lev Shestov to denounce him as a demolisher of hope in a famous essay, from which that phrase comes, had found his no-way-out in the land where the plague acquired such vitality as a metaphor as to survive war and the tedium of peace: moral plagues threaten us almost every day in Europe, according to the tabloids, even though microbial epidemics have long been a thing of the past.

As with his perilous journey to Sakhalin, Chekhov had ventured into a hermeneutical zone that might more obviously be associated with Dostoevsky.

He was unmistakably a dying man, but a man who lacked the rancour which Nietzsche, whom he read with interest around 1900, thought the sick foster against the living.

'I suffer: it must be somebody's fault': that was what the philosopher called *ressentiment*, the malign, histrionic, intensely social emotion he saw driving the moral economy in the modern age. It is the mechanism behind the pastiche fates laying in wait for Dostoevsky's self-proclaimed 'originals'; Chekhov's more discreetly wayward characters suffer a different kind of disillusionment.

He is unique as a writer in not intruding on his characters' motivations, their reasons for doing things: in not judging them he actually comes closer to the spirit of the Epistle to the Romans than the Christian apologist Doestoevsky. For judgement turns full circle and exposes critics as people in bad faith who desperately want to secure their own little plot of innocence. Judgement is always self-interested.

It must be said, however, that Chekhov stubbornly neglected his own reasons for doing things: his famous personal nonchalance had become, as his wife remarked, 'an almost reckless indifference'.

5

Chekhov, it seems, went to Germany largely at Olga's insistence. It was after seeing her doctor, Taube, that he felt he was in good hands: 'My advice, let Germans treat you … I have been tortured for twenty years!!!' he told his Yalta colleague Dr Sredin. His sister Masha opposed Olga's plan to take him to Berlin, where he was seen by a professorial chest specialist called Ewald: he examined Chekhov and left the room without saying a word, evidently appalled at the idea of a moribund man being shunted across Europe.

Chekhov was taking morphine, which eased his diarrhoea as well as his painful joints: he feared he had tuberculosis of the spine. As it happened, Dr Taube had a colleague called Schwöhrer who practised in Badenweiler and was married to a Russian woman called Zhivago, whom Olga had known in her school days. Nor was Chekhov the only writer to seek remission in Badenweiler. Only four years before, the young American writer Stephen Crane, author of *The Red Badge of Courage*, had gone to Badenweiler. He had the white disease, and wanted to get better. He was to die there too.

Despite asking around, I've never been able to determine whether it was ever German and Russian medical etiquette (as claimed by Donald Rayfield, Chekhov's most recent biographer) to open a bottle of champagne when a doctor attends a dying colleague, and all hope of remission has fled.

The man who downs a last drink as he dies turns up in Erasmus, who knew, like Rabelais, that 'with the aid of Bacchus, the spirits of human beings are borne aloft, their bodies clearly lightened, and what in them was earthy is rendered lissom' (*Quart Livre*).

At any rate, as Janet Malcolm says, Chekhov's death 'is one of the great set pieces of literary history'.

His hotel room has been getting more and more crowded since the contemporary newspaper report in the Russian daily *Russkie Vedemosti* and Olga's initial written account of 1908. Lev Rabeneck, a Russian student living in the hotel whom she woke with urgent instructions to fetch the doctor on the night of 2 July (the Julian calendar being thirteen days behind the rest of Europe), committed his own eye-witness account to paper even longer after the event: fifty-four years.

Olga remembered the following. Dr Schwöhrer felt Chekhov's pulse and ordered a bottle of the ethereal stuff. Anton sat up in bed and proclaimed, in German, 'Ich sterbe.' He emptied his glass, said, appreciatively, 'I haven't had champagne for a long time', lay down on his left side and died before Olga reached the other side of the bed.

That was how she remembered it in 1908; in her second account, in 1922, the 'dreadful silence' when he stopped breathing was disturbed 'only by a large moth which burst into the room like a whirlwind, beat tormentedly against the burning electric lamps, and flew confusedly around the room'.

Rabeneck's account differs from hers in significant details. But the most influential account of all, Malcolm notes, has actually been Raymond Carver's story *Errand*, which presents itself as fiction but is actually an embellishment of Olga's account. Carver has the methodical Dr Schwöhrer pushing the cork back into the neck of the champagne bottle, a quite impossible feat, at least with champagne corks, as anyone who has tried will know. He also invents a young porter with tousled blond hair, who brings in the silver ice bucket and tray with champagne glasses. And if this admixture of fact and fiction weren't galling enough, later biographers, in spite of their obvious duty towards history as objective record, have accepted the fictionalised account, and embellished Carver.

All very strange, since empirical doubt was second nature to Chekhov, whose view of knowledge as a lesser form of ignorance is close to the inert propositions in David Hume's *Dialogues*. 'It just isn't like that in life,' he exclaimed to the theatre director Stanislavsky as they watched a piece by Ibsen.

Chekhov's great secret as a writer is that he approached life not like a storyteller at all, and had only a limited confidence in the continuity of its larger themes, which was why he never assayed the novel. And why he seems so much our contemporary. Olga, after all, was an actress, a mimic, and she, too, had read her husband's stories: the large noctuid creature she mentions brushing into the room at the fatal moment and beating over the lamps must have been his soul flitting about in one of those offhandedly memorable deathbed scenes he wrote, in which mental images momentarily float free of the retina, like the distant darting reindeer spied by the dying Dr Ragin in *Ward Number Six*.

Only a few days after his death events did contrive, however, to become 'Chekhovian'.

Waiting at the central station in Moscow, the reception committee headed by Maxim Gorky that was to follow the cortège to the Novodevichii cemetery was greatly put out when Chekhov's body, sealed in its own bivalve, arrived in a refrigerated railway wagon marked 'For transportation of fresh oysters'.

Allegories of brine and firmament, tokens of closure and disclosure, nacreous bagnoires and vulgar spittoons, accretions of the sheer will to hang on – Chekhov's travelling companions must have been dredged not from the tidal beds of the North Sea but from primal ramparts on the slopes of the Black Forest. They were his last daydreams of refuge.

Iliad of Abject Europe

AIRWAR, LITERATURE AND COMPASSION

> *And it is different, different — you have understood*
> *Your world at last: you have tasted your own blood.*
> Randall Jarrell

I

A year ago, Germany's 'conscience' and grand old man of letters
Günter Grass published his boldest novel in years. *Crabwalk* tells
the story of the sinking, off what is now the Polish port of Gdynia,
of the Wilhelm Gustloff, a converted Kraft durch Freude
(Strength-through-Joy) cruise ship, by a Soviet torpedo in January
1945. Gustloff was a Nazi propagandist and intelligence officer in
Switzerland who had been shot in 1936 by a Jewish student from
the Balkans: the party promptly made him a martyr to the cause.
The ship launched with his name in 1937 carried workers on
mandatory state-financed holidays to Norway and the
Mediterranean: this was the socialist part of the Nazi programme.
In January 1945, having been transformed into a hospital ship, it
was crammed with refugees, some of them soldiers, fleeing the
advancing Red Army: about 9,000 people, many of them women
and children, lost their lives in the Baltic, making it the worst
maritime disaster ever. The central female character in the book,
Tulla Pokriefke, who survives the shipwreck in a state of advanced
pregnancy, bears the same name as Grass's own mother: her blunt,
canny and obdurate cast of mind, Stalinist leanings and all,
becomes a token of the kind of popular culture which survived
longer in the East than in the more politically correct West. For
Grass's book has a wider remit: it touches not just on the fate of
refugees like those of the Wilhelm Gustloff but on the misery of
the millions of 'Vertriebene' (expellees) driven from their homes

in the east. Hitler's legacy was double: not only the mass murder of the Jews but the destruction of ethnic German life outside of Germany. The end of the war saw the largest refugee flow in European history: in the last two years of the war five million Germans fled the advancing Red Army, and between 1945 and 1948 another seven million were driven out of their ancestral homes in Poland, Czechoslovakia, Romania, Yugoslavia and Hungary.

Grass is the first left-winger to develop what is claimed to be a taboo theme, or one which until recently had been identified with the 'Ewiggestrigen' – reactionaries and revisionists. Nobel laureate status and his various public engagements have made it possible for him to avoid the charge of moral equivocation. What he really seems to be arguing in his novel is the case against repression: deeply felt passions always return in some form or another, and the more stifled the less predictable their return.

Later in the same year the independent historian Jörg Friedrich published his 600-page work *Der Brand* (The Blaze), a detailed and unsparing account of the fate of civilians caught in the Allied bombing. As the economy (and exemplary social democracy) that absorbed so much energy after the war heads for deep depression, Friedrich's book seems to be in touch with a new mood in the country: it has been in the bestseller lists for months, and parts of it were serialised in the right-wing tabloid *Das Bild*. Only a few years ago Anglo-American historians had been accusing the Germans of being Hitler's 'willing executioners'; now for the first time the Germans are being invited to see themselves as victims of history too. In the same year as he was voted man of the century in Britain, Winston Churchill stood accused in Germany of a deliberate policy of airborne terror against civilians, and was even called a war criminal in *Bild*'s editorial pages.

In 1997, well before Friedrich's book, W.G. Sebald gave a series of four lectures in Zürich on the air war in Germany (and allegedly goaded Grass into taking his scuttle-step forwards). Born in the Allgäu in 1944, Sebald came as a lecturer to Manchester in 1966, and eventually ended up as Professor of European Literature at the University of East Anglia. After publishing a number of quite conventional if glum academic monographs in his native language (the title of one is *Describing Unhappiness*) he wrote four books in the 1990s which, in English translation, made him world-famous. *Vertigo*, *The Emigrants*, *The Rings of Saturn* and *Austerlitz* are part-memoir, part-travelogue, part-phantasmagoria, and go under the generic 'novel', it would seem, for want of a term more capacious. In an interview Sebald himself called the last 'a prose book of indefinite form'. His writings reveal that the mildly rebellious freebird rambling of the grandparents' generation (the Wandervogel movement, one of the first celebrations of youth as a social group, marked its centenary in 2001) has yielded to a craving for travel, a kind of fugue even, though Sebald is no Kaspar Hauser: if anything, he is rather more a type of Don Quixote, fated to spread the harm of which he is victim. He is a knight of doleful countenance longing to break out of the charnel-house we call Europe; a tourist to his own past in the manner of Stendhal's *Memoirs*, though rather more solemn: an enigmatographer. Grainy black-and-white photographs without captions garner Sebald's books and provide a kind of gestalt-show that harks back to earlier mixed-genre writers of the 1930s like Jünger and Duhamel. The reader is invited to move through a world of fact which has been removed to the limbo of fictionality – here be meaning, but not *determinate* meaning. Historical and public figures are evoked in a reverie that sounds like that of a man talking mostly to himself. Ironies float in from the edge of the visual field; try to focus on them, and they disappear. So his writings come to resemble the coast of the East Anglia that he knew so well; forever slipping away from exact definition.

While all four of his novels reflect on Europe seen from the outer circle of Hell, one issue overshadows everything else in *On The Natural History of Destruction*, which is a transcript of his Zurich lectures (published in German under the neutral title *Airwar and Literature*) padded out with essays on the German-language writers Alfred Andersch, Jean Améry and Peter Weiss: why has so little been written about the destruction of Germany, in which 131 towns and cities were levelled to the ground, 3.5 million homes destroyed, 600,000 people killed, and the RAF alone dropped one million tons of bombs? Why was there no great literary epic (*Epos*) of the 'total degradation'? Although the novelist Alfred Döblin is mentioned later and only in passing, Sebald is surely reaching back to a passage in the ageing novelist's autobiography *Schicksalsreise* (1968) when he returned to take a look at the country he had fled with his family in 1933: 'I read Jeremiah's lamentation on a city's destruction. The old prophet is grieving only for one city, though a particularly richly populated one that is holy to him. I am reminded of ancient events that still have not been forgotten today, of the volcanic destruction of the Roman cities of Pompeii and Herculaneum, devastation of mythological proportions. If people found this sudden destruction so monstrous that they have passed the story of it along from one generation to the next, then what name will be given to the levelling of the country that was once called Germany?' Well, whatever it would be called, it wouldn't be an epic, for, as Schiller wrote, epics only come in the youth of cultures, in their 'naïve' periods. Sebald's books themselves are chronicles of almost pure interiority.

Döblin goes on to remark: 'occasionally, one of their poets or wordsmiths will undertake to describe this calamity that passes all understanding, and will call upon apocalyptic images to that purposes. It has an artificial, shallow ring to it.' As someone writing in this spirit, Andersch is arraigned by Sebald for being an example of the type of false consciousness he feels afflicted the postwar Germans – 'a nation strikingly blind to history and lacking in tradition'. This figure of apparent integrity was, in reality, a deeply compromised man.

Here is the bitter, Oedipal argument that appears in Grass's book, where it is treated rather more dialectically: he accuses the 1968 generation that used to hold 'days of rage' against its complicit parents of overreacting, and fostering a mood of indifference among *its* children.

2

Born, like a generation of well-known filmmakers (Herzog, Fassbinder, Wenders) towards the end of the war, Sebald grew up in his little village under the Alps with almost no sense of what had happened to his country (although some Germans, such as the former Chancellor Helmut Kohl, were to dub this 'the grace of late birth'). The war was a terrible family secret. The vanquished were failed candidates for domination, and they knew it: their late Führer had led them not just into defeat, but had actually called down destruction. Eight-and-a-half million Germans had been card-carrying members of the Nazi Party. Their support gave a cult of violence twelve years of false transcendence. When the Reichstag went up in flames in 1933 Robert Musil noted in his diary: 'All the liberal fundamental rights have now been set aside without a single person feeling utterly outraged... One might feel most profoundly disappointed over this but it is more correct to draw the conclusion that all the things that have been abolished here are no longer of great concern to people.' In 1945, relieved to have survived the war but spouting Nazi phrases, as Sebald animadverts in his Andersch essay, young Germans proclaimed the moment Zero Hour (*Stunde Null*). Herald of what was to be a post-war trend towards a *gelenkte Sprache*, the term drew a blank over the deeply shameful past (wiping the past clean being a Nazi aspiration itself): 'The destruction... is reflected in works written after 1945 by a self-imposed silence, an absence also typical of other areas of discourse, from family conversations to historical writings.' Sebald wonders which did more to obliterate German history: the bombing of ancient medieval cities or the wilful erasure of memory: 'Even if you asked people directly,' says one of his characters in *The Rings of Saturn*, 'it was as if everything had been erased from their minds.'

German writers did, of course, write about the war. Completed in the unlikely setting of his Californian exile, Thomas Mann's *Doctor Faustus* (1947) compels German history to confront its ignominy in a tone not unlike Döblin's: 'There is no stopping it: surrender on all sides, everyone scattering. Our shattered and devastated cities fall like ripe plums. Darmstadt, Würzburg, Frankfurt have succumbed, Mannheim and Kassel, even Münster, Leipzig – they all obey strangers now… Among the régime's great men, who wallowed in power, riches and injustices, suicide rages, passing its sentence … Whatever lived as German stands now as an abomination and the epitome of evil. What will it be like to belong to a nation whose history bore this gruesome fiasco within it, a nation that has driven itself mad, gone psychologically bankrupt … a nation that cannot show its face?' Events had measured up to the wildest eschatological forecasts in a part of the world that, as Norman Cohn showed in his historical study *The Pursuit of the Millennium* (1957), was never short of visions of cities falling apart like ripe plums (nor in murderous anti-semitic thoughts masquerading as Christian virtue). One novel written directly about the effects of bombing raids, Heinrich Böll's *The Stone Angel*, remained unpublished until 1992. Other writers – Thomas Bernhard, Wolfgang Koeppen and Gert Hofmann – wrote obsessively about the social disruption caused by war, if not about the air war. Yet despite their work, and that of local and amateur war historians, the horrifying chapter, according to Sebald, 'never really crossed the threshold of the national consciousness'. One aspect of the problem is surely hindsight, which, as Grass's narrator says in *Crabwalk*, 'is always 20-20'.

Sebald, it seems, is after the blast of immediacy. Another novel recently translated into English, Gert Ledig's *Payback* (first published in German in 1956 and barely noticed at the time) is unremittingly radical in the way it depicts the horrors of a 70-minute bombing raid on an unspecified city in 1944: it leaves the reader, in the seventy minutes it takes to read it, in a state of lucid stupefaction. In his introduction to this book, Michael Hofmann states that the challenge of war as a subject 'is to get us to *feel* it, sharply and viscerally, nor merely to know it or think it, in a dull or droning way': psychic catastrophe and the dismantling of the everyday call for a kind of mimetic in which authenticity is guaranteed by people becoming sounding boards and broken strings themselves. This is the deadening of the emotions paradoxically required for the exquisitely heightened sensate perception in the Marquis de Sade's novels.

It is surely worth recalling that 'repressed' memories of bombing do return – and as a kind of sardonic exercise in self-justification – in the magnificently deranged trilogy of novels written by Louis-Ferdinand Céline in the 1950s. *D'un château l'autre*, *Rigodon* and *Nord* follow the despised 'collabo' (Céline was notorious in France for the repellent anti-Semitic pamphlets he published during the war) into exile, as he desperately tries to cross devastated Germany in the very last months of the war to reach the safe haven of Denmark. A rain of bombs was the proof positive demanded by Céline's paranoia: he had started off his writing career by portraying the first European war as a catastrophe brought about by a conspiracy of fools, only to envisage the second, when he came to write his trilogy in the 1950s, as an all-encompassing condition in which moral distinctions between opposing sides, not to speak of front line and home front, were quite beside the point. Epic? At the start of *Nord*, his narrator spits it out: 'chacun sa foireuse epopée!'

One of the episodes recreated by Céline in his Iliad of abject Europe (though he recounts it as happening in the last year of the war) was the obliteration of Hamburg. As he gleefully noticed, the violence of a full-scale bombing raid makes a shot to the head seems the act of a decent man; and it appears that those too badly wounded to be 'helped' were indeed summarily dispatched by the Gestapo. The firestorm raid of 27 July 1943, code-named (cynically enough) Operation Gomorrah, in which the RAF dropped 10,000 tons of high explosive and incendiary bombs on the city, can be seen, with the benefit of hindsight, as a dummy run for the nuclear bomb on Hiroshima. 'In bombers named for girls', fresh-faced young men, at some personal risk, destroyed one of the great cities 'learned about at school', wrote Randall Jarrell, one of the few poets to attempt to write about what air war meant. As Sebald writes: 'the fire, now rising 2000 metres into the sky, snatched oxygen to itself so violently that the air currents reached hurricane force, resonating like mighty organs with all their stops pulled out at once'. Fifty thousand people died – more than were killed by German bombing of Britain during the entire war. Panes of glass melted, families asphyxiated in their cellars, and anyone who tried to make a run for it sank into boiling asphalt. Corpses lay 'doubled up in the pool of their own melted fat'. Temperatures at the core of the firm-storms were over 1500 °C, and the intense heat climbed upwards so rapidly as to suck in cold air, and any kind of free-standing structure, including humans, at ground level: an entire district of a city became a howling crematorium furnace. It was RAF policy to concentrate bombing on poorly defended working-class areas in order to minimise casualties in the air and maximise them on the ground, although these areas, especially in Hamburg, were the heart of such anti-Nazi resistance as there was in Germany. (Hitler had refused to visit the city because it was noto-riously less than whole-hearted in its support for the Nazi cause.) More than a million people deserted the city in the weeks after the raid, some of them unhinged by what they had experienced. Sebald describes a woman's cardboard suitcase bursting open in the rush for a train and her carbonised baby falling out along with toys and a manicure case, ghastly relics of a life that had been intact just a few days before.

The destruction of that other city on the Elbe, Dresden, on 13, 14 and 15 February 1945 is perhaps better known because of the wide circulation of Kurt Vonnegut's novel *Slaughterhouse Five* (which goes unmentioned by Sebald). Two armadas of Lancester bombers, followed by a smaller group of American B-17s, dropped 2,690 tonnes of incendiaries and explosives on the city, destroying almost all of the poorly defended inner city: anti-aircraft guns had been sent east for use in the field against the Red Army. After a terrible firestorm, some thirteen square miles of the city lay in rubble; upwards of thirty-five thousand people lost their lives (the number is difficult to establish with certainty since the city was crowded with unregistered refugees and wounded soldiers). The event is described without any pathos at all in the remarkable diaries of Victor Klemperer, which were finely translated a few years ago by Martin Chalmers as *I Shall Bear Witness To the Bitter End*. Klemperer survived the various round-ups of Jews because he was married to an 'Aryan'; his wife Eva remained unswervingly loyal despite, as he notes, being subjected to 'insults, threats, blows and spittle' as well as incitements to divorce him. Gradually stripped of his rights – to teach, to publish (he was a Professor of Romance Literature at Dresden Technical University), to drive, to use the library, to own a pet, and to receive standard rations – he recorded, at great personal risk, how Germany was laid waste. (After the war he was to write another invaluable book, *LTI* or *Lingua Tertii Imperii*, a philological study of how the Nazis corrupted the language, in which he examines such pertinent issues as Goebbels' cult of the cold joke, a way of putting otherwise unmentionable ideas into circulation, or even the glaring fact, entirely overlooked by Sebald, that the Nazis themselves were smitten by the 'epic idea': the Niebelungenlied was used to justify the sacrifice of almost the entire Sixth Army at Stalingrad in 1942.) The day the bombers came Klemperer had been expecting to be rounded up for transfer to Theresienstadt, having had to deliver summons to the last remaining 'mixed-marriage' Jews in Dresden to report for labour duty on 15 February. In the resulting chaos, with SS squads burning thousands of the dead on huge pyres, he ripped the yellow star from his coat (an act punishable with death), and set off with his wife on a dangerous foot journey to Bavaria and, ultimately, liberation. Not only is his diary precious for its unique 'view from below', but for Klemperer's stubborn refusal – and his refusal refutes all simplistic mobilisations of the first person plural, before and after the war – to concede an inch of his pride in the achievements of German civilisation to the Nazi despoiling of it.

But Klemperer's dispassionate witness brings Sebald's question up again. When reality has been so cynically 'up for grabs', can anyone really expect an epic, a literary form which owes more to Apollo than it does to Dionysus?

After the bombs came the cargo cult of CARE parcels, Benny Goodman's swinging horns and Western movies. In 1945, if young Germans dreamed, they dreamed, even harder than their grandfathers before them, of America. Europe's proper epic was back in the Trecento, in Dante's concentric ultramundane city: somewhere in that great meditation on divine *fiat* and human *ingenium* might have been the sign to ward off the evil. But it would have been an ethical discovery, not the cadence of rising 'higher and higher through the circles of his spiralling prose', where Sebald is referring (in *The Rings of Saturn*) to Sir Thomas Browne and not Dante Alighieri, whose poem is perhaps more political than we can conceive or endure. A greater Muse is at work in the Divine Comedy, the same that holds the divine up to accusation in the Book of Job: it brings Dante to portray, in Mandelstam's unannealed words, 'betrayal, a frozen conscience, the ataraxia of shame, absolute zero'. Some of his contemporaries believed Dante bore the scorch-marks of Hell on his skin. They hadn't seen the effects of phosphorus on skin and bone.

Dante, in Erich Auerbach's words, moves '[to integrate] what is characteristically individual and at times horrible, ugly, grotesque, and vulgar with the dignity of God's judgement – a dignity which transcends the ultimate limits of our earthly conceptions of the sublime'. Mandelstam went the way of Orpheus too, though the psychedelic cartography of Hell as a cone with its summit at the centre of the earth and its base at the surface bore no earthly resemblance to the icy white infinity of Stalin's gulag, where Hell had no deep layers. He paid with his life for negating that other twentieth-century tyrant's attempt to monopolise the future. For the epic, it would seem, is intimately attuned to architecture, to the effort of constructing what Mandelstam called a 'verbal space', an abode in the world: industrialisation, having first triumphantly shown man that he is not at home in the world, has become so literal in its power as to annihilate actual edifices, not to speak of people. It is quite impossible to imagine Virgil saying to a contemporary author, as he does at the end of the *Purgatory* – 'Your will is free, erect, and whole.'

The house was utterly in ruins, as Adorno confessed. 'The destruction of European cities and the concentration camps merely continued the processes that the immanent development of technology decided for the houses long ago.'

3

The odd, Baconian title 'natural history of destruction' comes from Solly (later Lord) Zuckerman, whom Sebald interviewed in the 1980s. Anatomist turned weapons adviser, Zuckerman researched the effects of bombs on humans, their dwelling spaces as well as their body tissue, investigating, for instance, how high-velocity bomb fragments caused internal injuries by momentarily expanding body compartments to three times their normal size. Along with Frederick (Friedrich) Lindemann, later Viscount Cherwell, a German aristocrat and scientist who had become a naturalised British subject, Zuckerman was one of Churchill's most trusted advisers. In 1947, the year the poet W.H. Auden visited Darmstadt with other bombing research analysts of the American Strategic Bombing Survey to ask German citizens if they had minded being bombed, Zuckerman visited Cologne (in which there were 31.1 cubic metres of rubble per inhabitant) intending to write an article under that title for Cyril Connolly's *Horizon* magazine. Words adequate to describe what he had seen failed him. So it wasn't just a German phenomenon.

'How ought such a natural history of destruction to begin?' asks Sebald. 'With a summary of the technical, organisational and political prerequisites for carrying out large-scale air raids? With a scientific account of the previously unknown phenomenon of the firestorms? With a pathographical record of typical modes of death, or with behaviourist studies of the instincts of flight and homecoming?' Injuring, damaging, laying waste: these are the obsessive contents of war, but what is *natural* about the history of destruction? It is an adjective that seems to offer a derogatory clause: technology had created opportunities for destruction that were once available only to nature. Was that what Zuckerman was getting at? In those very years, Camus's novel *La Peste* (1947) was criticised as being morally evasive on the same grounds: why talk about the effects of Nazism as if it were a blind force of nature, a microbe loosed on the globe? Unless, of course, moral and natural evils are held to be the manifestations of a more radical evil that is instinct with the human condition. That was why Sartre tartly commented: 'Camus hates God more than he hates the Nazis.' But the point is worth labouring.

Familiar to all doctors, the phrase 'a natural history' suggests a disease process moving to its ineluctable end. But doctors learn about the natural history of diseases so that they can thwart or deflect them. Not so Sebald. 'Our species is unable to learn from its mistakes,' he rejoins, fatalistically, in the last words of his lectures. It remains to state the obvious that, however massive in its effects, policy is still decided upon by agents, even if they don't know much about their victims. Comparing conflicts to natural cataclysms is actually as political as that trivialising old Leninism about having to break eggs if you want to make an omelette. (It was that sense of evil tamed that drove Sade to spend most of his time in prison trying to call up a crime so horrific that nature itself would protest.)

Before contemporary warfare, only an earthquake could annihilate so many lives in such a short time. Voltaire was shocked by the Lisbon earthquake that killed tens of thousands of people in 1755 because his generation had turned God into the supremely rational guardian of a benign wonderland; one of the after-effects of the Lisbon disaster was the beginning of a modern conceptual distinction between natural and moral evils. Evil in the natural realm became meaningless: it was something to be dismayed about, but not something with a deeper meaning. Bad things happen, Rousseau told Voltaire, but then we build tall houses: we should only worry about evils we can *avert*. Rousseau, significantly, took things a step further. He shifted the burden of responsibility for evil from God not to us as individuals, but to our forms of being in society: the large social forces that, in the modern world, resemble the blind fates formerly associated with nature. Instead of theological despair he was offering hope in an attenuated form: sociological hope.

Lisbon therefore marks a conceptual watershed: Europeans had lost faith in the stability of the natural world, but not yet in the idea of justice under human administration. In the First World War, five per cent of deaths were civilian; in 1939–45 the proportion rose to 65 per cent. If anything, Sebald's book fails to present its moral case clearly enough. The bombing of Germany was not an earthquake; it was manifestly intentional. Goebbels promised total war; Heidegger, in his 1940 lectures, made Blitzkrieg 'a metaphysical act'; the Allies were willing to stretch the rules of war to include the mass killing of civilians. In fact, the British had been refining their techniques of aerial bombardment (and gas warfare) throughout the 1920s and 1930s between the Euphrates and the Tigris: Winston Churchill, Secretary of State for War and Air, estimated that reliance on the airforce would cut the numbers of British and Indian troops needed to control rebellious Iraq, then known as Mesopotamia and a creation of Britain's imperial ambitions, to less than a fifth. After the 1920 uprising, his economics were vindicated: military spending in Iraq fell from £23 million that year to less than £4 million in 1926. One of the men who developed bombing as a military strategy in Iraq, indeed invented the very idea of the heavy bomber (by having racks mounted on Vickers Vernon troop planes), was Arthur Harris, then an Air Commodore. 'The Arab and Kurd now know what real bombing means,' he wrote: 'within 45 minutes a full-sized village can be wiped out, and a third of its inhabitants killed or injured by four or five machines which offer them no real target, no opportunity for glory as warriors, no effective means of supply.'

That was shock and awe in the era before it became a tactician's slogan. What had happened to the principles of *jus in bello*? To Disraeli's 'purity of purpose'? To that most carefully cultivated sense of benevolence in high places even Joseph Conrad believed in, at least for a while? Sven Lindqvist's *A History of Bombing* (2000), a book which can be read either as a conventional linear narrative or as a labyrinth with, at its centre, the Atomic Minotaur, offers more insight into the twentieth century's cold psychology of killing at a distance than Sebald's lectures. Wars, it cannot be repeated enough, emerge not from political strength but from weakness. Shakespeare, who makes this point in *Troilus and Cressida*, has Ulysses come out with a famous line when he gives Agamemnon a vision of a world which has lost all sense of degree, and is dominated by mere oppugnancy:

> Force should be right – or, rather, right and wrong,
> Between whose endless jar justice resides,
> Should lose their names, and so should justice too.
> Then everything includes itself in power,
> Power into will, will into appetite;
> And appetite, an universal wolf,
> So doubly seconded with will and power,
> Must make perforce an universal prey,
> And last eat up himself.

4

Loss of degree: that was what Simone Weil seized on in her 1940 essay on the modern idolatry of force, as announced in *The Iliad*, and how it turns men into things: 'a moderate use of force, which alone would enable man to escape being enmeshed in its machinery, would require superhuman virtue, which is as rare as dignity in weakness'. Lindqvist cites the famous protest made against civilian bombing by George Bell, the Bishop of Chichester, in the House of Lords in 1944: 'What we do in war – which, after all, lasts a comparatively short time – affects the whole character of peace, which covers a much longer period.' There went a man of principle: his speech cost him his appointment as Archbishop of Canterbury.

Sebald acknowledges that, for the British in 1940, marginalised and cut off from the Nazi-dominated continent, bombing was 'the only way of intervening in the war at all'. In the first phase of the war, the British bombed by night, but more airmen were killed over Germany than civilians on the ground: the planes lacked the direction-finding equipment and bombing techniques which had made the Luftwaffe so effective at night. When Harris took over at Bomber Command in February 1942, the frontline strength of the bomber fleet was just 378 aircraft, of which only 68 were four-engined heavy bombers. Churchill and the Chiefs of Staff had already agreed on the new strategy of 'area targets' (i.e. bombing cities) in a directive of July 1941, and the directive was updated the week before Harris took over. The British had decided to do what, in the Blitz, had proved to be a gross miscalculation: seek to destroy the morale of the population. In spite of the loss of 40,000 lives, British resolve had actually been toughened by the Blitz. It was to be the same with the bombing offensives on Berlin, which were called off by Harris in March 1944 after the loss of 500 bombers: there would be no 'knock-out' blow from the air. But the grim advance of the bombing campaign was effective in pinning down the German airforce. In 1942, the Luftwaffe was able to send a fleet of a thousand bombers to 'soften up' Stalingrad; a year later 1,700 fighters had to be reserved to defend the airspace over Germany, leaving only 750 planes active on all its fighting fronts. After August 1944, however, with the Allies enjoying complete sovereignty of the air and delivering far more accurate attacks, the case for area bombing looks much shakier. Bomber Command was riding a period of what ethicists call 'military drift', which is a fancy term for things getting out of political control. (Even then, it is still something other than a natural history.) Harris conducted a *folie à deux* with the War Ministry in which the latter would not admit *in public* that the former was doing what it had instructed him to do behind closed doors: calculate, in the best utilitarian manner, how many people could be killed per bomb load. Churchill reacted to the devastated cities only after the bombing of Dresden (though Pforzheim and Wurzburg were, proportionately, dealt with even more harshly), sending a memo to his Chief of Staff that questioned the entire conduct of Allied bombing. Harris was furious, and protested that 'the feeling, such as there is over Dresden, could be explained by a psychiatrist. It is connected with German bands and shepherdesses'.

Though the new high-velocity V2 rockets (true rockets unlike the low-octane V1s, or 'doodle-bugs') were falling erratically on east London, there seems something vindictive about British policy in 1944–5: it is as if the realisation had sunk in that although the war was nearly won, it had cost the old lion all its teeth. So it showed its claws: the Soviets weren't that far from Dresden in the spring of 1945. Several years before, at the end of the war that started it all, Max Weber had suggested in his famous 1918 speech at Munich University, *Politik als Beruf*, that professional politicians (as opposed to the occasional ones we all are), who 'let themselves in for the diabolic forces lurking in all violence', ought to weigh their intentions against the consequences, foreseen and unforeseen, of what they set in motion, and not simply find their own motives beyond reproach because of the perceived 'ill-will' of their enemy.

It is greatly to the credit of many prominent Germans in the postwar period – and the most obvious example is the former chancellor Willy Brandt, who had actually fought Hitler's army out of Norway (and was not forgiven for having done so in some quarters) but assumed full responsibility for the war – that they were more concerned about what they had done to others than what others had done to them. Brandt was to sign treaties with Poland, Czechoslovakia and the USSR that formally settled the issue of the millions of expellees. While the Russians in 1945 stripped their share of Germany of all movables, the Marshall Plan (in opposition to the scheme devised by Henry Morgenthau, Roosevelt's Secretary of the Treasury, to depopulate what was left of Germany and turn it into a pastoral theme park) encouraged economic recovery as a way of preventing militarism. It was an act of good faith where it had been in short supply, though the generous terms of *pax americana* were not unrelated to the beginnings of the Cold War and the need to keep their own economy turning.

Many Germans even felt, after the event at any rate, that the rain of bombs was a form of retribution. *Wer Wind sät, wird Sturm ernten*, as the proverb says – sow the wind and reap the whirlwind. (Harris used this proverb, too, in a speech he gave in 1942.) That knowledge didn't dent the work-ethic. Döblin wrote: 'the destruction doesn't seem to depress them, it seems to intensify their work incentive'. It was easier to rebuild cities than wonder why they weren't there any more. The other knowledge took a lot longer to sink in. Although the historian Jan-Philipp Reemtsma recently claimed that the Germans became 'civilised' when they understood the true nature of the Nazi régime, the industrialised extermination of the Jews becoming more frenzied even as the country went up in flames, it has to be remembered that Auschwitz became a conceptual abomination only twenty years after war's end. Compassion itself is the product of history. It obliges us to know even as we feel. Even the worst atrocity has historical links with a wider reality. Sebald seems to be stricken instead by glimpses of the eschatological absolute: it is like looking down on one of those tormented and weirdly lit synoptic landscapes by the sixteenth-century master Albrecht Altdorfer that haunt his other works. Not only that: he is an unobliging historian, being thin on context and causes. And for once his sensitivity to language seems less than perfect. A number of the terms he adopts – 'Nationalerniedrigung' (national humiliation) or 'Vernichtungskrieg' (war of annihilation) – give pause for thought. Friedrich, in his substantially more forensic study, is downright reckless: he enlists Nazi jargon to describe the effects of Allied actions: choking bomb shelters become 'Krematorien' and Bomber Squadron 5 is an 'Einsatzgruppe', an SS term for the hunt-and-destroy commando units that killed so many civilians in the east. If Germany can be described as an 'extermination space' we are clearly being invited to consider that what the Allies did over Germany paralleled the Nazi dehumanisation of the Jews. Moral equivocation has a longer history than we might think: two days after the bombing of Dresden, Goebbels was the first person to speak of it as a 'war crime'.

Wary, above all in his novels, of the traps and pitfalls of this kind of outrage, in which left-wing moralising joins forces with right-wing grudges, Sebald's lectures on the air war seek to fit calamity into a larger logic. A kind of *ressentiment*, it would seem, in which the passage of time adds hitherto unsuspected details and provocations to the list of humiliations. The task of explanation in making sense of suffering is a fraught and dangerous one, as Sebald would have known from his reading of Jean Améry, who flatly contradicted Nietzsche's command that we should assent to reality just as we find it, carnage and all. 'Have you ever said Yes to a single joy? O my friends, then you said Yes to *all* woe. All things are entangled, ensnared, enamoured...' The violent realities of the twentieth century, as Améry experienced them, make Nietzsche's epic philosophy of the eternal recurrence of the Same look like a ghastly failure of the imagination. By the same token, those very historical realities demolish the grandiose claims Hegel made for the expectation that history might provide its own redemption: it takes a particular tactlessness (common enough among intellectuals perhaps) to still believe in the unfolding of reason through history when all its subtle corridors reek of the slaughterhouse. Now, as the last wisps of Romantic sublime slowly burn from the Channel, neighbour-nations have taken to bombarding each other with their griefs, and the shelf of human misery is sliding away from the mainland, much like the coast of

The Good European

Nietzsche's Counterculture

It cost him to travel: one day in the train and three to recuperate. He never visited Paris or London or Brussels, never went west to Madrid or Lisbon. He endorsed Herder's claim that German was Greek, but made no effort to cross the Balkans to the land that gave form not only to civic liberties but to the potent derivative concept of unenslaved inner freedom: the closest he came to Greece was the temple of Paestum, south-east of Sorrento, which he saw in the spring of 1877, or among the ruins of Sicily. He never visited Mozart's Prague, which was only a day's journey from Dresden: it was too far east. Nor did he pay much attention to that other German culture which had its capital in Vienna. What moved him was an instinct for the issues of glaciers and mountains, and stark shadowless sunlight. Lucid effort had to go into the election of a place: 'I can't allow myself to commit an error with regards to the weather. Do you know that the error of last winter (Santa Margherita and its dampness) very nearly cost me my life?' The wanderer above the clouds was forever on the lookout for a place where he could rediscover Goethe's great secret of living at peace with the world. There he might find the one place he could write, or take out his notebook and walk, as he did between Santa Margherita and Portofino where 'the bay of Genoa sings the last notes of its melody'.

No great traveller, our Herr Quidam was no adventurer either: while he was turning the pages of *Revue des Deux Mondes*, Rimbaud was running guns in Harar. Nietzsche was incapable of 'adding up' his dangers, as one of his later admirers, André Malraux, did;

but then Malraux managed to end his days as a cabinet minister and museum director. In the age of Pierre Loti and the great 'exotes', the first Thomas Cook excursions and the first travel magazines, Nietzsche followed a different schedule, attracted by the pagan springs of 'the old diluvian Europe' and his whim of setting up house in Tunis, Corsica or Spain. The axis of his world was the bar of the Alps: on one side the matriarchal North, from Naumburg down to Basle, the fogged Wagnerian landscape he grew to loathe; on the other the Ligurian and Piedmontese coast of Italy and France: Genoa, Turin and Nice, which he visited every year from 1883 until 1888. Zarathustra 'stole up on [him]' on the bay that stretches all the way from Santa Margherita to the promontory of Porto Fino, convincing him in a cold and damp *albergo*, with the high tide surging below his window and keeping him from sleep, 'that everything decisive comes about "in spite of"'. Out of gratitude, he hoped to bestow immortality on the village of Sils Maria ('perpetual heroic idyll': 8 July 1881): it should perhaps be considered as the furthermost salient of the Germanic world on the Latin, an Alpine balcony perched over the Mediterranean. This was where 'all fifty prerequisites for [his] meagre life' were united, where the idea of eternal recurrence was born one day in the woods beside the lake of Silvaplana '6,000 feet above the sea and higher still above all human things' (3 September 1883). Two tracks in his life met there: the trail above Rapallo and the forest road through the Engadine.

For all his poor arithmetic, Nietzsche was heroic in his isolation, and he knew it. The note of scorn in his writing is unmistakable: scorn for others who lacked, in his eyes, the courage to live their separateness. That was his self-mastery, which is to say morality. Being isolated meant getting to observe the doings of the domesticated. It gave him the urge to rush into the temple and overturn the money-changers' tables, which he did, though the columns of the temple ultimately fell in on Europe. Lyrical philosophy made for a poor anthropology. He even anointed himself with the ointment of great value when he claimed, in one fourth part of *Zarathustra*, and the Midi hymned the solar perfection of the world. In Venice a few weeks later, the weather proved to be magnificently clear and fresh, though everything pained him. He was enduring one of his recurrent migraines. He had gravitated to the edge of society, and some of his followers would have to go there to find him, too. New concepts of energy and power were beginning to gush into language; the buried solar energy of fossil fuels were already stoking the furnaces of industry in Nietzsche's lifetime. Nineteenth-century Europeans were reorienting themselves to the sun at the centre of culture, the source that cannot be gazed at. Years later, in the 1950s, Albert Camus decided, rather self-consciously, to redeploy Nietzsche's 'solar thought' when he insisted that a 'German ideology' had been allowed to triumph over the 'Mediterranean spirit' of those countries where the 'intelligence is the sister of the harsh light of the sun'. Nietzsche had said it before him: 'God, with the cynicism that is peculiar to him, lets his sun shine down particularly upon *us* more beautifully than upon the so much more reputable Europe of Herr von Bismarck.'

Nietzsche's debt to other writers was the familiar baggage of any central European thinker of his time: Pascal, Montaigne, Lichtenberg, Schopenhauer. He is seldom compared to thinkers and artists who might dent the myth of his originality, though much in his writing was anticipated by Mandeville, Spinoza, Rousseau (a comparison he always resisted), Hegel, Tocqueville, Heine, and above all Celsus, the second-century despiser of Christians. Nietzsche's calumny of Christianity is actually a kind of back-handed admiration, for he knows what Celsus did not: that the vulgar Christian habit of turning the cheek, of renouncing any kind of violence at all, had overcome not only the Roman Empire but the god of philosophy too. In following Celsus, Nietzsche fails to follow his own advice: 'The world-historical stupidity of all persecutors has lain precisely in their giving their opponents the appearance of honourableness – in bestowing upon them the fascination of martyrdom.' It is practically a confession. As for his famous notion of the Eternal Return, it is a classical idea. It was banished by Augustine: the incarnation could happen only once. His attitude to ethics goes as far back as Plato's Callicles, who considered the laws as a stratagem of the weak to dupe the strong. Shakespeare's Richard III comes out with it, too: 'Conscience is but a word cowards use,/ Devised at first to keep the strong in awe.' Dostoevsky made him want to learn Russian, but he never did; his English and Italian were poor, though he spent many of his most productive periods in Italy; only his French was halfway decent. His German, of course, was surefooted and nimble; and he surely never forgot the lesson he once inscribed in one of his notebooks – that the only real stylists were the Greeks and the French, who, regarding all other languages as cacophonous, made it a matter of pride not to learn them. Hardly enough, then, to be a good European today; though what Nietzsche had in mind with the term was something different.

The term 'good European' turns up again and again in his writings of the 1880s. It meant the liberty not to have to be German (didn't he insist in his last lucid piece of writing that he was 'a pure-blooded Polish nobleman, in whom there is no drop of bad blood, least of all German'?), but to allude freely to sources in Greek and Roman, French and Italian history. On the other hand, wanting to be what we are not, permanently convinced that 'life is elsewhere': what else are these but resentments? For the philosopher who, earlier in his career, had hoped for a New Greece born in Germany and seen it disperse in the cannon and cavalry of the New Prussia, it meant – ultimately – preferring the lightweight Bizet to that old thunderer, Wagner. 'What did I never forgive Wagner?... that he became *reichsdeutsch*.' The good European may well be an attenuation of the phrase that Jacob Burckhardt came up with during his professorship at Basle: *uomo universale*. It represented a cultural ideal; by 1860, when Burckhardt published his famous study on the culture of the Renaissance, the figure of the complete man was beyond recuperation. That union of experience and thought in one person was no longer an aspiration, it was a nostalgia.

The great prose stylist of modern German complains that for the Germans writing is wasted effort. Germany's gift to the world was music, 'the voice of the soul of Europe'. Indeed, Nietzsche actually composed some pieces which sound rather like Schumann. Without music, he wrote, life would be 'an error, an exhausting toil, an exile'. Zarathustra ought to be filed away with the symphonies, he wrote to his friend Peter Gast on 2 April 1883. 'As an old musician (which is what I really am) I have an ear for quarter tones,' he wrote to Georg Brandes, the Danish critic of Jewish origin, 'a good European and cultural missionary,' and the first academic to give serious consideration to Nietzsche's philosophy.

Germany had been the original Kulturnation, free from the scramble for colonies. Yet between 1848 and 1871, it went from being an agrarian economy to industrial might. Not having an empire, it was a German politician who came up with the idea of the welfare state; as a substitute for empire. The true concern of empire was always domestic. Empire absorbed misfits and malingerers; above all, it absorbed the resentment engendered by the passage from traditional to market society. Universal suffrage was the political expression of the markets expanding to include the colonising nations' entire workforce as consumers. Bismarck compelled Germany to ditch her old virtues, and enter the era of power politics. Only the state could provide a unified education in a part of Europe where culture had historically been seen as a realm distinct from, and superior to, the politics of social organisation. But where would Germany find the colonial slaves to maintain its programme of liberal expansionism? In Conrad's *The Heart of Darkness*, published as Nietzsche lay benighted in a bathchair in his sister's villa in Weimar, Marlow, slowly moving upriver to the source of the Congo in search of the symbolic figure of Kurtz ('All Europe contributed to the making of Kurtz'), is a civilised man learning the coils of his own 'internal savagery'.

For the Congo read the Rhine. Nietzsche himself had seen the effects of modern war on the front at Ars-sur-Moselle, near Metz.

In 1888, Nietzsche himself seems to have felt that his phrase 'the will to power', instead of being challenging his age, might actually be rather congenial to those it was meant to unseat. Walter Kaufmann at times describes it as an 'instinct for freedom', which makes it sound more acceptably a manifestation of Eros, an over-spilling of confidence, the kind of creative urge that, Nietzsche insists, is fulfilled only through self-discipline. But the confusion had been seeded. His antinomianism puts him very much at risk of being seen as a secret power-worshipper of the type so common in the 1930s that George Orwell talked about power being 'the new religion of Europe'. Now liberals fall over themselves to denounce all such 'wills' in the name of the wounded egalitarianism for which Nietzsche had such an implacable loathing: 'Eurocentrism' is one of them, though 'Europe' was only to emerge as a concept once the era of the great nation-states had ended. Power is the external counterpart to the internal happiness of virtue: the happy self is master of its circumstances. It festers in daily life as boredom, and releases itself in the great explosions called wars. (And by the time we get to Michel Foucault, it becomes clear that power in the social domain is the metaphorical equivalent of energy in the physical.)

Even here, though, Nietzsche is hardly original: the proud, magnanimous man who, in his grandeur, refuses to seek help because the taking of it would show him to be dependent on others was described millennia ago by Aristotle: this is the *megalopsychos*, the great-souled man who, with his 'slow movements, deep voice and calm speech' is something of an embarrassment to most virtue ethicists. Everyone seeks recognition, as the untold followers of Hegel insist; not so, rebuts Nietzsche, for what can be more servile and shallow than the person whose sense of self requires him to seek its worth in the eyes of others. 'Every valley shall be exalted, and every mountain and hill shall be laid low' was the Old Testament promise of ultimate levelling that was to be realised by the New: Nietzsche wanted to stand indomitably alone. David Hume had also attempted to 'redeem' pride, but made no secret of the fact that having dissolved all causal bonds solely by sceptical introspection he needed to play a round of backgammon with friends in order to restore him to equilibrium. Nietzsche, on the other hand, felt obliged to repudiate all qualities that implied mutuality: the most perfect enemy was the friend. Nietzsche's ethics are not at all concerned with what men do; it is what they *are* that counts: in a word, their character. He maintained an uncompromising individualism, admiring France for its tradition of philosophical egoism, though he was anything but that ruthless individual himself. Nietzsche extolled the victor, whose mercy comes from magnanimity and superabundance; in truth, the hapless Fritz was caught in a threeway emotional tangle with his mother Franziska ('meine alte Mutter') and above all his sister Elisabeth: her very person embodied the pietistic Naumburg inheritance that made him call himself 'the virtuoso of self-overcoming'. It is a vainglorious term for a monk who, dutifully throughout the 1880s, sent his emotions home for darning. Packages of biscuits, ham and sausages would come by return of post.

Truth was, Germany had already produced one good European, and that was Goethe, who 'did not cut himself off from life but put himself in the midst of it; he was not fainthearted but took as much as possible upon himself, over himself, within himself. What he wanted was *totality*; he fought the mutual extraneousness of reason, senses, feeling, and will (preached with the most abhorrent scholasticism by Kant, the antipode of Goethe); he disciplined himself into wholeness, he *created* himself' (*Twilight of the Idols*). This fabulous creature, a person of convinced realism, strongest instincts, self-overcoming, emancipation and tolerance – 'not out of weakness, but out of strength' – is clearly Nietzsche's own *Übermensch*. Indeed, the term itself comes from Goethe, when an earth-spirit conjured up by Faust rebukes him with it. Nietzsche considered the conversations with Eckermann to be the best German book ever. Goethe, as Nietzsche wrote in a brilliant phrase in a note on the older writer, was a 'stylised human being': an impetuous hotblood who as he aged into severe dignity cultivated a kind of steadfastness, the very opposite of the impetuousness of his earlier Romantic self.

It may well be the case that the modern era has only ever been fully inhabited by one or two supremely talented figures living at its very outset: Wilhelm and Alexander von Humboldt, explorers, anthropologists and linguists are perhaps the last modern men, certainly the last men to experience Europe as an informal republic of letters: the latter saw language not as an end-product but as a vital activity, not *ergon* but *energeia*, 'streaming outward from the heart's depths'. Our latter-day position is much closer to the frank remark made by Kafka, who allows himself a sigh of admiration, in his 1912 diary, at Goethe's physique. What he saw was probably the famous silhouette done by Lavater when he descended on the house at Weimar and subjected everyone he could lay his hands on to his truth-revealing pantograph. 'Simultaneous impression of repugnance when looking at this perfect human body,' Kafka writes, 'since to surpass this degree of perfection is unimaginable and yet it looks only as though it had been put together by accident. The erect posture, the dangling arms, the slender throat, the crook of the knees.'

We are all men of *ressentiment*, in other words, and Nietzsche's superman is the supreme disguise for Nietzsche's own sense of inadequacy. A superman could not even begin to think of himself in such terms: he would live in the conviction that his kingdom was not of this world. Nietzsche knew that too: that is why his explicitly pagan programmatic god cannot banish that 'innocent from the country' Jesus of Nazareth. Christianity remains the source of the deepest ethical insights of our society, including Nietzsche's own. As he himself wrote, 'if anything is unevangelical it is the concept of the hero'. Few of Nietzsche's followers have ever grasped what Nietzsche understood, for all his blindness to the material basis of his own experience: rejecting a world in which everything is transformed by exchange demands, in all logic, the refusal of the exchange-value generated by that act of rejection.

His writing was, finally, the only activity to which he attached absolute value; he would have agreed with Henry James that 'it takes a great deal of history to produce a little literature'. It was actually another American, Emerson, who had, in his essay 'The Over-Soul', given him the outline of the Overman; Emerson elsewhere defines the quality that attracted Nietzsche to the culture of the Mediterranean: 'No man ever states his griefs as lightly as he might.' Nietzsche never left Europe, yet the sea was his favourite metaphor: 'And where then would we go? Would we cross the sea? Where does this mighty longing draw us, this longing that is worth more to us than any pleasures? Why just in this direction, there where all the suns in human history have gone down too? Will it perhaps be said of us one day that we too, steering westwards, hoped to reach India – but that is was our fate to be wrecked against infinity?'

Nietzsche was more of a frontiersman than anyone has hitherto dared to suppose, more closely kin to the great American essayist he so admired. If the kingdom of God was anywhere it was at hand, in the hearts of men. Not only his antinomianism, but his suspicion of the state, are American instincts. Emerson had written: 'Society everywhere is in conspiracy against the manhood of every one of its members.' While the modern state for Hegel was the supreme manifestation of spirit, Nietzsche thought it merely a more complicated expression of the herd-instinct, an extension of man's animal nature: the only spirit that counted for Nietzsche was absolute, and its dividing line ran *through* the human species. Great men could write to each other across political borders, just as much as they could call out to each other down the ages. Walter Benjamin suggested that Goethe, for all that he foresaw the industrialisation of Europe in the second part of *Faust*, was unable 'to conceive of the state as a factor in history'; the comment applies with equal force to Nietzsche. As far as he was concerned the state was conformist; it was the arch-enemy of the individual's refashioning of his own nature. 'Nothing is at last sacred but the integrity of your own mind' (Emerson). But the all-out attempt to be honest about oneself is intimately related to a complete lack of interest in correctly representing others. What that genial pagan Whitman, who borrowed his word *cosmos* from Alexander von Humboldt, loved in American men and women was the resurgence of what Nietzsche once called the health of the race. But if we are looking for the American in Nietzsche, what of that odd, compelling figure Ambrose Bierce, who, in his late years, abandoned writing and went to seek 'the good, kind darkness' down in the Rio Grande? There was a civil war on in Mexico; and the Old Gringo vanished out of history. It was the end of a chapter in the annals of escapism: Americans wanted to escape from Europe, and here was Bierce trying to escape from history altogether.

Nietzsche once told Peter Gast that the landscape of Sils Maria wasn't Swiss, 'but something quite different, at least much more southern – I would have to go the high plateaux of Mexico overlooking the Pacific to find anything similar (for example, Oaxaca)'; and a couple of years later reminded the same friend that he hoped somebody would rescue him from what had been the worst winter in his life. He turns it into an escalating crisis: 'I regard myself as the victim of a disturbance in *nature*. The old Europe of the Great Flood will kill me yet; but perhaps somebody will come to my aid and drag me off to the plateaux of Mexico.' He wanted to go a ruined civilisation and rediscover, like an anthropologist from the future, its lapidary art of keeping the sun alive. To sit in a café in the airy *zócalo* of Oaxaca proselytising for the good life, waiving judgement, extolling cloudless skies and devising nutritious recipes; and perhaps even watching Europe's stately *danse macabre* (the one on Basle Cathedral) tear through the streets of Oaxaca on All Saints Day as a furious zapateado. Nietzsche knew that the outpouring of energy he extolled comes not from anything an individual good European might desire but from ritual cruelty. Going to Mexico was actually a fantasy of mortification.

A Lance for Hire

Four Hundred Years of Don Quixote

Miguel de Unamuno called it 'the Spanish Bible'; *Don Quixote* may not be holy writ, but like all great literature it describes us. Cervantes steps out of Spain when its golden age had waned so rapidly as to seem 'no more than an illusion' and tarries in ours. We, on the other hand, remain within its thousand pages and are unable to lift ourselves out of its rather plot-poor scenery to the vanishing point that would bring it wholly within our historical purview.

I mention the vanishing point advertantly, because Cervantes lived at a juncture in European history that had already witnessed not only the Iberian discovery of the globe in the search for precious metals and spices and the invention of the printing press in the Rhine Valley, but a ground-breaking shift in trade practices that would eventually to lead to the superseding of feudal Europe itself. The discovery of perspective in Florentine art and architecture accompanied the import of that dangerous cipher zero out of the east. Zero has no referent in nature; it exists only in the mind. But if God's creation was a plentitude, here was a culturally productive sign advertising its emptiness: zero's coming to Europe seemed a scandal, a revelation of such negative force that it was resisted for years by the Church. The Renaissance was therefore built on the liberating but perplexing discovery that the origin is the *product* of what it originates, a notion which explodes all crudely naturalistic links between systems of representation and the reality they purportedly represent. From this moment on, civilisation becomes more and more guided by desire. For if feudal Europe was essentially a barter system, money was to become the source of value in the world of activity and knowledge that came in its train: first precious metals, which only gradually gave way to paper, itself to be displaced on 15 August 1971, when President Nixon quietly annulled the gold standard, by virtual or xenomoney. Capital, in contradistinction to the institutional memory of the Church, is the power of forgetting. The realisation that goods could be made fungible on the promise of their future redemption by specie shocked Europe into a new kind of reflexive consciousness: it still finds its theatricality rather perplexing at times, and it has never entirely regained confidence in either the solidity of the objective world or the good faith of its social arrangements. Let it be said that self-reflexivity in literature is not a twentieth-century discovery.

Shakespeare and Cervantes died on the same day in 1616; *Don Quixote: Part One* appeared under the imprint of Juan de la Cuesta in Madrid in 1605, the year in which *King Lear* received its first performance in London. Lear offers the paradoxical spectacle of a vain and capricious feudal king who tries to do a deal on his kingship, to transact its subtle distinctions in the arithmetic that cannot represent them. Numbers, he discovers to his chagrin, are a tyranny worse by far. It is Gloucester who gets his eyes plucked out in Shakespeare's play, but Lear is blind too, blind to the workings of language. He reads things awry. Similarly, Don Quixote de la Mancha, our hidalgo nearing fifty, with his rusty armour, bookish education, guilelessness and pride, 'who took to reading books of chivalry with such relish and enthusiasm that he almost forgot about running his property' and decides 'for his honour and the common good' to become a knight errant. Burgesses don't risk their lives, they *invest* in them: the limited risk company was later invented precisely to stop poor investments destroying the living substance. The knight errant, on the other hand, sets out for glory by doing great deeds and by triumphing over whatever trials and tribulations lie in his way. Prudential thinking hardly comes into it. The innkeeper who humours him at the time of his first departure and arranges for Quixote to be knighted asks him if he has any money to pay for his board and lodging: 'Don Quixote replied that he didn't have as much a single penny, for he'd never read in the histories of the knights errant of anyone who had.'

Don Quixote sees the world minus its most important element. It is Sancho who gets to carry the purse. Sancho Panzo is the guarantor of Quixotism.

In setting out into the world on his nag Rocinante, in believing that the world of the Romances is real, Quixote actually surrenders his prerogative as an individual: self-determination. He *mirrors* the exploits of Amadis of Gaul. This is the paradoxical core of the novel: Cervantes asks us to acknowledge that imitation is the force behind cultural integration as well as the craving that threatens to engulf it. Two aldermen run over the mountains, braying, in search of a missing donkey: their mimicry is so convincing that one keeps rushing up to the other, convinced he has found the lost animal. (It has been devoured by wolves.) Quixote can hardly be faulted for his devotion: even when the famous episode with the windmills gives way to the comedy of the barber's basin doubling as Mambrino's helmet or the savage demolition of Master Peter's puppet-show, he perseveres. He perseveres through 124 outrageous chapters, and not once in his long persecution does he receive a word of commiseration or compassion from his author. This may be the origin of Flaubert's famous saying that a writer should be in his work like God in the creation: neither seen nor heard. G.K. Chesterton called Quixote 'the greatest caricature in all of literature', and meant the word caricature, more commonly used to describe the shape of a personality flattened out, as an accolade to Cervantes' ability to portray the truly essential features of his hero's nature. Don Quixote is a decent, warm and intelligent man, except when he hears the call of chivalry. An instinctive conservative, we might say, quite happy to accept things the way they are except when they stand in the way of his ambition. The truly exalted thing about him is his will, the will to be a man of distinction; and it has to keep him going through some pretty savage humiliations and rough adventures. Lucidity keeps breaking in on the dusty roads of Castille; it breaks in the crushingly belated disillusionment of his deathbed when the Don repudiates the vanity of his wish to be a hero. In Chapter LXXIV, the last episode of Part II, he dies. Sanity has been hard-won. But along the way desire has become contagious: Don Quixote's simple manservant Sancho Panza ('Paunch') is no longer at the bidding of his unreflecting peasant appetite for food or wine: he wishes to see himself governor of the island his master had promised him, though when he is tricked by two aristocrats in Book Two into thinking he is 'Governor of the Isle of Barataria', he good-naturedly renounces the title, convinced he just wouldn't be up to the job. Cervantes seems to be showing us that this strange human quality we call desire, as distinguished from animal appetite, is always aroused by another person's; it is never unprompted. And when his master dies as Alonso Quixano the Good – 'and one of the signs that led them to conclude that he really was dying was the ease with which he had turned from a madman into a sane man' – it is the village squire who promises to continue the adventure and discover the peerless lady Dulcinea (whom we never meet) 'behind some bush or other'.

The inheritor of the faith is Sancho Panza. Not the rational faith of Christianity, but the emulative faith inspired by the reading of 'profane histories'.

A new kind of humour, it would seem, enters literature with Cervantes and the invention of the novel. Not belly-laughter, or the mockery or satire of Shakespeare, but a gravely serious species of the comic that renders ambiguous what it touches: everything in this paper world has been brushed by the ambiguity of signs. Humour sweetens the relationship between the knight with his anachronistic fantasies and the plebeian realism of his increasingly resourceful servant. For Shakespeare, self is the man: most of the friendships in his plays are treacherous or deceitful, at best sardonic – just look at Falstaff and Master Slender. The description of friendship in Cervantes' novel has few parallels in literary history. If Prospero and Caliban offer a dramatisation of the mind-body split, in a relationship that rapidly degenerates, Don Quixote and Sancho Panza, contrariwise, find each other's company a perpetual source of diversion and solace. More than any other work, Cervantes' merits being called a 'recreation'. For if the whole novel is about the most Christian madness of Don Quixote preparing to forsake the world, then he most certainly needs a neighbour to love as himself, whoever *he* might be.

Books and the printed word are everywhere in *Don Quixote*. In the second part of the book Cervantes shows us his hero bumping into people who've read the first part. In Chapter VI, the point at which Cervantes realised he himself has entered the world of Don Quixote rather being the author of the short moral fable he had intended to write, some of the characters are allowed to discuss *Galatea*, one of his own pastoral romances and just the kind of thing Cervantes mocks his hero for liking. By Chapter VIII (the encounter with the windmills), all the stock situations have been exhausted. Eight hundred pages later, Sidi Hamet, the Moorish chronicler whose account Cervantes is supposedly paraphrasing, is still lamenting the 'unendurable toil of confining himself to such a dry, cribbed story'. In the famous game of tennis recounted to Don Quixote by the duchess's maid Altisidora, and the chapter which Vladimir Nabokov thought the pinnacle of Cervantes' art, the devils are returning not balls but books, and as they do so they grumble and curse — with every volley the number of books increases. On his deathbed, Don Quixote instructs his auditors to ask the author of *Second Part of the Exploits of Don Quixote*, should they ever make his acquaintance, to forgive him (the fictional creation) for having provided the motive (to the author) for 'writing all the gross absurdities contained in that book'. We read a novel to discover that reading novels can drive us crazy, just as happens to Arabella, in Charlotte Lennox's *The Female Quixote* (1752), a novel written in the manner of Fielding, who was as much a fervent admirer of Quixote as those other great initiators of the English novel, Steele, Addison, Smollett, Sterne and Swift.

Flaubert read bits of Cervantes' novel every Sunday and despaired of ever being able to match it. Yet Cervantes insists that the world of print is a delirium and that literature and life are coextensive: literature imitates life (who could deny it?) but life imitates literature, too. The protagonists of *Quixote* are also its readers: that must be why Cervantes craves our indulgence 'not for what he has written but what he has left unwritten'. Hamlet's play within a play offers analogous paradoxes of self-inclusion. In 1614, an unknown writer in Tarragona called Alonso Fernández de Avellaneda (he has never been identified) published a 'false' *Don Quixote* in response to Cervantes' flippant invitation at the end of Book One for someone else to continue the story; Cervantes vents his anger at being so poorly imitated – as if all he had written had been a piece of buffoonery – in the Prologue to the Reader (which was the last section of Book Two to be written) but slyly works the appearance of the impostor Quixote into the closing chapters of his own book, which was published the following year. As Jorge Luis Borges suggests, Cervantes was reaching towards a further vertiginous possibility: that the characters of a fictional work are the true readers, while we its putative readers are fictitious.

Who would ever expect the steadfast Dr Johnson to offer a self-diagnosis in terms made explicit by Don Quixote? Yet we have it in the letter written by Dr Thomas Percy to Boswell when the latter was gathering material for *The Life of Samuel Johnson*, informing him that when Johnson was a boy, 'he was immoderately fond of reading romances of chivalry, and he retained his fondness for them through life... Yet I have heard him attribute to these extravagant fictions that unsettled turn of mind which prevented him ever fixing in any profession.'

Hegel even managed to propel Don Quixote into the bourgeois era when he writes in his *Lectures on Aesthetics* that the novel is chivalry become serious again: 'the contingency of outside life has been transformed into the secure order of civil society and the state, so that the forces of law and order, courts and political government replace the chimerical ends which the knights errant set before themselves'. Indeed, *Don Quixote* is a kind of advance guard for those newfangled forms of ethical selfhood in the century that fought to establish the rights of the individual even though it had abandoned the unique person so familiar to (and so taken for granted by) the schemers of the eighteenth century. Cervantes, who lost his left hand – 'for the greater glory of the right' – at the battle of Lepanto, in which the two hundred and fifty vessels of a combined Christian fleet under Don Juan of Austria defeated the somewhat larger Ottoman navy in 1571, and only a few years later was captured and imprisoned by Barbary pirates, knew that the idea of the hero as lone fighter was as outdated as feudalism itself: wars would increasingly be decided by drilled formations and mass deployments, as they had been in Roman times. The soldiers of the future would be anonymous but rigorously trained Sancho Panzas: after all, a foot soldier could, with a musket, bring down the most noble knight at no great risk to himself, and at the same time deny his distinguished opponent any opportunity for valour. In due time, with entire citizenries mobilising in defence of the glorious romantic pageant of their nations, and suffering a terrible disillusionment at Flanders and Verdun, it would be the Sancho Panza perspective – the view of the humble retainer who sees through all dreams of castles in the sky and merely wishes to save his skin – that asserted itself. In August 1914 the principle that had governed European politics for three centuries fell apart: the belief that to engage in politics meant to control events. Sancho Panza's perspective was universalised in the trenches as the Good Soldier Schweik principle: muddling through. It even became an intellectual strategy in the Weimar era, exemplified by Bertolt Brecht and his sardonic gutter-idiom commentary on the higher school of equestrianism, *viz.* Thomas Mann, who thought culture 'a manifestation of the nobility of the spirit'. As far as Brecht was concerned, theatre was a school for survival. Somewhere along the line, he had perceived that, uncoupled from the proletarian good sense of Brother Sancho, the Knight of Doleful Countenance had turned into that excessive Romantic paragon: the Martyr of

Wounded Vanity. In nursing his nostalgia like a badge of rank he had lost the most precious thing of all, the trust of his friend and companion: Sancho Panza doesn't believe in the call of chivalry, but he trusts in Don Quixote.

Personally, I still admit to a sneaking admiration for the figure of Don Quixote, and not just for lessons in the art of jousting. Who else would dare to play St George to a world so firmly in the grip of systems, not least the overarching system made in the image of the supreme idol of capital, money, which mimics the redemptive structure of Christianity, though in reverse? Every system, as Kierkegaard wrote, is plebeian. Only literature remembers what it means to be an aristocrat: it calls him the outcast. Perhaps the fantastic truth about Cervantes' hero is that we can't begin to understand him unless we saddle ourselves with his adjective — even now, especially now, in the age of the digital windstream. Failure is guaranteed, but it is the kind of failure that underwrites our civilisation. As Erich Auerbach wrote in his great book *Mimesis*, 'There are probably few lovers of literature who do not associate the concept of ideal greatness with Don Quixote. It may be absurd, fantastic, grotesque; but it is still ideal, unconditional, heroic.' I would go further and suggest that the greatest quixote of modern times was Friedrich Nietzsche, who set out with the passionate intensity of a true believer to tell Europe its institutional religion was as dead as chivalry, and in so doing negated the ethic which made him possible: it was surely one of Rocinante's distant ancestors he embraced the day he lost his mind in Turin. Like Prince Myshkin, the innocent adrift in Dostoevsky's *The Idiot*, that imperfect great novel about lost absolutes, the Quixote he played was a desperado, a man suffering not just for the sake of what he reads but for what he writes.

Working in a modest capacity as a freelance myself, it struck me recently that, although doing your own thing has an irresistible appeal to those unhappily secure in office jobs (everything he knew of hell, according to Kafka, or 'half-man half-desk' as an international bureaucrat once described himself to me), the word itself is all about being *beholden*. Freelancing is an archaism loose in the modern exchange system. For the original freelance was a lance for hire selling his services to a lord, the upholder of a moral codex inherited from knight errantry and mindful to a fault of honour and conviction, talent and beauty, glory and virtue — notions so old-fangled as to be non-price-indexable. But the freelance can't wear his valour on his sleeve: he might wish to appear to be a man on a mission for the examined life but in the ever widening orb of money's venalities what he actually resembles is a mercenary.

Now the dilemma is clear: if you want to give yourself airs as a uniquely awakened consciousness you'll have to put yourself on the lance-for-hire market.

And nobody, but nobody, will carry your purse.

All the Glory of his Father's House

Bruno Schulz's Drawings and Writings

Bruno Schulz was born in 1892 in the Galician town of Drohobycz, a station of the Austro-Hungarian Empire. His father Jacob ran a haberdashery; the family was decently well-off, and although Bruno regularly attended the synagogue with his elder brother and sister the family was not religiously conservative. In 1915, Schulz's father died, and Drohobycz's marketplace, including his father's shop, was flattened by the Russian army. This was the great divide in Schulz's life. Unlike Kafka, to whom he bears some resemblance, he doted on his father. One of the fetish images he carried through his life was 'of a child carried by its father through the spaces of an overwhelming night, conducting a conversation with the darkness'. It is, as he recognised, the story of the father who tries to shelter his sick son from harm as they ride through the night, wind and wood in Goethe's poem of frightened eroticism 'Der Erlkönig'. With one difference: the roles are reversed. All his writings were to become a mythological consecration of his father's cabalistic speculations in the backroom to his shop, literary returns on what the Book of Isaiah calls 'all the glory of his father's house'. Double-entry bookkeeping has rarely been described so enticingly: 'The Book lay in all its glory on my father's desk, and he, quietly engrossed in it, patiently rubbed with a wet fingertip the top of decals, until the blank page grew opaque and ghostly with a delightful foreboding and, suddenly, flaking off in bits of tissue, disclosed a peacock-eyed fragment.' The obvious is a most terrible enigma.

At war's end in 1918, Drohobycz became Polish (it is now in

western Ukraine). Schulz went on to earn his living as an arts and crafts teacher, having initially studied architecture at the University of Lvov in 1911, a course of study he was compelled to abandon because of poor health. His elder brother Izydor, an executive in the Polish oil industry, died suddenly in 1935, leaving Bruno to support his semi-invalided sister and her family. After hostilities broke out in 1939, Drohobycz was occupied first by the Nazis, then the Red Army, and, after Operation Barbarossa, the Germans again: for the local Jews it was a life lived in the constant expectation of being rounded up and sent to one of the camps. In November 1942, Schulz was shot in the back of the neck by a Gestapo officer who bore a grudge against his protector Felix Landau, a Viennese Nazi who had commissioned him to paint fairy-tale frescos in various parts of town and for that purpose granted him the temporary reprieve of being a 'useful Jew': Schulz's safe-conduct band was intended to prevent his being summarily rounded up with the less useful. It clearly didn't count for much. His murderer triumphantly announced to Landau, who was himself responsible for exterminating most of the Jews of Drohobycz: 'You killed my Jew – I've killed yours.' This dismal death, on a day on which 100 Jews were executed in the ghetto in what amounted to a shooting spree, was nothing at all like the splendidly orchestrated end of the world announced in his long story *The Comet* when 'the curtains blew out far into the night and the rows of rooms stood in an all-embracing, incessant draught, which shot through them in violent, relentless alarm'.

Schulz was not forgotten, though almost all traces of his life and his unpublished writings, including many of his letters and the only work he wrote in German, *Der Heimkehr* (Homecoming), disappeared. Jerzy Ficowski, a young Polish poet, first read his stories in the year Schulz was killed: it is thanks to his unstinting efforts, over sixty years, that we owe much of our knowledge of Schulz's work. In his most recent book on Schulz, he tells us that the polychromes done for Landau, which were thought to be lost or defaced, turned up accidentally in 2001, hidden beneath whitewash and plaster, and were filmed by a German team making a documentary on the writer. Shortly after their discovery and authentication by experts from the Polish National Museum the wall paintings were pried from their supports, a process which damaged or mutilated some of their friable boards and surfaces, and secretly conveyed to the Yad va'Shem museum in Israel. A spokesman for the museum later claimed it was the proper place to preserve them. Nobody had consulted Schulz himself, who wrote that Drohobycz was his 'one and only town on earth'.

Schulz was a bashful and sexually complicated man, to judge from his weirdly compelling and theatrical drawings, which show dwarfish males who, as in Masoch's notorious novel *Venus in Furs* (1870), take their pleasure by prostrating themselves before elegantly bored young girls who 'wear their hair ribbons in a characteristic way and flounce on their slim legs with a peculiar gait, an impure expression in their eyes that foreshadows their future corruption'. His drawings are Goya's *Caprichos* redone as tales of the boudoir. Men beg to be oppressed by the female leg, preferably sheathed in silk and armed with a stiletto; on the other hand, Schulz's precise graphic observation of carriage and bearing suggests an author uniquely open to the pleasures of 'damselling' – experiencing a feminine life imaginatively from the inside: 'sanctified by it, bodies become distinctly more beautiful, and feet, already shapely and graceful in their spotless footwear, speak eloquently, their fluid, shiny pacing monologue explaining the greatness of an idea that the closed faces are too proud to express'. In a 1935 essay about his graphic work, he notes that he is drawn to certain recurrent images such as the cab and carriage horse – 'its schizoid anatomy, sprouting antlers, whorls, knotholes, outcroppings at every extremity... and the wagon is a schizoid structure, too, derived from the same anatomical principle – multi-articulated, fantastic, made up of sheet metal warped into flipper shapes, of horse hides and huge clattering wheels'. He chastely omits to mention his other obsession.

In fact, while confessing it in terms of cabs and carriage horses, matter itself takes on the same allure as the female body. As Father says in the story 'Treatise on Tailors' Dummies, or the Second Genesis', 'there is no dead matter. Lifelessness is only a façade concealing forms of life unknown to us.' This is the wild rational efflorescence of Leibniz's monadology, in which what we perceive at the phenomenal level as bodies and entities actually consists of an infinite number of animate and inanimate monads. Evil is a mere imposture of appearance. The proliferation of objects from fatherly substrates in Schulz's writing amounts to a parodic but exact elaboration of Leibniz's central metaphysical conviction: this universe is the most perfect possible, and that for God to allow living beings to have bodies *only* at the level that constitutes our phenomenological familiarity with them would be a waste of possible perfection. His stories are an inventory of the attributes of God.

While Schulz needed another person to share his writing – 'What for one person is a risk, an impossibility, a caprice stood on its head, when reflected in two pairs of eyes becomes a reality,' he wrote to the novelist Tadeusz Breza in 1934 – he was singularly diffident about getting the finished articles published. It was only through the intervention of literary friends that Schulz's stories were collected at all, in the volumes *Cinnamon Shops* (1934) and *Sanatorium under the Sign of the Hourglass* (1937). Fame was not a formula for writing. Indeed, most of his stories emerged in direct correspondence with a single trusted interlocutor, Debora Vogel. The most rewarding aspect of being in the literary limelight, which otherwise froze him in its glare, was the extensive correspondence it opened up with other key figures of Polish letters, principally the novelist, critic, theoretician, essayist, painter, dramatist and catastrophist Stanisław Ignacy Witkiewicz (Witkacy) – his arch expression for Schulz's graphics was 'poems of pedal atrocity' – and the future literary enigma Witold Gombrowicz, whose three-volume diary, much of it written in his wartime exile in Argentina, is one of the indispensable guides to literary life outside the mainstreams of the twentieth century. In 1961, he recalled Schulz as 'a tiny gnome with a macrocephalic head, seemingly too scared to dare exist, he was ejected from life and crouched along its peripheries... He was superfluous. He was extraneous. It is possible that his masochism also had a different aspect. I don't know, but it most certainly was homage paid to the powers of being that were trampling him.'

Schulz made little progress with the novel he was purportedly working on in the latter thirties, *The Messiah* – 'I'm getting nowhere with it,' he writes in 1936; although Cynthia Ozick was to follow up his lead with her *The Messiah of Stockholm*, in which the long-lost manuscript of Schulz's novel, turns up, like the Messiah himself, when people have stopped looking. Ozick's imagined Messiah is a project of Schulz's imagination, being in the form of a giant book 'with several hundred wing-like sails'. But what would a real Messiah be doing in a century of false ones? David Grossman, whose novel *See Under: Love* also pays tribute to Schulz, commented: 'He wrote so very little. Yet sometimes I think: an entire novel by Bruno Schulz. They would have to sew its covers together to keep it from overflowing at night. Life explodes on every page he wrote.'

Various attempts at marriage came to nothing, including to the woman to whom his second book was dedicated, Józefina Szelinska. He fell out with Gombrowicz (who was already making literary expeditions into hitherto unexplored regions such as juvenility and the Polish inferiority complex and how art looks to people who don't like art) when he insisted that for the 'doctor's wife from Wilcza Street' (a Philistine of his invention), Schulz was a 'pervert or poseur' and, anyway, his stories were 'just pretending'. In an open reply Schulz averred that though he might find it difficult to resist 'the charm of her legs', such a reader was constitutionally incapable of appreciating his stories, her vitality being simply 'her heavy passive mass'.

When Schulz is not writing in the baroque, sarcastic mode that also characterises the 'experimental Polish prose' of Witkacy and

Gombrowicz, in which history is conditional and unachieved (his reference to the 'thirteenth month, supererogatory and in some sense superfluous' is, in the politicised condition of the times, surely a rebuff to the Marxists who thought they were doing history's bidding), he can sound very late Romantic: in a letter to the critic Andrzej Plésniewicz in 1936, he avowed that wanting to 'mature' into childhood was his artistic aim. 'Were it possible to turn back development, achieve a second childhood by some circuitous road, once again have its fullness and immensity: that would be the incarnation of an "age of genius", "messianic times" which are promised and pledged to us by all mythologies.' There is a touch of the rapt stamp collector about Schulz. Walter Benjamin's lyric aside on the hypotactic universality of the postal system might have been intended for him: 'like Gulliver the child travels among the lands and peoples of his postage stamps. The geography and history of the Lilliputians, the whole science of the little nation with all its figures and names, is instilled in him while asleep. He takes part in their dealings, attends their purple assemblies, watches the launching of their little ships and celebrates with their crowned heads, enthroned behind judges, jubilees.'

Proust, of course, set out with a similarly nostalgic agenda, but found that his real task as an artist was to show how the closed childhood world of Combray survived, both intact and dispersed, in the folded paradoxes of adulthood. Rather than dissect the strange errors of perception resulting from the loss of a unified world (for there is only one Proust and 'lost time' cannot be salvaged in Proust's manner), Schulz turns modest Drohobycz into a fantasy 'Babylon the great': his stories are dominated by preternatural seasons, the peculiar splendours of provincial life, and a parental home where every door might be the secret passage to the archives of the cosmos. 'The inhabitants of the city are quite proud of the odour of corruption emanating from the Street of Crocodiles', their concession to 'modernity and metropolitan corruption'. This is no ordinary zoo. Schutz's imagination was a unique meld of wisdom literature, Linnaean Latin and biblical allusions (extended by his repeated readings of Thomas Mann's *Joseph and his Brothers*, a novel he held in the highest esteem), a teeming nursery of new species in which he, the heresiarch of dreams, enjoys, like his father in his shop, a partial existence 'under the sign of the hourglass'. No wonder that in his imagined city people go outdoors with an umbrella not as protection against the rain but to ward off Cantor dust and other debris from the rings of Saturn.

With that kind of Babylonian calendar to keep the time, Schulz returns in almost every story to the same small cast, not least the enigmatic, impractical figure of Father dreaming of demiurges among his bales of cotton, musty Bibles and disintegrating ledger files. The entire house is an extended pathetic fallacy: 'The wallpaper began in certain places to imitate his habitual nervous tic; the flower designs arranged themselves into the doleful elements of his smile, symmetrical as the fossilised imprint of a trilobite.' Dispersing sense in an eccentric orbit seems to be father's way of preparing the family for his demise; it is a sure method for provoking the wrath of his archenemy, the housemaid Adela, who is efficiency with a broom. In the background are Bianca, the unattainable beloved, and Mother, the guarantor of normality, who presides over what she thinks is a family and gets small thanks for her sanity. If she'd looked over her writing son's shoulder she would have seen metaphors going on the rampage, and sucking up all the mundane air: 'In an atmosphere of excessive facility, every whim flies high, a passing excitement swells into an empty parasitic growth; a light grey vegetation of fluffy weeds, of colourless poppies sprouts forth, made from a weightless fabric of nightmares and hashish. Over the whole area there floats the lazy licentious smell of sin, and the houses, the shops, the people seem sometimes no more than a shiver on its feverish body, the gooseflesh of its febrile dreams. Nowhere as much as there do we feel threatened by possibilities, shaken by the nearness of fulfilment, pale and faint with the delightful rigidity of realisation. And that is as far as it goes.'

'Father's Last Escape', the ultimate story in his second collection, borrows its surrealism of scale from Jonathan Swift and its insect imagery from Franz Kafka. But where metamorphosis in Kafka's stories is indissociable from moral repugnance and social ostracism, the bodily transformations undergone by Father are seemingly void of consequence, at least within the inner family. Though 'definitely dead', he has become a crustacean. Repulsiveness is his mark of distinctiveness. 'It was sad and pitiful to see him desperately moving all his limbs and rotating helplessly around his own axis. We could hardly force ourselves to look at the conspicuous, almost shameless mechanism of his anatomy, completely exposed under the bare articulated belly. At such moments, Uncle Charles could hardly restrain himself from stamping on Father.' One day, Father slips into the family pot and gets boiled with the stew. A horrified family puts him on a dish out of further harm's way. He lies there like a baby, with his limbs in the air. And even then, after several weeks of immobility in the sitting room, 'although boiled and shedding his legs on the way, with his remaining strength he had dragged himself somewhere to begin a homeless wandering, and we never saw him again'.

Making off through teeming jungles of indestructible monads (which the son describes as if they were plants and vegetables in a well-tended patch behind the house), Father finally scuttles into the regions of the great heresy, one more escapee from life's irrepressible biological comedy. But Schulz's heresy, in the century when Europe did away with its fathers, including those who honoured them, is actually that old conciliatory orthodoxy, the one that vexed Voltaire: all that happens happens for the best in the best of all worlds.

The Road Not Taken

Arriving at the former edge of the known world by plane almost entirely disqualifies me from writing from Santiago de Compostela, although I can plead one mitigating circumstance for my aberrant choice of transport. My gazetteer — 'in a new English translation, from the original Latin of the twelfth-century Pilgrim's Guide to Santiago de Compostela, the earliest account of the pilgrim routes through France and Spain to the shrine of St James' — is so bulky it couldn't possibly fit into a knapsack. Imagine the ignominy of collapsing somewhere under the weight of a book as big as a paving stone! Stones clutter the landscape for an exceedingly long time and don't need to shorten the life of those beneath them.

Anyway I'm forgetting; this is a book not just about Santiago, but about the places where the trail originates in France: St-Denis, Vézelay, Le Puy and Arles. These are the tributaries that converge like a reverse delta on Puenta la Reina to form the Camino de Santiago which picks its way across northern Spain. In fact, this book is a photographic epic of Romanesque Europe, in which the same iconography repeats itself from place to place: depictions of the angels, the Twenty-Four Elders, Signs of the Zodiac, the Wise and Foolish Virgins, the various personifications of the Liberal Arts. I've seen the Tree of Jesse and the Labours of the Months, the Expulsion from Paradise and Christ in Majesty with the Four Evangelists, Adam and Eve covering their genitals with their hands, prophets and pygmies and fishermen and monsters, and great winged angel holding scales for the weighing of souls: in short, the entire mystic mill of cosmological and earthly doings in the minds of Carolingian and Romanesque architects.

The original guide was written in Latin and published by an unknown Frenchman in the twelfth century, when the Church was more afraid of heretics than infidels. Perhaps the elders of the Church were uncomfortable with the notion that their orthodoxy had itself started out as a heresy within Judaism, and that the enduring conditions needed to ensure the elaboration of religion as a social institution were vulnerable to those who might spread the call for mystic renunciation of the world. So many pilgrims were already coming to the region that the rebuilding of the cathedral had been started in 1070, and was still going on when this unknown writer entered it by the French Gate. It describes what reads like a perilous journey through dangerous regions, where miracles are just as likely to happen as roads blocked with bellowing animals and peasants dispensing small kindnesses. Caspar, Melchior and Balthasar never had to be frightened by the men of Navarre sharpening their knives, and rushing out to rob them of their convictions. (The author so disliked the Navarrese that he says their name derives from *non verus* – 'not begotten as the true offspring of a legitimate race', which is a periphrastic way of being Anglo-Saxon about them.) Pliny's world of monsters has not entirely been forgotten. Nor have the Saracens in Andalucia. The hospitality industry of the Middle Ages was just as inventive at fleecing the unsuspecting as today's tourist services. Relics multiplied themselves. People didn't understand Basque any better then than they do now. Greedy innkeepers, rapacious bandits and polluted water were deep worries, especially for pilgrims with mules or horses. Snow in the Pyrenees could hold you up for weeks, or for ever. When the light failed, night was true night. To think that the end of the world lay beyond all those villages caked in drabness! The transcendent realms are vast, and just waiting to swallow a man should he slip. These days, all you need is a pair of good Salomon boots to see you along the road of the blessed James.

The view takes in: the paths winding through the green fields, the folds of the fallow field of the star, the sense of the medieval, of Rome and even Jerusalem, the colonettes and towers and baroque statues of the city and even the autostrada to La Corunna. By now it's obvious, even to me, that I'm not lost in the other Galicia, the Polish one with the oilfields.

Santiago has forty churches, and their bells are all in regular communication. Bronze is smitten, and the stone walls and granite blocks of the pavement leading through the walled city pick up the message and trundle it down the narrow streets. The granite gleams when it rains, heightening the melancholic atmosphere that hangs over the centre of the town with its scores of ecclesiastical buildings. Black-frocked seminarians flit batlike from church to cloister, in imitation of those endearingly comic photographs of clerics at play by Giacomelli. The surge of car horns and traffic is as far off as the sea. The only thing to do is prepare for that after-noon-long festival called lunch. Then sleep it off in the whitewashed hotel room with its sun-bleached curtains, stiff with the dust of the ages, and ponder the fact that the Spanish, long feared for their enmity towards anything foreign, have become Europe's most hospitable people.

Even outside of the High Mass celebrated every year on 25 July, Saint James' feast day, the great cathedral is jam-packed, the air breath-wrinkled and thick with incense trailing from the massive *botafumeiro*, a silver censer that swings the length of the transept on ropes pulled by six vergers. All cathedrals are ships, but not ocean liners: they are vessels of space that drift among the people, even if they batten on the figure of Christ on the cross: the long nave and chevet and, on each side, the outstretched transepts. They are adorned with chevrons and modillions, corbelled arches and span-drels, words you get to use only once in a lifetime; and that feeling for the eternal that comes from the marriage of light, space and structure. If everything about Christianity is anthropomorphic, Spanish ecclesiastical architecture brooks no exception. Cathedrals are constructed on the template of the human being, who measures 'eight palms': the length of the Cathedral of Santiago is fifty-three human statures. The other side of anthropomorphism is theomorphism, which is being told that we are created in God's image. How does that fit with the fierce instruction not to worship idols at all, which seems to push us to the edge of unbelief in order to have us fly?

When I walk back through the spires of the city myself, having admired the portals bustling with as many stone figures – the work of Master Mateo in the twelfth century – as the cathedral holds live ones, I find myself mingling with a crowd of backpackers and pilgrims replete with staff and scallop-shell, drop-outs and 'liminars' who tell me they've left their normal lives behind for a few months to be able to walk to Santiago from Geneva or Mainz or Paris. Geoffrey Chaucer once satirised the mixed motives of people who go on pilgrimage, but few of the ones I meet are penitent, grief-stricken or saddled with grave illnesses: most seem to have gone to Santiago on their way from the office job to retirement. What was it St Augustine once said? Time takes no holiday. They all press down into the Praza do Obradoiro, which is one of the most beautiful town squares in the world. Once you reach Santiago you've earned the right to enter your name in the great ledger-book held in the office in the Praza das Platerías, and to rest from your labours for three nights in the palatial Hostal dos Reis Católicos. In the old days it took fifteen weeks to walk from Paris to Santiago. These days the roads are better. You can even start off from Hamar, in Norway. But nobody lingers too long in Santiago: life is a forest, as in Dante, and we are called to follow the Way, to move through the world weighed down or ecstatic, as pilgrims of our own puzzlement. The only thing that doesn't change is the horizon, which always stretches beyond the moment in which we experience ourselves walking towards it. The horizon is never a goal, it's an incentive. Does a pilgrim worry about losing himself in the crowd? I don't know. I don't know whether I'd recognise myself if I ever came back here on foot.

But let me tell you what I'd find beyond the French Gate. God will be creating Adam and Eve from clay on the embrasures of the portal. King David will be about to draw his bow across the three-stringed instrument tucked beneath his chin in praise of the Lord. Daniel will be smiling indulgently at the dulcet Esther, having forgotten the words he put in the mouth of Francis Bacon: *plurimi pertransibunt, et multiplex erit scientia*. And there will be an angel with scales.

Now I ought to leave this paving stone of a book behind. Perhaps someone will use it as a pillow.

Afterword

This book brings together various essays and reviews, most of which were first written in response to commissions from periodicals and small magazines: I am grateful to their editors for the chance to reprint them here. All of them, in one way or another, straddle the gulf between the institutional developments and shared economic practices that have taken form since the end of the Second World War and the apparent lack of any clear or meaningful idea of what Europe is. Some adopt chivalresque or even Carlylean postures of hero-worship in homage to the the time when the word 'Europe' merely had to be pronounced for it to sound like a deep and ultimate promise. It was Friedrich Nietzsche's passionate example, as the professor who resigned from his post to tramp the mountains around the bay of Genoa, which convinced enlightened Europeans that the fully developed individual life (made possible by a developing market society) was not a turning away from reality but ethics in action. What Nietszche had discovered, in fact, was the baleful cultural weight of suspicion or resentment: the negative that recognises itself, but knows nothing, since it distorts the reality of what it sees. The subtle contemporary sense of connoisseurship that allows us to feel so right about our badness or sadness, especially when we happen to be educated Europeans, also derives from Nietzsche: he was the first writer to discover that being a producer of high cultural goods offered a certain protection against the boundlessness of an all-too-Christian compassion. Eventually, Nietzsche tried to hide the victims entirely from view: that was his contribution to the events of the twentieth century.

A smaller number of perhaps more candid pieces survive as testimony to other occasions on which either impatience or curiosity got the better of me. These, as the Bible suggests, are very nearly the same thing. Their amalgam is, at any rate, a quality literature thrives upon, along with caprice and a feral skittishness; as John Gross wrote in his indispensable book *The Rise and Fall of the Man of Letters*, 'even the most intensely serious literature needs to be approached with a certain lightness of heart, if it is to yield its full intensity'. Nietzsche aspired to that sentiment. He suggested that his future readers ought to read him against the grain, being 'monsters of curiosity'. The earliest piece in this book was written in November 1989 when I visited Berlin for the first time in the company of my father-in-law, a German journalist of some repute: photographic record shows me reaching my hand through a hole in the Wall. I had begun a career of metaphysical border trafficking, an avocation that was to intensify when curiosity (rather than design) brought me to live in old ergotic Europe, where Strasburg runs out of its gate to the north. Many years later, I was to discover, to my delight, that it was the same monstrous curiosity, as related by Laurence Sterne in Slawkenbergius's Tale in Volume IV of *Tristram Shandy* (which appears as the prologue to this book) that did for the city as a proudly independent part of the Holy Roman Empire and made it an eastern outpost of Louis XIV's France.

Strasburg is still a half-timbered town where the Genius of Europe lingers on. It is the capital of aboriginal Europe, the Europe of humanism, printing and the Book, the Europe of city-states in opposition to the nation-state, Schlaraffenland and the Romantic reaction to Enlightenment. A marbled young Goethe, who, when studying law in the city, spurred the Germans into a nation through his readings of Shakespeare, still stands on his plinth outside the Palais universitaire; and my notebook records Thomas Jefferson's nearly contemporaneous visit to the city in 1788: 'At Strasbourg I sat down to write to you, but for my soul I could think of nothing at Strasbourg but the promontory of noses, of Diego, of Slawkenburgius his historiaga, & the procession of the Strasburgers to meet the man with the nose.' Now that Europe's days of recklessness are past, the city is inhabited by the feckless – quires of bureaucrats and professional Europeans who, when asked, have almost nothing intelligible to say about it at all. Whatever Europe may become, it cannot be a kind of nationalism writ large. Not unless we think we know everything there is to know about what makes for not just good Europeans but ultimately successful human societies. Recent history gives the lie to that logic.

My friends know who they are, and I have no wish to blow their cover. However, I would like to thank a number of people who have provided succour and support over what was a difficult period for me, as a British doctor expatriated to what seemed at times like a no-man's-land: curiosity is not always mutual. John Western and Raymond Bach, successively directors of the Syracuse University Program in Strasbourg, provided me with a teaching platform: I still treasure that brief period of contact with young American students discovering the continent. Peter McCarey in Geneva helped me, perhaps advertantly, to understand better his adopted city, one that casts its shadow all the way from Edinburgh to Philadelphia. Chris Harvie in Tübingen taught me to appreciate George Orwell's empirical approach to what the Germans calls 'Landeskunde'. István Janos Schütz, a polyglot Hungarian friend who now teaches Icelandic in Budapest, first quickened my interest, in the days before the Velvet Revolution, when spies lurked around his bookshop, in elaborate Gothic fantasias. Bruce Charlton's correspondence has always kept me awake. Christine Thayer turned up when the cupboards were bare and showed me how (to make) ends meet in Papua. Patrick and Monika Garruchet, whose marriage also straddles a European frontier, made their house a refuge; so, too, did Keith Noble and Tania Dennis at Mission Beach in the far north of Queensland. But my greatest thanks go to my wife Cornelia, whose concern

Notes and Acknowledgements

The Continuing Adventures of Mr Ross Hall, Esq. (& Madam Zell)
First appeared in *PN Review* 169. Two indispensable accounts of the life and times of Jean-Jacques Rousseau are Maurice Cranston's three-volume biography (Chicago, 1983, 1991 and 1997) and *Jean-Jacques Rousseau: La transparence et l'obstacle* by Jean Starobinski (Paris, 1971).

A Critical Consciousness
First appeared as a review of Heinrich von Kleist, *Selected Writings*, edited and translated by David Constantine (London, 1997), in *Times Literary Supplement*, 2 October 1998.

Being Nice to Nietzsche
First appeared as a review of *Nietzsche in Turin: The End of the Future* by Lesley Chamberlain (London, 1996), in *Times Literary Supplement*, 14 February 1997. It was read in conjunction with Christopher Middleton's indispensable translations of the *Selected Letters of Nietzsche* (Chicago, 1969).

Shelf-Life
Previously unpublished. The best guide to a literary and philosophical appreciation of the aphorism is *Lichtenberg: A Doctrine of Scattered Occasions* by J.P. Stern (Bloomington, Indiana, 1959).

Scheherezade in Vienna
First appeared as a review of *The Tale of the 1002nd Night* by Joseph Roth, translated by Michael Hofmann (New York, 1998), *New York Times Book Review*, 15 November 1998.

Berlin Diary
Previously unpublished; written in Berlin in November 1989.

A Jolly Good Show
First appeared as a review of *Ornamentalism: How the British saw their Empire* by David Cannadine (London, 2001), in *Quadrant*, No. 385, April 2002.

Overwhelmed by Aura
Previously unpublished. The retrospective in question was Eugène Atget, le pionnier, Hôtel de Sully, Paris, July–September 2000.

Politics and Aesthetics
'The Red Count': first appeared as a review of *The Diaries of Count Harry Kessler (1918–1937)*, by Harry Kessler, translated and edited by Charles Kessler (New York, 2000), in *New York Times Book Review*, 2 July 2000. 'The Word at War': first appeared as a review of *Man from Babel*, by Eugene Jolas, edited by Andreas Kramer and Rainer Rumbold (New Haven, 1998), in the *Times Literary Supplement*, 12 March 1999. 'The Usual Business': first appeared as a review of *The Hothouse* by Wolfgang Koeppen, translated by Michael Hofmann, in *New York Times Book Review*, 1 July 2001.

You Must Change Your Life
First appeared as 'A Letter from Kakania' in *Quadrant*, No. 369, September 2000.

Bile with Style
First appeared as a review of *Extinction* by Thomas Bernhard, translated by David McLintock (London, 1995), in the *Times Literary Supplement*, 6 October 1995.

The Future of the Walk
My thanks are due to Dr John Gillies who kindly invited me to deliver a paper on the medical and literary aspects of the peripatetic at the 6th World Conference on Rural Health Care in Santiago de Compostela, Spain, September 2003, from which this essay derives.

Cinema Verities
Part one first appeared as a review of *The Film Explainer* by Gert Hofmann, translated by Michael Hofmann (Evanston, Ill., 1996), in the *New York Times Book Review*, 1 September 1996. Part two first appeared as a review of *Der Untergang*, a film by Bernd Eichinger, 2004, in the *British Journal of General Practice*, February 2005.

Candour and Hygiene
First appeared as an essay-review of Philippe Alméras, *Entres Haines et Passion* (Paris, 1994), and Henri Godard, *Céline Scandale* (Paris, 1994), in the *Times Literary Supplement*, 17 March 1995.

Third Person to Herself
First appeared as a review of *Marguerite Duras: A Life* by Laure Adler, translated by Anne-Marie Glasheen (London, 2000), in *Quadrant*, No. 379, September 2001.

Believing in Architecture
First appeared as a review of *Berlin: A Modern History* by David Clay Large (New York, 2001), in *The Lancet*, 3 November 2001.

The Last Culture Broth
First appeared as a commentary article on the exitus of Bernard Pivot's long-running book programme *Bouillon de Culture*, in the *Times Literary Supplement*, 24 August 2001.

Kafka and America
First appeared as a review of *Amerika (The Man who Disappeared)* by Franz Kafka (New York, 2002), in *New York Times Book Review*, 26 January 2003; expanded in *PN Review* No. 155, January 2004.

Paris, France
First appeared as a literary portrait of Mavis Gallant in *PN Review* 130, November 1999.

Russia and the End of Time
First appeared as an essay-review of *Natasha's Dance: A Cultural History of Russia* (London, 2002), in *Quadrant*, No. 402, December 2003.

Next Year in Jerusalem
First appeared as a review of *One Palestine, Complete: Jews and Arabs under the British Mandate* by Tom Segev, translated by Haim Watzman (New York, 2000), in *Scotland on Sunday*, October 2001.

The Life and Times of Tomi Ungerer
First appeared as an essay on Tomi Ungerer's children's books in *London Review of Books*, 19 July 2001. See, in particular, *Tomi: A Childhood under the Nazis*, 1998, *Die Gedanken sind Frei*, 1993, and *A la Guerre comme à la Guerre*, 1991.

A Stuttered Essay on the French
Previously unpublished.

Five Postcards from Badenweiler
First appeared on the centenary of Chekhov's death in *PN Review* 158, July 2004.

Iliad of Abject Europe
First appeared as an essay-review of *On The Natural History of Destruction with Essays on Alfred Andersch, Jean Améry and Peter Weiss* by W.G. Sebald, translated by Anthea Bell (London, 2003), in *Quadrant*, No. 403, January 2004.

The Good European
Previously unpublished.

A Lance for Hire
First appeared in a shorter version in celebration of four hundred years of quixotism in *PN Review* 165, August 2005.

All The Glory of His Father's House
First appeared as a review of Jerzy Ficowski, *Regions of the Great Heresy: A Biographical Portrait of Bruno Schulz*, translated by Theodosia Robertson (New York, 2003) in *Quadrant*, No. 403, January 2004. Citations are from *The Street of Crocodiles* and *Sanatorium under the Sign of the Hourglass* by Bruno Schulz, translated by Celina Wienewska (London, 1980).

The Road Not Taken
Previously unpublished. See *The Pilgrim's Guide to Santiago de Compostela, A Gazetteer* with 580 illustrations, Annie Shaver-Crandell and Paula Gerson (London, 1995).

Index